BOOK
–MARKS

DISTANZ

acb
Kisterem
Vintage

Gábor Altorjay_Gábor Attalai
Imre Bak_ Miklós Erdély
Tibor Hajas_Károly Halász
György Jovánovics_Tamás Kaszás
Ilona Keserü_Ádám Kokesch
Katalin Ladik_László Lakner
Little Warsaw_Dóra Maurer
István Nádler_Géza Perneczky
Société Réaliste_Tamás Szentjóby
Dezső Szabó_Péter Szalay
Endre Tót_Gyula Várnai

2015

Hungarian Neo-Avant-Garde
and Post-Conceptual Art from
the Late 1960s to the Present

Neo-Avantgarde und postkonzeptuelle
Positionen in der ungarischen Kunst
von den 1960ern bis heute

Katalin Székely

BOOKMARKS

Neo-Avantgarde und postkonzeptuelle Positionen in der ungarischen Kunst von den 1960er Jahren bis heute
Hungarian Neo-Avant-Garde and Post-Conceptual Art from the Late 1960s to the Present

Zur Zeit der Wende 1989/90 war die Akademie der Bildenden Künste Budapest ein Ort revolutionärer Ereignisse. Die Studenten demonstrierten, revoltierten gegen das Ethos des Akademismus in der Lehre und die staatssozialistische Struktur der Institution. Unter anderem wollten sie erreichen, dass die „neuen Medien" Teil des Curriculums werden. Sehr viel wichtiger aber war ihre Forderung nach Lehrfreiheit, nach der Möglichkeit, frei einen Professor zu wählen. Sie konnten sogar die Künstler benennen, bei denen sie studieren wollten. Ihre Forderungen blieben nicht ungehört. Als Folge der Studentenbewegung wurde der Lehrstuhl Intermedia ins Leben gerufen, und zahlreiche neo-avantgardistische Künstler, die bis dahin größtenteils in den Hintergrund gedrängt worden waren (wie etwa György Jovánovics, Dóra Maurer, Zsigmond Károlyi und Tamás Szentjóby), erhielten eine Professorenstelle an der Akademie.[1]

Die von den Galerien acb, Kisterem und Vintage organisierte Ausstellung *Bookmarks* kann keine umfassende Übersicht über die letzten fünfzig Jahre ungarischer Kunst geben, sie zeigt nur eine Auswahl aus den Werken zweier Generationen: der Künstler der Neo-Avantgarde der Sechziger und Siebziger sowie der Künstler, die ihre Laufbahn nach der Wende begannen. Auch wird keine lineare Entwicklungsgeschichte verfolgt, vielmehr blickt die Ausstellung aus heutiger Sicht auf die künstlerischen Positionen zurück, die als direkter oder indirekter Einfluss eine grundlegende Rolle in der zeitgenössischen ungarischen Kunst von heute spielen.

• • •

Die Wortführer der Studentenrevolte von 1989/90 wandten sich den prominentesten Persönlichkeiten der Neo-Avantgarde durchaus bewusst zu. Die alternativen Kunstkurse, die Miklós Erdély und Dóra Maurer in den Siebzigern und Achtzigern in den Kulturhäusern der Budapester Außenbezirken gaben, sollten die jüngeren Künstlergenerationen nachhaltig prägen.[2] Doch für die Studenten war das kunstpädagogische Programm zur Förderung kreativen Denkens nicht der einzige Grund, warum sie Künstler der Neo-Avantgarde zum Unterrichten einluden.[3] Durch sie und mit ihnen schien es den damaligen Studenten möglich, Anschluss an die internationale Kunstszene zu finden und die immer wieder unterbrochene Tradition einer progressiven ungarischen Kunst fortzusetzen. Die Kunst der

At the time of the political changes of 1989–90, revolutionary events took place in the Academy of Fine Arts in Budapest. The students began a series of demonstrations to protest against the academic teaching ethos and socialist state structure of the institution. Among other aims, they wanted "new media" to become part of the curriculum, but what was more important was their demand for academic freedom and the possibility to choose their own teachers. They went so far as to name artists with whom they wanted to study. Their demands did not fall on deaf ears. As a result of the student movement, the Intermedia Department came into being, and the teaching body of the Academy was joined by numerous artists from the neo-avant-garde generation who – mostly – had previously been pushed into the background, such as György Jovánovics, Dóra Maurer, Zsigmond Károlyi, and Tamás Szentjóby.[1]

The exhibition "Bookmarks," organized by the galleries acb, Kisterem, and Vintage, does not aim for a comprehensive overview of the past fifty years of art in Hungary. Instead, it offers a selection of the works of these two generations: the neo-avant-garde artists of the 1960s and '70s, and the artist generations that started their careers after the political changes. What follows is not a linear developmental history; instead, the aim is to look back with today's eyes at those artistic positions that directly or indirectly, through their influence, play a fundamental role in contemporary Hungarian art today.

• • •

It was not by chance that the spokespeople of the 1989–90 student revolution turned towards the most prominent personalities of the neo-avant-garde. In the seventies and eighties, the alternative artistic courses held by Miklós Erdély and Dóra Maurer in suburban houses of culture were a formative experience for new generations of artists.[2] But for the students, an art educational program able to prepare them for creative thinking was not the only reason for inviting the neo-avant-garde artists to be their teachers.[3] They believed that through and with them, it would become possible to connect to the international art scene, and that they would be able to carry on the tradition of progressive Hungarian art, which had been continuously interrupted. To their minds, the art of the seven-

Siebziger war für sie allerdings eine Welt der Legenden. Mehrere Mitglieder der Neo-Avantgarde lebten damals gar nicht in Ungarn (so etwa Tamás Szentjóby), und die Werke der meisten hatten die jungen Künstler gar nicht sehen können, sondern kannten sie nur vom Hörensagen. Die Neo-Avantgarde konnte damals noch nicht Teil der Kunstgeschichtsschreibung werden, eine Revision setzte erst in der Wendezeit ein und ist im Grunde bis heute nicht abgeschlossen.

Die Neo-Avantgarde hatte seinerzeit ihren Platz in einer ähnlich zersplitterten Tradition gesucht und ihre Mitglieder die Freundschaft zu jenen älteren Künstlern, die sich ebenfalls in einer marginalisierten Position befanden. Ein solcher Bezugspunkt war der vielseitig talentierte, herausragende ungarische Avantgardist Lajos Kassák (1887–1967), der weniger mit seinen konstruktivistischen Werken als vielmehr aufgrund seiner Person den jungen Künstlern als Vorbild diente. Daneben waren vor allem die Mitglieder der Europäischen Schule (Európai Iskola), einer in den Jahren nach dem Zweiten Weltkrieg wirkenden, progressiven künstlerischen Gruppe (der unter anderen Endre Bálint, Tihamér Gyarmathy und Dezső Korniss angehörten), von großer Bedeutung für die heranwachsenden Generationen ungarischer Künstler – und nahmen mit ihrer geistigen Haltung und ästhetischen Einstellung ebenfalls eine Vorbildfunktion ein.[4] Ähnlich wie sie konnten die jungen Künstler nicht einfach so an Ausstellungen teilnehmen oder künstlerische Anerkennung innerhalb des offiziellen institutionellen Systems erlangen.

Éva Körner, eine der bedeutendsten Kunsthistorikerinnen jener Zeit, schrieb im Jahr 1974 über die „neue Avantgarde", und ihre Feststellung lässt sich praktisch Wort für Wort auf die Künstlergenerationen nach der Wende übertragen: „[…] Als die junge ungarische Kunst nach Vorbildern suchte, wollte sie keineswegs die offiziell und in der breiten Öffentlichkeit anerkannte ungarische Kunst weiterspinnen, sondern versuchte, die Fäden aufzunehmen, die zuvor wiederholt mit Gewalt zerrissen worden waren. Der Ausgangspunkt, den sie suchten, war nur zum Teil stilistisch […], viel eher war er geistiger Natur: Es reizte sie ein Beispiel, das analog zu ihren eigenen existenziellen Problemen war, jene Art von Progressivität, die sich immanent, aber in vielen Fällen auch in einem präzise bestimmten gesellschaftlichen Programm äußerte, und ihre gemeinsame Bedingung war die Position, die sich in Ungarn für sie zwangsläufig herausgebildet hatte und die sie hier einnahmen."[5]

Um die marginalisierte Situation verstehen zu können, in der sich Lajos Kassák und die Europäische Schule – wie auch die jungen Künstler – in den Sechzigern befanden, muss man beachten, dass der Modernismus in den verschiedenen zentral- und osteuropäischen Ländern durch die

ties was a world of legend. At that time, many of the members of the neo-avant-garde generation no longer lived in Hungary (such as Tamás Szentjóby), and most young artists had not had the chance to encounter their works first hand and only knew them by word of mouth. The neo-avant-garde had not yet become part of art historical accounts, since the process of retrospective revision only began after the system change and, in fact, has still not come to an end.

In its own time, the neo-avant-garde generation had similarly sought its place within a fragmented tradition. They sought the friendship of those older artists who were in the same marginal position as themselves. One of these points of reference was the multi-talented and exceptional representative of the Hungarian avant-garde, Lajos Kassák (1887–1967), who had been an influential figure for the younger generation not so much for his Constructivist artworks, but through his personal example. Apart from Kassák, it was mainly the members of the European School (Európai Iskola), a progressive artists' group active in the years after the Second World War that included Endre Bálint, Tihamér Gyarmathy, and Dezső Korniss, who constituted, through their spiritual strength as well as their ethical and aesthetic opinions, an example for the rising generation of Hungarian artists to follow.[4] Similarly, the young artists did not find straightforward ways to take part in exhibitions or win recognition of any kind within the official institutional system of Hungarian art.

The words Éva Körner, one of the most important art historians of the period, wrote in 1974 about the "new avant-garde" could also be applied word for word to the generation of artists who started their careers after the political changes: "…When young Hungarian art sought predecessors, it did not wish to continue to weave the fibers of the official, widely accepted Hungarian art, but rather to take up those threads that had been broken earlier and with such violence. The starting point they sought was only partly stylistic […] and far more spiritual: the examples that attracted them were those that were analogous to their own existential problems, the kind of immanent progressivity that in many cases was manifest in precisely defined social programs, where a common condition was the position of necessity they occupied in Hungarian life."[5]

In order to understand the marginal situation that Lajos Kassák and the members of the European School (and, indeed, the young artists starting their careers) faced in the sixties, it is necessary to take into account the fact that communist regimes in Central and Eastern European countries treated modernism in very different ways. While abstract art was accepted as early as the late fifties in Poland, and

kommunistischen Regimes unterschiedlich bewertet wurde. Während die abstrakte Kunst in Polen bereits in der zweiten Hälfte der Fünfziger erlaubt war, und in Jugoslawien bereits Anfang der Fünfziger statt des sozialistischen Realismus eine modernistische Ästhetik die Rolle der offiziellen Kunst übernahm, konnte man in Ungarn (mit wenigen Ausnahmen) bis Ende der Sechziger offiziell keine modernistischen Werke ausstellen. Kassák hatte zum Beispiel erst 1967, im Jahr seines Todes, eine eigene Ausstellung, jedoch nicht an einem großen staatlichen Ausstellungsort, sondern in der kleinen Adolf-Fényes-Halle, in der Künstler sogenannte „eigenfinanzierte" Ausstellungen organisieren konnten. (Die ansonsten übliche staatliche Unterstützung wurde ihnen also verweigert.) Die ungarische Neo-Avantgarde wandte sich auch nicht in dem Maße gegen ihre Vorgänger, wie es in Polen oder Jugoslawien üblich war. Die Kunsthistorikerin Éva Forgács nennt als Grund den Umstand, dass Kassák und die mit seinem Namen verknüpfte Tradition damals noch immer die Opposition zur offiziellen Kunst darstellte. Dies habe es unmöglich gemacht, Kassák zu verleugnen und gegen das Erbe der Avantgarde der Zwanziger offen zu polemisieren.[6] Der polnische Kunsthistoriker Piotr Piotrowski erklärt unter anderem damit, dass die ungarische Neo-Avantgarde beispielsweise im Gegensatz zu den polnischen und jugoslawischen Künstlern, die stärker auf die Kunstwelt und die großen Vorgänger reflektiert hätten, sehr viel politischer gewesen sei.[7]

In den Sechzigern herrschte in der offiziellen Kulturpolitik die figurative, darstellende, mimetische Kunst vor. Jede Form von Abstraktion wurde strikt abgelehnt. Dass dazu im Vergleich Pop Art, Fluxus oder Happening als geradezu systemfeindlich galten, liegt auf der Hand. Die zeitgenössische Kunst tauchte in keinster Weise in der Kunsterziehung auf, die Mehrzahl der Professoren tat so, als ob die Kunstgeschichte mit dem Beginn des 20. Jahrhunderts endete. Aus diesem Grund nennen alle Schriften aus der Zeit dieselben Quellen, aus denen sich die jungen Künstler neben der in der künstlerischen Lehre alleinherrschenden realistisch-figurativen Malerei ihre Informationen zu den aktuellen internationalen künstlerischen Trends beschafften. Eine Reise in den Westen war daher in den Lebensläufen der Künstler von besonderer Bedeutung.[8] Manchmal boten aber auch Reisen nach Osteuropa echte Überraschungen. Bei einer von der Akademie organisierten Studienreise im Jahr 1961 sahen beispielsweise Imre Bak und István Nádler das erste Mal Bilder von Cézanne, Picasso, Gauguin, Matisse, Léger oder Kandinsky in den Lagerräumen der Tretjakow-Galerie, der Eremitage oder des Puschkin-Museums.[9] Tamás Szentjóby und

modernist aesthetics replaced Socialist Realism in the role of official art in Yugoslavia in the early fifties, in Hungary it was not possible to officially exhibit modernist works (with very few exceptions) until the late sixties. Kassák, for example, wasn't allowed to show until 1967, the year of his death, and the exhibition did not take place in a major state exhibition space, but in Fényes Adolf Terem, a gallery where artists could put up so-called "self-financed" exhibitions (that is to say, they were denied the otherwise customary state support). The Hungarian neo-avant-garde, therefore, did not turn against its predecessors, as happened in Poland or Yugoslavia. Art historian Éva Forgács remarks that the reason for this was the following: "The fact that Kassák and the tradition attached to his name was still the enemy of official art made it impossible to reject Kassák or to be openly polemical about the legacy of the avant-garde of the twenties."[6] The Polish art historian Piotr Piotrowski also cites this fact as an explanation for why the Hungarian neo-avant-garde was much more political in tone than, for instance, the Polish or Yugoslavian artists who preferred to reflect on the art world and their great predecessors.[7]

The dominant role in the official cultural politics of the sixties was played by figurative, descriptive, mimetic art, while all forms of abstraction were sharply rejected. It is not hard to imagine that in comparison Pop Art, Fluxus, and happenings were viewed as a direct opposition to the system. Contemporary art did not feature in any form in art education, as the majority of teachers acted as though art history had come to an end at the beginning of the twentieth century. This is why all memoirs of the period concur concerning the domination of realistic figurative painting in artistic teaching and the sources from which young artists were able to obtain information about relevant international artistic trends of the period. This is also why, in their artistic biographies, each individual trip to the West is accorded a prominent role.[8] At the same time, travels to Eastern Europe could also turn into real journeys of discovery. During a trip to the Soviet Union organized by the Academy in 1961, for instance, Imre Bak and István Nadler saw paintings by Cézanne, Picasso, Gauguin, Matisse, Léger, and Kandinsky for the first time in the storage rooms of the Tretyakov, Hermitage, and Pushkin Museums.[9] Tamás Szentjóby and Gábor Altorjay, on the other hand, traveled frequently to an essentially far more free-spirited Poland between 1963 and 1967, which seemed to their eyes like a "cultural Mecca."[10]

• • •

Gábor Altorjay hingegen reisten zwischen 1963 und 1967 oft in das unter diesem Gesichtspunkt sehr viel freiere Polen, das in ihren Augen als „kulturelles Mekka“ galt.[10]

• • •

Gemäß eines Parteibeschlusses aus dem Jahr 1958 „öffnet die Partei der nicht realistischen, aber humanistischen, unserer gesellschaftlichen Ordnung gegenüber nicht feindlich gesinnten, nicht zerstörerisch wirkenden Kunst den Weg“, was zugleich aber auch bedeutete, dass gewisse Stilrichtungen automatisch der „Sackgasse bürgerlicher Dekadenz“ zugeordnet wurden und bestimmte Werke rein auf der Grundlage ihrer Stilmerkmale als Werke von zerstörerischer Wirkung eingestuft werden konnten.[11] Gemäß dieser Direktive wurden Kunstwerke regelmäßig durch die Jury von Ausstellungen ausgeschlossen. Man konnte auf diese Weise Ausstellungen schließen und ein ausgedehntes Netz von Informanten im Kreis der als „systemfeindlich“ eingestuften avantgardistischen Künstler unterhalten. Wie der Historiker János M. Rainer bemerkt, war im Laufe der Sechziger „im geistigen Leben ohne jegliche Deklaration, manches Mal sogar entgegen einer solchen ein gewisser Pluralismus und eine Offenheit in Erscheinung“ spürbar. Diese von vielen begrüßte Entwicklung brach allerdings in der ersten Hälfte der Siebziger ab. „Ab Anfang der Siebziger wurde zunächst (ab 1972) in der Wirtschaftspolitik, dann (ab 1973) auch im geistigen, kulturellen Leben ein Teil der Mitte der Sechziger deklarierten und stillschweigenden Reformen und Korrekturen ‚zurückgenommen‘.“[12]

Daher waren im Verlauf der Sechziger und Siebziger die wichtigsten Kunstschauplätze nicht die offiziellen Ausstellungsorte, sondern Ateliers, Privatwohnungen, Kulturhäuser in den Außenbezirken und Säle des Kommunistischen Jugendverbandes (KISZ). Der Kunsthistoriker Lajos Németh schreibt: „Halboffizielle oder private Präsentationen boten den wirklich wichtigen Kunstwerken Raum, an die Öffentlichkeit zu gelangen, doch nur ein begrenztes Publikum konnte sie dort kennenlernen. Sie lebten in Beschreibungen, ihr Ruf verbreitete sich auf dem Weg der Mundpropaganda.“[13] Anfang der Sechziger war ein solcher Schauplatz die Wohnung des Malers Sándor Molnár, in der sich die später als „Zuglóer Kreis“ benannte Gruppe von Freunden zwischen 1958 und 1968 traf. Mitglieder wie Imre Bak, István Nádler oder Gábor Attalai betrachteten es als ihre Hauptaufgabe, die ungarische und internationale Avantgarde-Kunst kennenzulernen. Der als eine Art autodidaktischer Zirkel funktionierende, lockere Freundeskreis interessierte sich in erster Linie für die lyrische Abstraktion Frankreichs. Daneben studierten sie die Kunst von

According to a party resolution of 1958, “the party opens the way to non-realist, but humanist, art that is not opposed to our social system and does not have destructive effects,” a position that at the same time meant that certain stylistic tendencies were automatically consigned to the “blind street of bourgeois decadence,” and that certain artists could be evaluated as having a destructive influence purely on the basis of stylistic characteristics.[11] In the spirit of this directive, works were excluded from juried exhibitions, exhibitions were closed down, and a network of informers spread through the circles of avant-garde artists regarded as “anti-system.” As the historian János M. Rainer observes, over the course of the sixties “in intellectual life, without any particular declaration, and even against such declarations, a certain pluralism and openness appeared.” This process, which was welcomed by many, broke off in the first half of the seventies. “From the beginning of the seventies (from 1972) in economic policy, and then (from 1973) in intellectual and cultural life, a part of the declared and implied reforms and corrections of the mid-sixties were ‘taken back.’”[12]

This is another reason why, over the course of the sixties and seventies, the main venues of art were not the official exhibition spaces, but rather studios, private flats, suburban houses of culture, and communist youth halls. As art historian Lajos Németh wrote: “Half-official or private presentations provided the space for truly important artworks to reach their public, and at the time only a narrow audience saw them. They lived through descriptions, and news of them spread by word of mouth.”[13] At the beginning of the sixties, one of these important venues was the flat of the painter Sándor Molnár, where the group of friends later known as the “Zugló Circle” got together between 1958 and 1968. The members of the group, which included Imre Bak, István Nádler, and Gábor Attalai, viewed their main task as getting to know the work of the Hungarian and international avant-garde. This loose group of friends operated as a kind of self-educational circle and directed its attention primarily towards French lyrical abstraction. They also studied the art of Klee, Kandinsky, and Malevich, got in touch with members of the older avant-garde generation, and contacted the equally marginalized Béla Hamvas, whose esoteric philosophy had influenced numerous young artists of the period, for example Szentjóby and Altorjay, who organized and carried out the first Hungarian happening (*The Lunch. In memoriam Batu Khan*, 1966). They, on the other hand, belonged to the circle of the radiologist and concrete music composer, Dr. László Végh, who introduced the young artists that gravitated to his circle to contemporary music and to a radically free lifestyle.[14]

Klee, Kandinsky und Malewitsch, nahmen Kontakt zu älteren Avantgardisten und zu dem ebenfalls an den Rand gedrängten Béla Hamvas auf, dessen esoterische Philosophie in dieser Zeit zahlreiche junge Künstler beeinflusste. So auch Szentjóby und Altorjay, die als Erste in Ungarn ein Happening (*Das Mittagessen. In memoriam Batu Khan,* 1966) organisierten und durchführten. Beide gehörten zum Kreis um den Röntgenarzt und Komponisten konkreter Musik Dr. László Végh, der die jungen Künstler, die sich um ihn gruppierten, unter anderem in die zeitgenössische Musik einführte und ihnen einen radikal freien Lebensstil nahebrachte.[14]

Diese geistige Freiheit, die auch dem relativen Tauwetter der Sechziger zu verdanken war, zeigte sich in der seitdem legendären I. und II. IPARTERV-Ausstellung, die im Prunksaal des gleichnamigen staatlichen Unternehmens für industrielle Gebäudeplanung stattfand. Die Künstler der IPARTERV-Ausstellungen wagten in dem ideologisch betäubten institutionellen Umfeld einen großen Schritt und gründeten eine eigene Plattform.[15] So schrieb der Organisator der Ausstellung, Péter Sinkovits, in dem zusammenfassenden Katalog mit dem Titel *dokumentum 69–70*: „Diese jungen Leute führten die Traditionen nicht unmittelbar fort, sondern versuchten, sich in dem derzeitigen Zustand der internationalen Kunst zu orientieren, Schritt mit den fortschrittlichsten avantgardistischen Bestrebungen zu halten. Ihr Ziel war es, die Bande zu zerreißen, die sie an die traditionellen, gelösten, aufgearbeiteten künstlerischen Formen ketteten und die kreative Gesten bremsten. Sie versuchten, frei über die Erscheinungen der Welt nachzudenken, suchten neue Formen zum Ausdruck ihrer Erlebnisse."[16] Die neuen Ausdrucksformen führten die meisten hier ausstellenden Künstler zum Konzeptualismus.[17] Auf diese Weise rückte ab Ende der Sechziger das Foto als Medium beispielsweise in den Arbeiten von Miklós Erdély, László Lakner und Dóra Maurer in den Vordergrund. Ab Anfang der Siebziger gehörte Károly Halász als Mitglied der Pécser Werkstatt zu den Pionieren der Land Art in Ungarn; Endre Tót und Géza Perneczky schlossen sich dem internationalen Network der Mail Art an. Ab Anfang der Siebziger waren Gábor Attalai und Katalin Ladik aus Novi Sad sowie in der zweiten Hälfte des Jahrzehnts Tibor Hajas die bedeutendsten ungarischen Vertreter der Body Art.[18]

Die Konzeptkunst war bestens geeignet, den begrenzten institutionellen Raum auszugleichen. In den Siebzigern konnte beispielsweise der bedeutende Kunsthistoriker László Beke ausländischen Gästen die wichtigsten ungarischen Kunsttrends in seiner eigenen Wohnung präsentieren, da diese Werke leicht zu sammeln und aufzubewahren waren, unter anderem seine Dossier-Sammlung *Elképzelés*

This intellectual freedom that had been made possible by the relative thaw of the sixties was evident at the now legendary first and second IPARTERV exhibitions held in the assembly hall of the state architecture office for industrial planning bearing the same name. In the sedated institutional environment of the sixties, the artists of the IPARTERV were able and dared to take a major step and bring their own platform into being.[15] Exhibition curator Péter Sinkovits wrote in the summary catalogue of the exhibitions, *dokumentum 69–70*: "these young people did not directly continue traditions, but rather tried to inform themselves about the current state of art in the world and to step forward in tandem with the most progressive avant-garde endeavors. They attempted to break from the bonds that tied them to the traditional, well-trodden, already worked out artistic forms that acted as a brake on their creative gestures. They tried to think freely about the meaning of the new world and to express their experiences through new forms."[16] The new forms of expression for the artists exhibiting here necessarily meant conceptualism.[17] In this manner, from the end of the sixties, photography came to the fore as a medium, as for example in the work of Miklós Erdély, László Lakner, and Dóra Maurer. From the beginning of the seventies Károly Halász, as a member of the Pécs Workshop, was one of the pioneers of Land Art in Hungary; Endre Tót and Géza Perneczky joined the international network of Mail Art. From the beginning of the seventies, Gábor Attalai, Katalin Ladik from Vojvodina, and in the second half of the decade Tibor Hajas were the most significant Hungarian representatives of body art.[18]

Conceptual art was also suitable as a means to counterbalance the narrow institutional frame. In the seventies, for instance, the leading art historian of the period, László Beke, was able to present the most important artistic trends to his foreign guests in his own flat, as these works could easily be collected and preserved. This was also the case with his dossier-collection *Imagination/Idea*, which was made up of works contributed in answer to his 1971 call for submissions and included emblematic pieces of Hungarian conceptual art.[19] The most important venue for new artistic practices, however, was the Balatonbolglár studio chapel run by György Galántai, which between 1970 and its closure by the authorities in 1973 became one of the most important centers of neo-avant-garde art.[20] As Beke put it in his remembrances about the Balatonboglár chapel exhibitions: "…conceptual art had a kind of political tone. This resulted firstly from its very being and strangeness, secondly from its communicational effectiveness – because it used a lot of channels that were unsupervised –, and thirdly because of the emphatically political character of

(Vorstellung / Idee), die aus Werken bestand, die auf seinen gleichnamigen Aufruf im Jahr 1971 hin eingetroffen waren und unter denen sich emblematische Stücke der ungarischen Konzeptkunst befanden.[19] Der wichtigste Schauplatz der neuen künstlerischen Praxis war aber das von György Galántai geführte Kapellenatelier in Balatonboglár, das von 1970 bis zu seiner Schließung durch die Behörden 1973 das bedeutendste Zentrum der Neo-Avanatgarde-Kunst darstellte.[20] Wie Beke in seinen Erinnerungen an die Kapellenausstellungen von Balatonboglár formulierte: „[…] die konzeptuelle Kunst hatte eine Art politische Färbung. Dies hing einerseits mit ihrer Existenz und Merkwürdigkeit, andererseits mit ihrem kommunikativen Geschick zusammen – weil sie eine Menge solcher Kanäle nutzte, die unbewacht waren –, drittens aber mit den ausgesprochen politisch gearteten Arbeiten, Werken.“[21] Miklós Haraszti bezeichnet dieses künstlerische Denken in seinem als Samisdat erschienenen Buch *Der Staatskünstler* als „dissident“, denn es betrachtet die Spielregeln für sich nicht als verpflichtend. Er fügt hinzu: Ein solcher Künstler „kann ganz bis dorthin aus dem Ästhetikum hinausgeschoben werden, wo er bereits als politischer Protestler erscheint“, oder er wird von vornherein als feindlich betrachtet, „denn er lehnt die Staatskultur grundlegend ab: er bricht das Monopol“. Die von Haraszti beschriebenen „dissidenten Künstler“, die jede Form der Zensur – inbegriffen die Selbstzensur – abzulehnen versuchen, verzichten auf die Privilegien angepasster Künstler (Stipendien in Künstlerhäusern, staatliche Aufträge, Ausstellungsmöglichkeiten) und zielten darauf ab, arme Künstler zu sein, um frei sein zu können.[22]

Es wäre jedoch ein Fehler, hier zu verallgemeinern und die künstlerischen Erscheinungsformen der Neo-Avantgarde mit einem heroischen Kampf zwischen Widerständlern und der Macht zu vergleichen.[23] Nicht nur weil in den letzten Jahren bekannt wurde, dass einige Ikonen für den Staatssicherheitsdienst spioniert hatten, wie der Regisseur Gábor Bódy oder Dr. László Végh, der als Vaterfigur der Neo-Avantgardisten bekannt war. Sondern auch, weil die verschiedenen Ebenen der Öffentlichkeit, das heißt die offizielle Kultur und die nicht-offizielle Underground-Kultur, durchlässig waren. Beispielsweise im Fall von Miklós Erdély, der zeitgleich zu seiner avantgardistischen Kunstpraxis mit großformatigen Fotomosaiken an öffentlichen Plätzen einer der visuellen Pioniere der damals einsetzenden Werbeindustrie Ungarns war.

Erdély sagte bei seiner *Optimistischen Vorlesung* 1981 am Lehrstuhl für Ästhetik der Budapester Universität ELTE: „Ich will nicht auf die Konzeptkunst eingehen, denn meiner Meinung nach ist das eine Periode, die vorbei ist – und unter Vorbeisein verstehe ich nichts Pejoratives –, sie ist bereits

the works exhibited there.”[21] Miklós Haraszti, in his samizdat book, *The Velvet Prison: Artists under State Socialism*, uses the term “maverick artist” for the type of artistic thinking that does not accept the rules of the game, adding that such artists “are exiled from the world of aesthetics,” or they are automatically regarded as enemies, since a maverick artist “rejects state culture at its foundations. He disrupts the smooth operation of the machinery of monopoly and provokes independent activity.” The “maverick artist” is described by Haraszti as someone who tries to refuse all forms of censorship – including self-censorship – and renounces the privileges granted to conformist artists (art residencies, state purchases, exhibition possibilities), aiming “to be a poor artist in order to remain a free one.”[22]

It would, however, be a mistake to make generalizations, or to describe neo-avant-garde artistic phenomena as a heroic struggle between resistance fighters and power.[23] Not only because it has come to light in recent years that several iconic figures wrote reports for the secret police, such as the filmmaker Gábor Bódy or the father figure of the neo-avant-garde artistic generation, Dr. László Végh. But also because there was an exchange between the various levels of the public sphere, that is to say between official and non-official or underground culture, as for example, in the case of Miklós Erdély, who was one of the visual pioneers of the Hungarian advertising industry in tandem with his avant-garde artistic practice, which gave rise to large-scale photo mosaics in public space.

In 1981, during the *Optimistic Lecture* he held at the Department of Aesthetics at ELTE University, Erdély made the following statement: “I don’t want to expatiate upon conceptual art, as I think that the moment of this period has passed – and with its passing, I don’t mean to suggest anything pejorative – it simply passed away, and it did so because it has renounced the sensual, immediate, and total effect, an effect that has always been used in the communication of art. Today art is once again in search of visual and sensual effects.”[24] In the eighties in Hungary, new painting, or as art historian Lóránd Hegyi called it, “New Sensibility,” also came to the foreground. According to Hegyi, in contrast to the modernity, expansionism, and conceptualism of the avant-garde, the artists of the “New Sensibility” made works that were resigned, introverted, and aimed at sensitivity. A lot fits into this category: radical eclecticism, new wild painting or *heftige Malerei*, and many tendencies that grew out of conceptual art. In Hungary the new approach left its mark on the work of both young artists at the beginning of their careers and the older neo-avant-garde artists. Among the representatives of the New Sensibility with

Vergangenheit, und zwar, weil sie zu sehr auf die sinnliche, unmittelbare, totale Wirkung verzichtet hat, derer sich die Kunst in der Kommunikation immer bedient hat. Die Kunst sucht erneut nach visuellen und sinnlichen Wirkungen."[24] In den Achtzigern rückte auch in Ungarn die neue Malerei in den Vordergrund, oder, wie der Kunsthistoriker Lóránd Hegyi sie nannte, die „Neue Sensibilität". Nach Ansicht Hegyis schaffen die Künstler der „Neuen Sensibilität" entgegen der Modernität, dem Expansionismus und Konzeptualismus der Avantgarde resignierte, introvertierte, nach Sinnlichkeit strebende Werke. Darin hat sehr viel auf einmal Platz: der radikale Eklektizismus, die heftige Malerei und zahlreiche andere Tendenzen, die aus dem Konzeptualismus entstanden sind. In Ungarn prägte diese neue Anschauung die Arbeiten der jungen Künstler zu Beginn ihrer Laufbahn ebenso wie die der älteren Künstler der Neo-Avantgarde. Vertreter der Neuen Sensibilität von internationaler Bedeutung waren zu dieser Zeit unter anderem Imre Bak, Károly Halász, Zsigmond Károlyi, Ilona Keserü und István Nádler. Aber wie Dóra Maurer sagte: „Die Konzeptkunst ist nicht nur hierhergekommen, sondern auch hier geblieben, sie war ein echter globaler Paradigmenwechsel, und seitdem denken wir anders über Kunst. Die Konzeptkunst hat die kreative Reflexion, die auf egal welche Erscheinung gegeben werden kann, befreit. Der bessere Teil der zeitgenössischen ungarischen Kunst kann (meiner Meinung nach) als postkonzeptuell bezeichnet werden."[25]

• • •

Erzsébet Tatai merkt in ihrem Buch zur neo- oder postkonzeptuellen Kunst nach der Wende an: „Die quasi Fortsetzung der früheren konzeptuellen Kunst ist erkennbar, ihre Quelle ist bei uns in erster Linie in der Lehre zu entdecken und nur in geringerem Maße in der Rezeption der Werke und Publikationen."[26] Da die Neo-Avantgarde in Ungarn erst in jüngster Zeit verstärkt in das Zentrum der Aufmerksamkeit (von Institutionen, Forschung und Kunstmarkt) gerückt ist, sind es in der Tat die persönlichen Beziehungen, die Verbindungspunkte zwischen den verschiedenen Generationen der letzten 25 Jahre bieten könnten. Von den Künstlern der Ausstellung besuchten beispielsweise András Gálik (Little Warsaw) und Ádám Kokesch die Klasse von Dóra Maurer, Ferenc Gróf (Société Réaliste) und Tamás Kaszás studierten hingegen – als Studenten des Faches Intermedia – bei Szentjóby. In die Klasse für Malerei von Zsigmond Károlyi, der in der zweiten Hälfte der Siebziger seine Laufbahn mit konzeptuellen Fotoarbeiten und Filmen begründete, gingen Bálint Havas (Little Warsaw) und Dezső Szabó.[27]

international significance in this period were Imre Bak, Károly Halász, Zsigmond Károlyi, Ilona Keserü, and István Nádler. But as Dóra Maurer noted: "conceptual art not only arrived in Hungary, but also stayed here. It was a true global paradigm shift, and we have been thinking differently about art ever since. Conceptual art liberated creative reflection and was applicable to any phenomenon in the world. The better examples of contemporary Hungarian art (at least in my opinion) could be called post-conceptual."[25]

• • •

As Erzsébet Tatai notes in her book about neo- or post-conceptual art since the political changes: "the quasi continuity with earlier conceptual art in Hungary derived primarily from teaching, and only to a small degree through the reception of artworks and publications."[26] As neo-avant-garde art in Hungary has only become the center of attention – for institutions, for scholarship, and for the art market – very recently, it is indeed the personal relations that have offered points of connection between the different generations during the last two and a half decades. Among the artists participating in the exhibition, András Gálik (Little Warsaw) and Ádám Kokesch studied in Dóra Maurer's department, while Ferenc Gróf (Société Réaliste) and Tamás Kaszás – at the Intermedia department – were students of Szentjóby. Bálint Havas (Little Warsaw) and Dezső Szabó went to the painting department of Zsigmond Károlyi, who began his career in the second half of the seventies with conceptual photo works and films.[27]

If we seek more concrete, thematic, or stylistic points of connection between the art of the sixties/seventies and that of the new millennium that are relevant to the exhibited works, it is worth noting that among the young artists exhibiting here, the neo-avant-garde generation appears as a theme most distinctly in the work of Little Warsaw. Through installations, films, and re-enactment actions, they attempt to restore the missing pieces to the puzzle of Hungarian neo-avant-garde art.[28] Their works in this exhibition, however, investigate the possibilities for a contemporary reinterpretation of small avant-garde sculptures produced between the two world wars. In recent years, the avant-garde of the twenties, particularly Kassák's utopian modernism, has also become an important research territory for Tamás Kaszás – partly through the intermediation of the neo-avant-garde generation. His kiosk models made from waste materials provide an exceptional critique of faith in utopias and in modernism. The revolutionary avant-garde of the time of the Republic of Councils (for exam-

Sucht man konkretere thematische oder stilistische Anknüpfungspunkte zwischen der Kunst der Sechziger und Siebziger und jener der Nullerjahre, die auch für die ausgestellten Werke Gültigkeit zeigen, dann muss unbedingt angemerkt werden, dass die Neo-Avantgarde als Thema unter den jüngeren Künstlern der Ausstellung vor allem für die Arbeit von Little Warsaw kennzeichnend ist. Sie streben mit Installationen, Filmen und Reenactments von Aktionen danach, die fehlenden Stücke des Puzzles der ungarischen Neo-Avantgarde zu ergänzen.[28] Ihre Arbeit bei der jetzigen Ausstellung untersucht jedoch die Möglichkeit, die avantgardistische Kleinplastik der Zwischenkriegszeit zeitgenössisch neu zu interpretieren. Ebenso wurde die Avantgarde der Zwanzigerjahre, ganz konkret der utopistische Modernismus von Lajos Kassák, für Tamás Kaszás zu einem wichtigen Forschungsgebiet der vergangenen Jahre – zum Teil aufgrund der Neo-Avantgarde, die das Thema ebenfalls behandelt hatte. Seine aus Abfallmaterial gefertigten Kiosk-Modelle sind jedoch bereits eine gnadenlose Kritik am Glauben an die Utopie und den Modernismus. Die revolutionäre Avantgarde der Zeit der Räterepublik (beispielsweise das berühmte Plakat von Mihály Bíró mit dem den Hammer schwingenden Mann) wird auch in der kultur- und politikgeschichtlichen „Kuriositätensammlung" der Société Réaliste häufig heraufbeschworen.

Die den Fluxus kennzeichnende Bricolage-Ästhetik lebt in den aus gefundenen Gegenständen angefertigten Klanginstallationen und Mobiles von Gyula Várnai sowie in den ebenfalls auf dem Prinzip des Objet trouvés aufbauenden konzeptuellen Objekten von Péter Szalay weiter. Die Heimwerkerobjekte von Ádám Kokesch führen den Betrachter zwar schon eher in die Welt des industriellen Designs und der wissenschaftlichen Fantasie, doch seine Objektauffassung zeigt Verwandtschaft zu Dóra Maurers in den Raum hinausgreifenden, geformten Leinwänden.

Dezső Szabó gelangte als Student von Zsigmond Károlyi über die analytische monochrome Malerei zur Tradition der konzeptuellen Fotografie. Seine neuesten, auf der Grundlage von Modellen angefertigten Fotografien lassen sich durchaus als Erben des auch bei Miklós Erdély präsenten wissenschaftlichen Denkens auffassen.

Doch wie die Vertreter der Neo-Avanatgarde führen auch diese Künstler nicht „unmittelbar die Traditionen weiter", sondern blicken von ihrem eigenen, zeitgenössischen Blickwinkel auf die Arbeit früherer Künstlergenerationen zurück. Auch das gemeinsame Projekt von Little Warsaw, Dezső Szabó und Gábor Erdélyi mit dem Titel *Die Gegenständliche Welt* ist nicht eine einfache Hommage an den einstigen

ple the famous figure with a hammer on Mihály Biró's poster) is referred to in various ways in Société Réaliste's "collection of curiosities" of cultural and political history.

The bricolage aesthetic of Fluxus lives on in the sound installations and mobiles of Gyula Várnai, as well as in the conceptual objects likewise built on the principle of the "objet trouvé" of Péter Szalay. On the other hand, the DIY objects of Ádám Kokesch lead more towards the world of industrial design and scientific fantasy. In spatial terms, however, they are related to Dóra Maurer's shaped canvases that jut out into the exhibition space.

It was in Zsigmond Károlyi's department that Dezső Szabó reached across through analytical monochromatic painting to the tradition of conceptual photography. His most recent photographs based on models can also be seen as heirs to the scientific thinking that was present in Miklós Erdély's work.

However, just as with the members of the neo-avantgarde generation, these artists also do not "directly continue traditions," but rather look back to the work of earlier artistic generations from their own contemporary viewpoints. The project *The World as Objectness* by Little Warsaw with Dezső Szabó and the painter Gábor Erdélyi is not just an homage to their former master, but also poses relevant questions concerning the role of the artist, the essence of the art object, the mechanisms of the art market, and essential issues surrounding the ownership of an art object.

1 Among the most vocal figures of the student movement are internationally known artists from a generation around fifty years old today, such as Attila Csörgő, Róza El-Hassan, Tamás Komoróczky, and Zoltán Szegedy-Maszák. These events were examined by Little Warsaw in the research and publication project *Rebels '89* (2006-2015).

2 *KREATIVITÁSI GYAKORLATOK, FAFEJ, INDIGO. Erdély Miklós művészetpedagógiai tevékenysége 1975–1986 [Creativity Exercises, Fantasy Developing Exercises (FAFEJ), and Inter-Disciplinary Thinking (InDiGo). Miklós Erdély's art pedagogical activity, 1975–1986].* Edited by Sándor Hornyik Sándor and Annamária Szőke (Budapest: MTA Művészettörténeti Kutatóintézet – Gondolat Kiadó – 2B Alapítvány – Erdély Miklós Alapítvány, 2008). An exhibition presenting these creative exercises was held as *Kreativitätsübungen* in the GfZK in Leipzig in 2014 and was curated by Dora Hegyi and Franciska Zólyom.

3 They could not invite Miklós Erdély, as he passed away in 1986.

4 Piotr Piotrowski, *In the Shadow of Yalta, Art and Avant-Garde in Eastern Europe, 1945–1989* (London: Reaktion Books, 2009), pp. 34 – 41.

5 Antik Cs. Asztalos [Körner Éva], "No ism's in Hungary," *Studio International,* 1974, No. 3. [Translated from the Hungarian edition, Éva Körner, "Magyar avantgárd – izmusok nélkül," in: *Avantgárd Izmusokkal és Izmusok nélkül, Válogatott cikkek és tanulmányok [No ism's in Hungary. Selected writings]* (Budapest: MTA Művészettörténeti Kutatóintézet, 2005), pp. 397–408.]

6 Éva Forgács, "A kultúra senkiföldjén – Avantgárd a magyar kultúrában" [In the No Man's Land of Culture – The Avant-garde in Hungarian Culture]. In: Hans Knoll (ed.), *A második nyilvánosság, XX. századi magyar művészet [The Second Public Sphere.*

Meister, sondern formuliert überaus aktuelle Fragen zur Rolle des Künstlers, zum Wesen des Kunstobjekts, zu den Mechanismen des Kunstmarktes sowie zur Besitzbarkeit eines Kunstgegenstandes.

1 Unter den Wortführern der Studentenbewegung sind auch international anerkannte Künstler der Generation der heute etwa Fünfzigjährigen zu finden (Attila Csörgő, Róza El-Hassan, Tamás Komoróczky oder Zoltán Szegedy-Maszák). Die Ereignisse hat Little Warsaw in dem Forschungs- und Publikationsprojekt *Rebels '89* (2006–2015) aufgearbeitet.

2 *KREATIVITÁSI GYAKORLATOK, FAFEJ, INDIGO. Erdély Miklós művészetpedagógiai tevékenysége 1975–1986. [Kreativitätsübungen, FAFEJ („Holzkopf", Abkürzung für Phantasie-fördernde-Übungen) INDIGO (Abkürzung für Interdisziplinäres Denken) Die kunstpädagogische Tätigkeit von Miklós Erdély 1975–1986].* Zusammengestellt von: Sándor Hornyik und Annamária Szőke. Budapest: MTA Művészettörténeti Kutatóintézet – Gondolat Kiadó – 2B Alapítvány – Erdély Miklós Alapítvány, 2008. Eine Ausstellung, die diese Übungen vorstellte, war unter dem Titel *Kreativitätsübungen* 2014 in der Leipziger GfZK zu sehen, kuratiert von Dóra Hegyi und Franciska Zólyom.

3 Miklós Erdély konnte nicht mehr eingeladen werden, da er 1986 verstorben war.

4 Piotr Piotrowski, *In the Shadow of Yalta, Art and Avant-Garde in Eastern Europe, 1945–1989.* London: Reaktion Books, 2009. S. 34–41.

5 Antik Cs. Asztalos [Éva Körner], „No ism's in Hungary", *Studio International,* 1974. Nr. 3. [Übersetzt nach der ungarischen Ausgabe. Körner, Éva, „Magyar avantgárd – izmusok nélkül", In Dies., *Avantgárd Izmusokkal és Izmusok nélkül, Válogatott cikkek és tanulmányok.* Budapest, MTA Művészettörténeti Kutatóintézet, 2005. S. 397–408.]

6 Éva Forgács, „Kultur im Niemandsland." In: Hans Knoll (Hrsg.), *Die zweite Öffentlichkeit. Kunst in Ungarn im 20. Jahrhundert.* Dresden: Verlag der Kunst, 1999. S. 4–57.

7 Piotr Piotrowski, „Mapping the Legacy of the Political Change of 1956 in East European Art." *THIRD TEXT,* Bd. 20, Heft 2, März, 2006. S. 211–221.

8 Ab 1963 konnte man alle drei Jahre in den Westen reisen (das Reisebudget durfte 70 Dollar nicht überschreiten), doch die Ausgabe des Reisepasses war an verschiedene Genehmigungen geknüpft, in vielen Fällen wurde sie verweigert, beispielsweise Szentjóby, der von 1969 ganz bis 1975 keinen Reisepass erhielt. Später erzwangen die Behörden allerdings seine Emigration. Siehe Klara Kemp-Welch, *Antipoltics in Central European Art 1956–1989. Reticence as Dissidence under Post-Totalitarian Rule.* London: IB Tauris, 2013. S. 140.

9 Gábor Bellák, „Beszélgetés Bak Imrével" [Gespräch mit Imre Bak] In: Ildikó Nagy (Hrsg.), *Hatvanas évek – Új törekvések a magyar képzőművészetben. [Die Sechzigerjahre – Neue Bestrebungen in der ungarischen bildenden Kunst]* (Ausstellungskatalog), Budapest: Képzőművészeti Kiadó–Magyar Nemzeti Galéria–Ludwig Múzeum, 1991. S. 175–183.

10 Klara Kemp-Welch, (wie Anm. 8) S. 105.

11 *Az MSZMP határozatai és dokumentumai 1956–62. [Die Beschlüsse und Dokumente der MSZMP, 1956–1962]* Budapest: Kossuth Könyvkiadó, 1973. S. 268.

12 János M. Rainer, „ A 'Hatvanas évek' Magyarországon. Politikatörténeti megközelítések." [Die „Sechzigerjahre" in Ungarn. Politikhistorische Denkansätze], in: ders. (Hrsg.), *„Hatvanas Évek" Magyarországon. Tanulmányok. [Die „Sechzigerjahre" in Ungarn. Aufsätze.]* Budapest: 1956-os Intézet, 2004, S. 11–30.

13 Lajos Németh im ersten Katalog der Ausstellungsreihe *Tendenciák 1970–1980 [Tendenzen 1970–1980]* mit dem Titel *Új Művészet 1970-ben. Tendenciák 1970–1980, I. [Neue Kunst im Jahr 1970. Tendenzen 1970–1980, I.]* Auswahl, Text und Redaktion: Katalin Keserü und Ildikó Nagy, veranstaltet von: János Frank, Budapest, Fővárosi Tanács Óbudai Galéria, 1980. o. S.

14 Vgl. Kürti Emese, „Generations in Experiment. The Cage Effect int he Early Sixties of Hungary", In: Katalin Székely (ed.), *The Freedom* *Art in Hungary in the 20th Century]* (Budapest: Enciklopédia, 2002), p. 55 [in German: *Die zweite Öffentlichkeit. Kunst in Ungarn im 20. Jahrhundert* (Dresden: Verlag der Kunst, 1999)].

7 Piotr Piotrowski, "Mapping the Legacy of the Political Change of 1956 in East European Art." *THIRD TEXT,* Vol. 20, Issue 2, March, 2006. pp. 211–221.

8 From 1963, it was possible to travel to the West three times a year (the travel budget could not exceed 70 dollars), although various permissions were necessary to get a passport, which in many cases was refused, for example in Szentjóby's case, who from 1969 to 1975 was not issued a passport. At that point he was essentially forced to emigrate by the authorities. Cf. Klara Kemp-Welch, *Antipolitics in Central European Art 1956–1989. Reticence as Dissidence under Post-Totalitarian Rule* (London: IB Tauris, 2013), p. 140.

9 Gábor Bellák, "Beszélgetés Bak Imrével" [Interview with Imre Bak] in: Nagy Ildikó (ed.): *Hatvanas évek – Új törekvések a magyar képzőművészetben [Sixties: New Endeavours in the Hungarian Visual Arts]* (exhibition catalogue) (Budapest: Képzőművészeti Kiadó – Magyar Nemzeti Galéria – Ludwig Múzeum, 1991), pp. 175–183.

10 Klara Kemp-Welch, op. cit., p. 105.

11 *Az MSZMP határozatai és dokumentumai 1956–62 [Decisions and Documents of the Hungarian Social Workers' Party (MSZMP) 1956-62]* (Budapest: Kossuth Könyvkiadó, 1973), p. 268.

12 János M. Rainer, "A 'Hatvanas évek' Magyarországon. Politikatörténeti megközelítések." [The Sixties in Hungary – some historical and political approaches.] In János M. Rainer (ed.): *"Hatvanas Évek" Magyarországon. Tanulmányok [The Sixties in Hungary. Essays]* (Budapest: 1956 Institute and Oral History Archive, 2004), pp. 11–30.

13 Lajos Németh in the first catalogue of the exhibition series *Tendenciák 1970–1980.* Published in *Új Művészet 1970. Tendenciák 1970–1980, I., [New Art 1970. Tendencies 1970–80],* the catalogue was written and edited by: Katalin Keserü and Ildikó Nagy and organized by: János Frank (Budapest, Fővárosi Tanács Óbudai Galéria, 1980).

14 Kürti Emese, "Generations in Experiment. The Cage Effect in the Early Sixties of Hungary," In: Katalin Székely (ed.), *The Freedom of Sound. John Cage behind the Iron Curtain* (Budapest: Ludwig Museum, 2013), pp. 134–151.

15 Among the Bookmarks exhibitors, Bak, Jovánovics, Keserü, Lakner, Nádler, and Tót all took part in the first IPARTERV exhibition of 1968, as well as the second in 1969, while Szentjóby only took part in the second. Erdély's work can be found in the catalogue of the IPARTERV exhibitions, *dokumentum 69–70,* although he did not take part in the exhibition.

16 Péter Sinkovits [Introduction], *dokumentum 69-70,* (Budapest, 1970). Quoted in: Ivet Ćurlin et al. (eds.), *Art always has its consequences: Budapest, Łodź, Novi Sad, Zagreb, 2008–2010* (Zagreb, Budapest: WHW, Tranzit Budapest, 2010), p. 47.

17 In Eastern European art, in contrast to "conceptual art," which is seen as a closed historical category (which in the sixties and seventies referred to a narrowly defined conceptual art, so to speak), the term "conceptualism" is more useful, since it is an essentially broader notion in terms of the geography, history, and artistic practices it covers. Cf. László Beke, "Conceptual Tendencies in Eastern European Art," in: *Global Conceptualism: Points of Origin, 1950s–1980s,* Queens Museum of Art, New York – Walker Art Center, Minneapolis, Miami Art Museum [exhibition catalogue] (Miami: Philomena Mariani, 1999–2000), pp. 41–51, and Zdenka Badovinac et al., "Conceptual Art and Eastern Europe: Part I–II," *e-flux journal,* Vol. 40 (December 2012) and Vol. 41 (January 2013).

18 Miklós Peternák, *concept.hu / koncept. hu. A konceptuális művészet hatása Magyarországon / The Influence of Conceptual Art in Hungary* (Budapest, Paks: Paksi Képtár – C³ Alapítvány, 2014).

19 Dóra Hegyi et al. (eds.), *Imagination/Idea. The Beginning of Hungarian Conceptual Art. The László Beke Collection, 1971* (Zürich: JRP Ringier, 2015).

20 Júlia Klaniczay, Edit Sasvári (eds.), *Törvénytelen avantgárd. Galántai György balatonboglári kápolnaműterme 1970–1973 [Illegal Avant-garde.*

of Sound. John Cage behind the Iron Curtain. Budapest: Ludwig Museum, 2013. S. 134–151.

15 Unter den Künstlern von Bookmarks nahmen Bak, Jovánovics, Keserü, Lakner, Nádler und Tót sowohl an der ersten IPARTERV-Ausstellung 1968 als auch an der zweiten 1969 teil, Szentjóby nur an der zweiten. Von Erdély ist zwar ein Werk im Überblickskatalog zu den IPARTERV-Ausstellungen, *dokumentum 69–70*, vertreten, an den Ausstellungen hat er jedoch nicht teilgenommen.

16 Péter Sinkovits, [Einleitung], *dokumentum 69–70*, Budapest, 1970. Vgl. Ivet Ćurlin et al. (eds.), *Art always has its consequences: Budapest, Łodź, Novi Sad, Zagreb, 2008–2010.* WHW, Tranzit Budapest, 2010. S. 47.

17 In der osteuropäischen Kunst ist es zweckmäßiger, den Terminus des „Konzeptualismus" entgegen der „konzeptuellen Kunst" als geschlossene geschichtliche Kategorie (die in den Sechzigern und Siebzigern auf eine sehr eng gefasste konzeptuelle Kunst verwies) zu verwenden, denn dieser Terminus ist sowohl geografisch als auch historisch sowie hinsichtlich der künstlerischen Praxis, die er umfasst, sehr viel weiter gefasst. Vgl. László Beke, „Conceptual Tendencies in Eastern European Art", In: *Global Conceptualism: Points of Origin, 1950s–1980s*, Queens Museum of Art, New York – Walker Art Center, Minneapolis, Miami Art Museum, [exhibition catalogue], Miami: Philomena Mariani, 1999–2000. S. 41–51; und Zdenka Badovinac et. al., „Conceptual Art and Eastern Europe: Part I–II. ". *e-flux journal*, Bd. 40 — (Dezember 2012) u. Bd. 41 (Januar 2013).

18 Peternák Miklós, *concept.hu / koncept. hu. A konceptuális művészet hatása Magyarországon / The Influence of Conceptual Art in Hungary.* Paksi Képtár – C³ Alapítvány, 2014.

19 Dóra Hegyi et al. (eds.), *Imagination/Idea. The beginning of Hungarian Conceptual art. The László Beke Collection, 1971.* Zürich: JRP Ringier, 2015.

20 Klaniczay Júlia, Sasvári Edit (Hrsg.), *Törvénytelen avantgárd. Galántai György balatonboglári kápolnaműterme 1970–1973. [Illegale Avantgarde. Das Kapellenatelier von György Galántai in Balatonboglár 1970–1973.*] Budapest: Artpool-Balassi, 2003.

21 ebd. S. 205.

22 Miklós Haraszti, *A cenzúra esztétikája*, Budapest: AB Független Kiadó, 1981/1986. S. 66. [auf Deutsch: *Der Staatskünstler.* Übersetzung Molli Sauer, Rotbuch Verlag, Berlin 1984]

23 Zu dem Zusammenhang von Underground-Kunst und politischem Samisdat siehe z. B.: László Beke, Edit Sasvári, „‚Ungarn kann dir gehören'. Die Künstler des Underground". In: Wolfgang Eichwede (Hrsg.), *Samizdat. Alternative Kultur in Zentral- und Osteuropa: Die 60er bis 80er Jahre.* Bremen: Edition Temmen, Bremen 2004. S. 168–171.

24 Miklós Erdély, „Optimista előadás [Optimistische Vorlesung]", In: Id., *Művészeti írások [Schriften über die Kunst]*, hrsg. von Miklós Peternák. Budapest: Képzőművészeti Kiadó, 1991. S. 147.

25 Maurer Dóra (Hrsg.): *KONCEPT KONCEPCIÓ, szemelvények [Konzept Konzeption, Auszüge].* Budapest, Nyílt Struktúrák Művészeti Egyesület / OSAS, 2008. o. S.

26 Erzsébet Tatai, *Neokonceptuális művészet Magyarországon a kilencvenes években [Neokonzeptuelle Kunst in Ungarn in den Neunzigerjahren].* Budapest: Præsens, 2005. S. 60.

27 Der jüngste ausstellende Künstler, Péter Szalay, studierte an der Universität Pécs, Gyula Várnai hingegen hat keine offizielle Kunstausbildung absolviert.

28 In ihrem Projekt *Tableau Vivant* präsentierten sie das Reenactment der Aktion *Kizárásgyakorlat. Büntetésmegelőző autoterápia [Exklusions-Übung. Autotherapeutische Übung zur Vorbeugung gegen Bestrafung]* von Tamás Szentjóby (1972 in Balatonboglár), die sie mit der Hilfe des Künstlers rekonstruierten (2005). Die IPARTERV-Generation und der dort ausstellende Grafiker und Konzeptkünstler János Molnár waren die Hauptakteure ihrer Installation *Crew Expandable*. Im Projekt *Spiel der Wandlungen* aus dem Jahr 2009 baten sie ebenfalls Künstler der Neo-Avantgarde, sich an ihr eigenes Ich vor vierzig Jahren zu erinnern: Zsigmond Károlyi konfrontierte sie mit einer Filmaufnahme von 1971 (dem experimentellen Film *Der Dritte* von Gábor Bódy). Ebenfalls im Rahmen dieser Reihe präsentierten sie 2009 im Museum Abteiberg das Reenactment der berühmten Aktion *Ausstellung von Jochen Gerz neben seiner photographischen Reproduktion* (1972/73) mit Jochen Gerz selbst.

The Balatonboglár Chapel Studio of György Galántai 1970–1973] (Budapest: Artpool-Balassi, 2003).

21 Ibid. 205.

22 Miklós Haraszti, *The Velvet Prison: Artists under State Socialism* (London: Tauris, 1988), pp. 150–152.

23 For the connections between underground art and political samizdat, cf. for example: László Beke, Edit Sasvári, "'Ungarn kann dir gehören.' Die Künstler des Underground" in: Wolfgang Eichwede (ed.): *Samizdat. Alternative Kultur in Zentral- und Osteuropa: Die 60er bis 80er Jahre* (Bremen: Edition Temmen, 2004), pp. 168–171.

24 Erdély Miklós, "Optimista előadás" [Optimistic Lecture], in: Id., *Művészeti írások [Writings on Art]*, ed. by Miklós Peternák (Budapest: Képzőművészeti Kiadó, 1991), p. 147.

25 Dóra Maurer (ed.): *KONCEPT KONCEPCIÓ, szemelvények [Concept Conception. Extracts]* (Budapest: Nyílt Struktúrák Művészeti Egyesület / OSAS, 2008), n. p.

26 Erzsébet Tatai, *Neokonceptuális művészet Magyarországon a kilencvenes években [Neoconceptual Art in Hungary in the Nineties]* (Budapest, Præsens, 2005), p. 60.

27 The youngest exhibiting artist, Péter Szalay, went to Pécs University, while Gyula Várnai did not participate in official artistic training.

28 In the course of their *Tableau Vivant* project, for example, they reconstructed, with the help of Szentjóby himself, his action from Balatonboglár in 1972, *Expulsion Exercise. Punishment – Preventative Autotherapy*. The Iparterv generation, and the graphic and conceptual artist János Major who exhibited there, was the main figure in their installation *Crew Expandable* from 2007. In their 2009 project *Game of Changes* they again asked neo-avant-garde artists to reflect on how they were forty years ago. Thus, they confronted Zsigmond Károlyi with 1971 film footage (with Gábor Bódy's experimental film *The Third*). It was also within the framework of this series that they showed in Museum Abteiberg a reenactment of Jochen Gerz's action from 1972/73, *Exhibition of Jochen Gerz Next to His Photographic Reproduction*.

Gábor ALTORJAY

Budapest, 1946

Gábor Altorjay organisierte mit Tamás Szentjóby das erste Happening in Ungarn (*Das Mittagessen. In Memoriam Batu Khan*, 1966) als Auftakt der neuen Avantgarde der Sechzigerjahre. Die Geschichte des Happenings verweist auf die Besonderheit des ungarischen Aktionismus, denn im Gegensatz zur Ontologie relativ zeitgleich stattfindender zeitgenössischer Phänomene lässt es sich nicht aus der Aktionsmalerei, sondern aus der experimentellen Praxis der beiden Dichter ableiten. Altorjay, dem diese internationale Synchronizität bewusst war, nahm unmittelbar nach dem Happening Kontakt zu den Vertretern des zeitgenössischen Aktionismus, Wolf Vostell, Dick Higgins und dem tschechischen Theoretiker Jindřich Chalupecký, auf. Als er im Herbst 1967 – auch aufgrund von Repressionen durch die Polizei wegen des Happenings – nach Deutschland emigrierte, setzte er seine Tätigkeit im Kreis um Wolf Vostell fort. Nachdem er Bekanntschaft mit den Künstlern um den Sammler Hanns Sohm gemacht hatte, schloss er sich der von Vostell gegründeten Kommune und Ausstellungsort Kombinat 1 an, wo sie mehrere gemeinsame Aktionen realisierten. Seine erste Einzelausstellung fand im Februar 1968 in der Stuttgarter Galerie Senatore statt. Hier zeigte er – entgegen der Praxis im Kunsthandel als vervielfältigtes Multiple – seine die charakteristischen Merkmale des Fluxus aufweisenden Objekte, zum Beispiel das ursprünglich für ein Event in Ungarn angefertigte *Schach-Kompott* (1967/68) oder seine Objekte aus dem Jahr 1968, *Vostell in Milch* und *Anti-Apotheke Bakunin* (mit dem Porträt von Marx). Altorjays internationale, avantgardistische Tätigkeit entwickelte sich organisch aus den Verbindungen zwischen Fluxus und seiner ungarischen Praxis, wobei er besonderes Augenmerk auf die bewusste Repräsentation des „östlichen Aktionismus" legte. Die Collage *Mein Weg in die Freiheit* (1967) verweist auf den Moment der Grenzüberschreitung – also auf zwei Weltordnungen –, und der Begriff „Freiheit" bezieht sich aufgrund der Verhältnisse in Ungarn eindeutig auf die Idealisierung des „ersehnten Westens". In Deutschland fand sich Altorjay im kritischen Umfeld der Neuen Linken und inmitten der 68er wieder, was sich auch auf seine eigene politische Einstellung auswirkte: Dies wird im Objekt und Foto *La Strada* (1969) deutlich, das im Zuge einer politischen Protestaktion entstand und bei dem ein Stück Zitrone ursprünglich das von der Polizei eingesetzte Tränengas neutralisieren sollte.

Gábor Altorjay, together with Tamás Szentjóby, organized and conducted the first Hungarian happening (*The Lunch. In memoriam Batu Khan*, 1966), as the first event of the new avant-garde of the sixties. The history of the happening reflects the particular character of Hungarian Actionism, in that – contradicting the ontology of contemporary phenomena that took place around the same time – it derived not from Actionist painting, but from the experimental praxis of the two poets. Nevertheless, Altorjay, well aware of the international synchronicities, made contact directly after organizing the happening with representatives of contemporary Actionism, namely Wolf Vostell, Dick Higgins, and the Czech theoretician Jindřich Chalupecký. When in the autumn of 1967 – in the face of police harassment due to his happening activities – he emigrated to Germany, he continued his activities in the circle of Wolf Vostell. After he got to know the artists belonging to the circle of collector Hanns Sohm, he joined the commune and exhibition space Kombinat 1, founded by Vostell, where numerous collaborative actions were realized. His first solo exhibition was shown at the Galerie Senatore in Stuttgart in February 1968. In this exhibition, presented in the form of reproduced multiples and thus in opposition to the usual practices of the art market, he showed the *Chess Compote* (1967–68), which had originally been made for a Hungarian event and bore the characteristic signs of Fluxus; *Vostell in Milk*; as well as an object from 1968 titled *Anti-Pharmacy Bakunin* that incorporated a portrait of Marx. Altorjay's international avant-garde activities developed organically from the connections between Fluxus and his Hungarian practice, an important part of which was the deliberate representation of "eastern Actionism." His collage *My Way to Freedom* (1967) refers to the moment when he stepped over the border between two countries and two world orders, at which point the concept of "freedom," seen from beyond the conditions prevailing in Hungary at the time, was necessarily connected to an idealization that lacked experience in the "wild west." In Germany, however, Altorjay found himself in the company of followers of New Left criticism in the wake of 1968, which also made his own political attitude more articulate: this is suggested by the object and photograph *La Strada* (1969), which arose in the course of a political protest action, with a piece of lemon originally serving to counteract the effects of police tear gas.

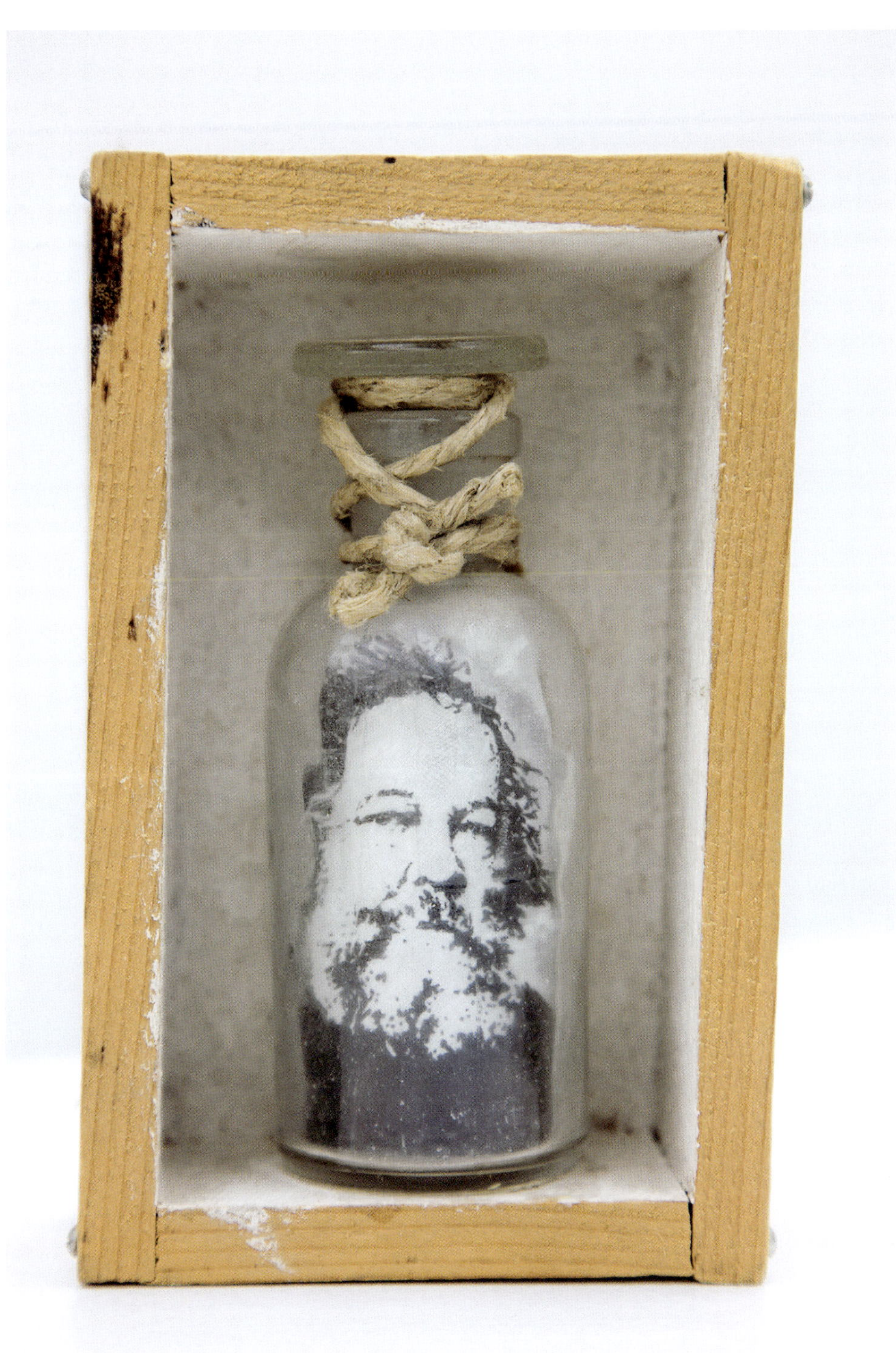

Anti-Apotheke Bakunin / Anti-Pharmacy Bakunin, 1968

Gábor ATTALAI

Budapest, 1934 – Budapest, 2011

Gábor Attalais Lebenswerk erklärt sich in erster Linie durch jenes internationale Umfeld, zu dem er – mangels progressiver künstlerischer Einrichtungen im eigenen Land – Kontakt aufgebaut hatte. Er sagte selbst, dass er zwar in Ungarn lebte, aber „nach außen funktionierte". Seine spezielle Position gründete auch darin, dass er – im Gegensatz zu den meisten Vertretern der Neo-Avantgarde – seinen Abschluss an der Hochschule für Angewandte Kunst im Fach Textil absolviert hatte. In den Sechzigern und Siebzigern schenkte die Kulturpolitik der Textilkunst keine allzu große Aufmerksamkeit, sodass sie zu einem wichtigen Experimentierfeld des freieren künstlerischen Ausdrucks werden konnte. Attalais in den Sechzigern angefertigten Filzplastiken brachen mit dem Paradigma der „angewandten Kunst". Sie waren autonome Werke, in denen er das Verhältnis von Material und Form, die „Eigengesetzlichkeit" des Textilmaterials untersuchte. Das Hard Edge, das er durch Reproduktionen und im Zuge seiner Reisen nach Westeuropa kennenlernte, bedeutete für den Künstler eine wichtige Quelle der Inspiration, doch weisen seine Installationen Ende der Sechziger (mit Luft beziehungsweise Wasser gefüllte Plastiktüten-Skulpturen wie *Air Work; Water Sculpture,* 1969) bereits auf den Konzeptualismus in seiner Kunst hin. Werke wie *Antagonistic Relations between the Time-Numbers and the Time-Names* (*Antagonistische Beziehungen zwischen Zeit-Nummern und Zeit-Namen,* 1972) untersuchen mit den untereinander, nebeneinander oder auch übereinander gedruckten Datumstempeln die philosophischen und bildtheoretischen Zusammenhänge von Raum und Zeit.

Die in der ersten Hälfte der Siebziger entstandenen, unter freiem Himmel installierten hängenden Gurtplastiken sind sowohl als ephemere Textilskulpturen wie auch als Land-Art-Arbeiten zu verstehen. Unter seinen mit Sand und Schnee ausgeführten Land-Art-Aktionen wurde *Negativer Stern* (1970–71) zu einem der emblematischsten Werke jener Zeit. Der am Budapester Donauufer aus dem Schnee ausgegrabene fünfzackige Stern beleuchtete – neben seinen politischen Konnotationen – die Möglichkeiten einer Ausweitung der geometrischen abstrakten Malerei.

Seine Aktionen im engen Freundeskreis können auch als Body Art gedeutet werden, doch meist fanden sie ausschließlich vor dem Fotoapparat statt. Attalais Aktionen (z. B. platzierte er eine Sacknadel zwischen Lid und Gesicht oder rasierte sich eine Warze ab) spiegeln die Einflüsse des Wiener Aktionismus wider. Sein Ziel war dabei allerdings nicht die Überschreitung von Grenzen. In diesen Aktionen, wie beispielsweise in seiner Serie *Idiotic Manner* (*Idiotisches Verhalten*, 1973) ist die ironische Selbstreflexion ausschlaggebend, mit der er auf seine eigene Situation, auf das eingeschränkte Dasein als osteuropäischer Künstler verweist.

In the first place, the artistic career of Gábor Attalai should be understood and evaluated in the international context with which he established contact in the absence of progressive artistic institutions. As he himself said, he lived in Hungary, but "worked towards the outside." Attalai's particular position was also determined by the fact that, in contrast to most members of the neo-avant-garde generation, he'd graduated from the Textile Department of the University of Applied Arts. In the sixties and seventies, the area of textile art did not attract much attention on the part of cultural politics, which is why it was able to become an important field for a freer and more experimental artistic expression. Attalai's felt-tip works of the sixties also broke with the paradigm of "applied art." These were autonomous works in which the artist examined the connection between material and form, questioning the "autonomous" character of textiles. Hard edge painting was an important source of inspiration for the artist, which he'd encountered through reproductions and subsequently in the course of his travels in Western Europe, but the installations he made at the end of the sixties (plastic bag statues filled with air or water, such as *Air Work* and *Water Sculpture,* 1969) already marked the appearance of conceptualism in his work. With date stamps underneath, next to, or above one other, his *Antagonistic Relations between the Time-Numbers and the Time-Names* (1972) examined the philosophical and art theoretical connections between space and time.

The sculptural works made from straps and installed in public space in the first half of the seventies can be interpreted both as ephemeral textile sculptures and examples of land art. Among his land art actions made with sand and snow is *Negative Star* (1970–71), which became one of the most emblematic works of the period. Along with its political connotations, the five-pointed star dug out of snow on the banks of the Danube in Budapest also examined the possibilities of the expansion of geometric abstract painting.

His actions, which he carried out for a close circle of friends, or more frequently realized in front of the camera, can also be understood as body art. While his actions (for example, placing a sack-sewing needle between his eyelids and his face, shaving off a wart) reflect the influence of Viennese Actionism, the aim of these gestures was not to stretch boundaries. In these works and in the series *Idiotic Manner* (1973), ironic self-reflection plays the main role, pointing to his own situation and the limits of his existence as an Eastern European artist.

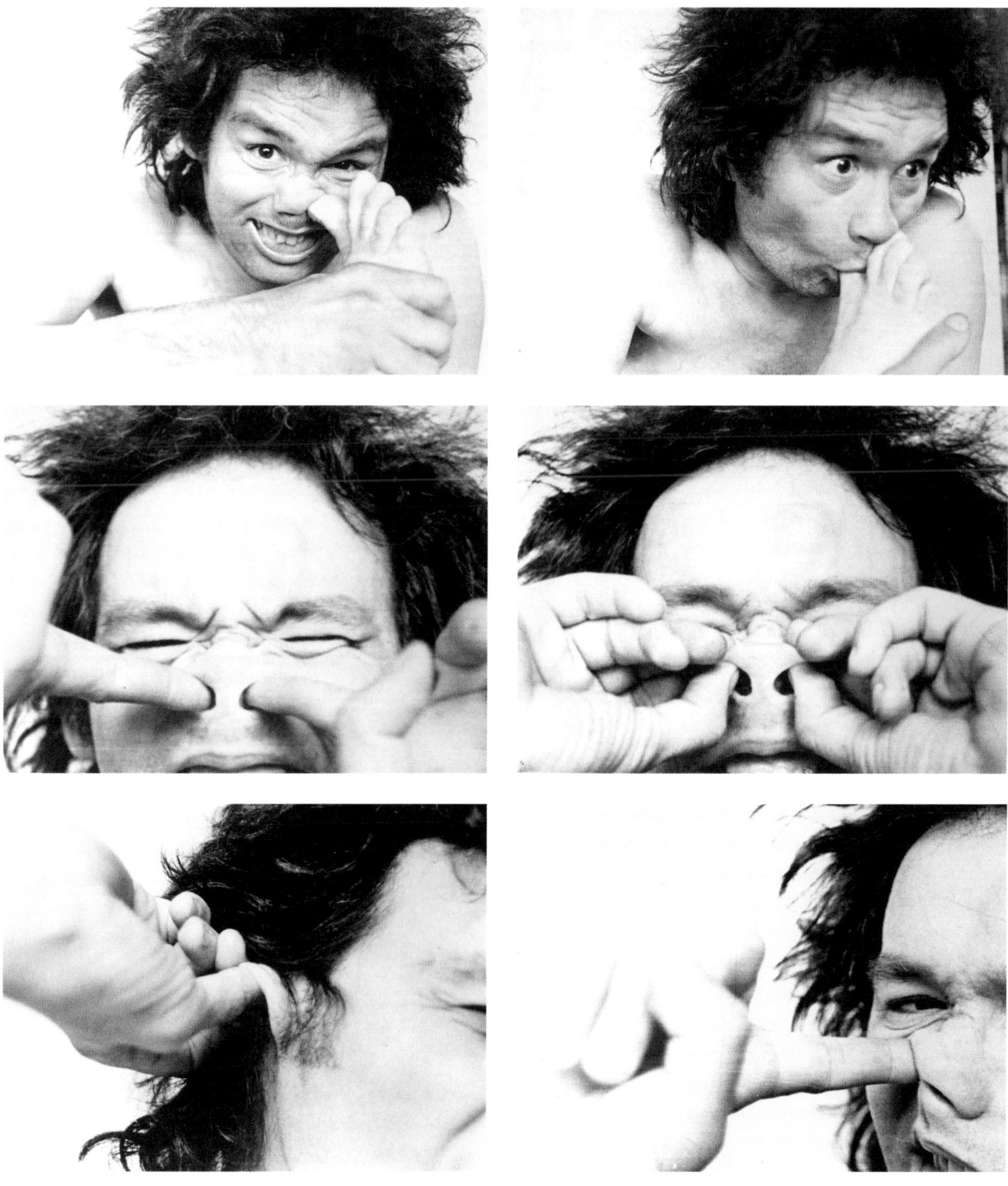

Idiotic Manner I–VI, (Idiotisches Verhalten I–VI), 1973

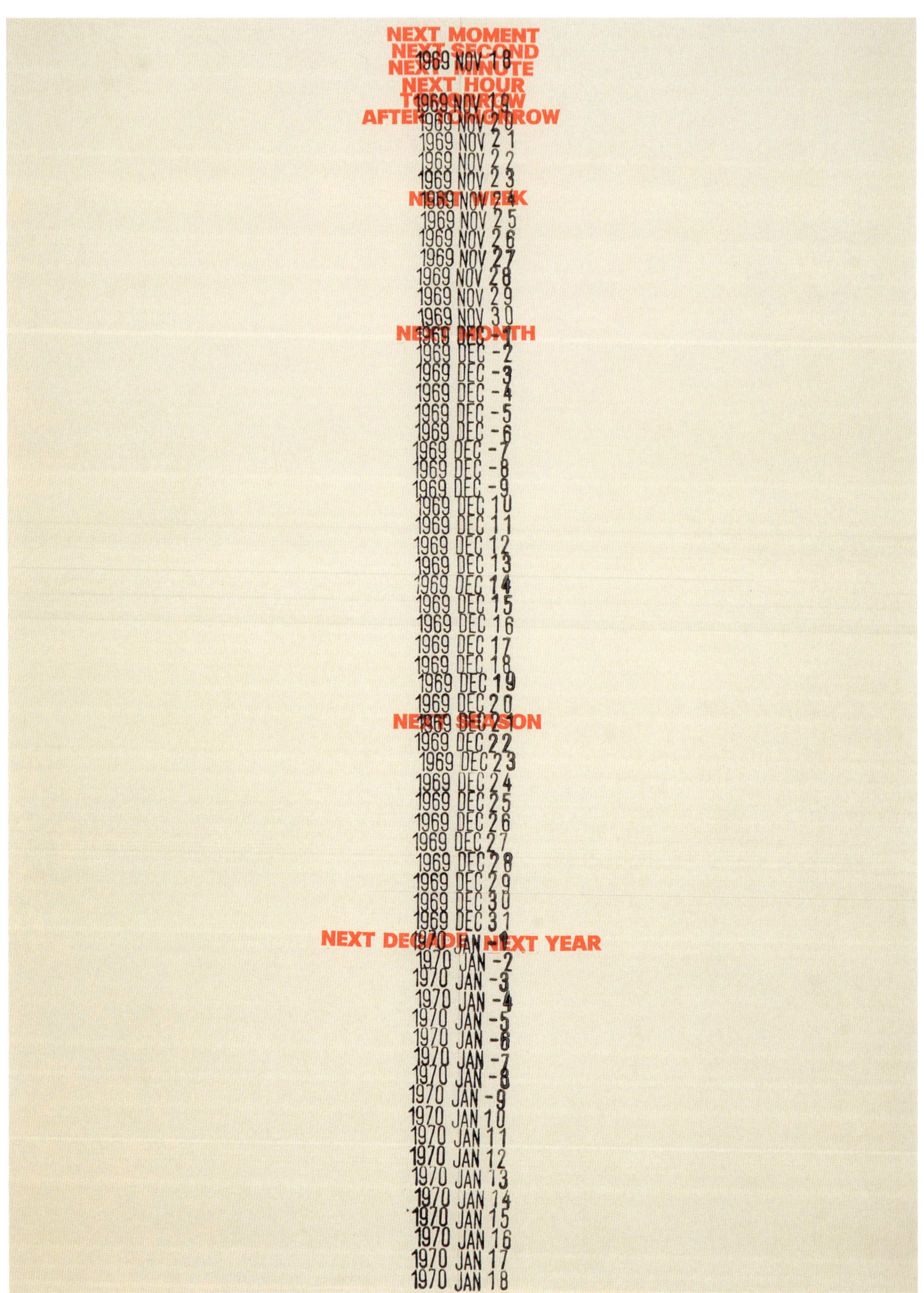
NEXT MOMENT
NEXT SECOND
1969 NOV 18
NEXT MINUTE
NEXT HOUR
TOMORROW
1969 NOV 19
AFTER TOMORROW
1969 NOV 20
1969 NOV 21
1969 NOV 22
1969 NOV 23
NEXT WEEK
1969 NOV 24
1969 NOV 25
1969 NOV 26
1969 NOV 27
1969 NOV 28
1969 NOV 29
1969 NOV 30
NEXT MONTH
1969 DEC -1
1969 DEC -2
1969 DEC -3
1969 DEC -4
1969 DEC -5
1969 DEC -6
1969 DEC -7
1969 DEC -8
1969 DEC -9
1969 DEC 10
1969 DEC 11
1969 DEC 12
1969 DEC 13
1969 DEC 14
1969 DEC 15
1969 DEC 16
1969 DEC 17
1969 DEC 18
1969 DEC 19
1969 DEC 20
NEXT SEASON
1969 DEC 21
1969 DEC 22
1969 DEC 23
1969 DEC 24
1969 DEC 25
1969 DEC 26
1969 DEC 27
1969 DEC 28
1969 DEC 29
1969 DEC 30
1969 DEC 31
NEXT DECADE
NEXT YEAR
1970 JAN -1
1970 JAN -2
1970 JAN -3
1970 JAN -4
1970 JAN -5
1970 JAN -6
1970 JAN -7
1970 JAN -8
1970 JAN -9
1970 JAN 10
1970 JAN 11
1970 JAN 12
1970 JAN 13
1970 JAN 14
1970 JAN 15
1970 JAN 16
1970 JAN 17
1970 JAN 18

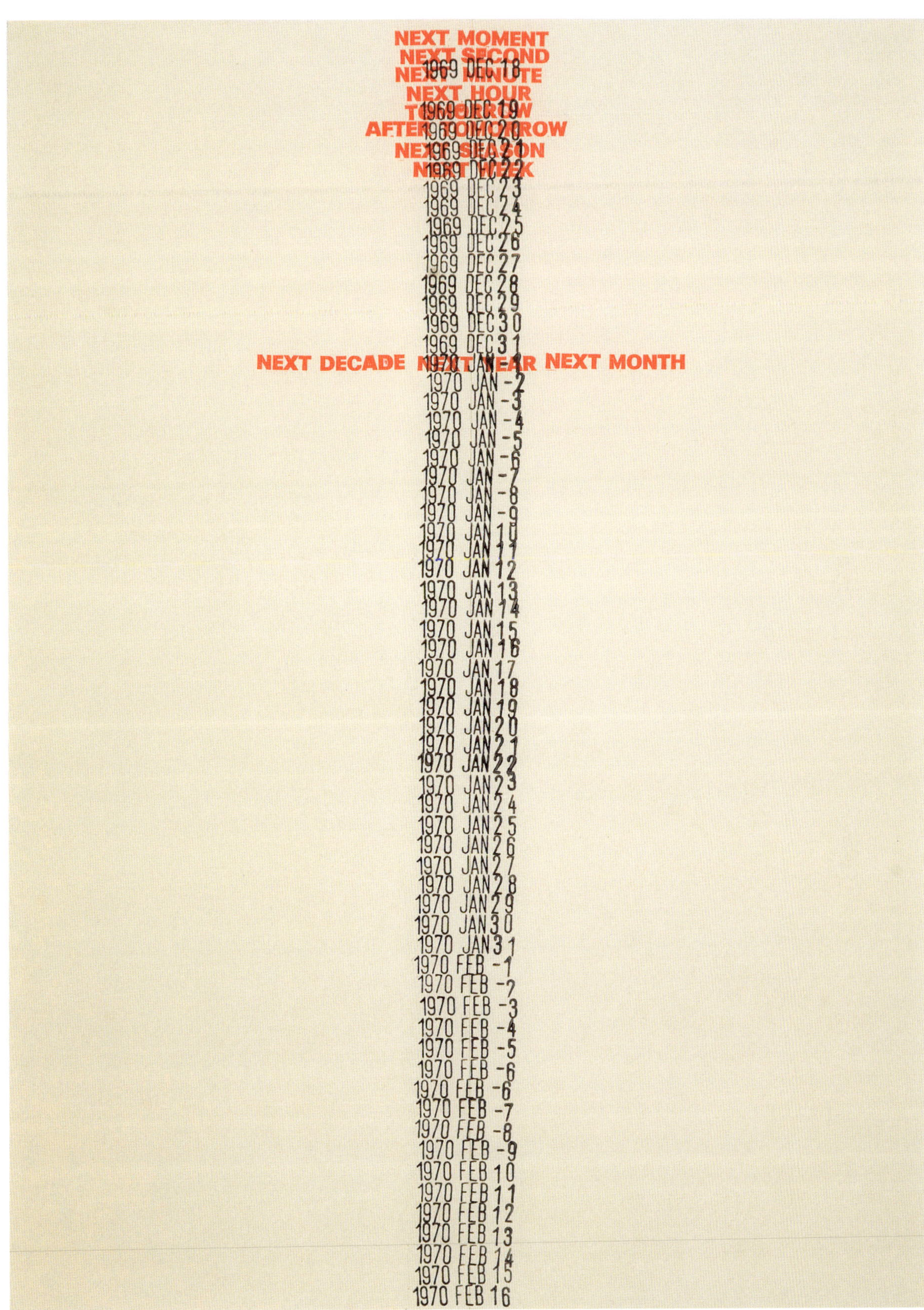

Antagonistic Relations between the Time-Numbers and the Time-Names I–II.
(Antagonistische Beziehungen zwischen Zeit-Nummern und Zeit-Namen) I–II., 1972

Imre BAK

Budapest, 1939

Imre Bak gehörte zu jener Zeit zu den engagiertesten Protagonisten der Abstraktion, als der „gegenstandslosen" Kunst die stärkste Ablehnung zuteilwurde. Als Mitglied des Freundeskreises, der später unter dem Namen „Zuglóer Kreis" bekannt wurde, beschäftigte ihn in erster Linie die Kunst der École de Paris. Ein wichtiger Orientierungspunkt war für ihn aber auch die ungarische künstlerische Tradition der Avantgarde, die in den Fünfziger- und Sechzigerjahren an die Peripherie gedrängt worden war.

Bak entdeckte für sich die Kunst des amerikanischen Hard Edge und der deutschen Neuen Abstraktion in der Stuttgarter Galerie Müller. Persönlich machte er unter anderem mit Karl Pfahler Bekanntschaft, eine Begegnung, die zu einem Wendepunkt in seiner Kunst führte. Die organische, gewebeartige Oberfläche seiner früheren Gemälde wurde durch genau passende, mit scharfen Konturen abgegrenzte Formkonstruktionen abgelöst. 1965 entstanden im Herzen der einst so bewunderten Pariser Schule, in einer Pariser Mansardenwohnung, seine ersten Hard-Edge-Bilder. Zeitgleich mit der ersten IPARTERV-Ausstellung im Jahr 1968 fand seine erste bedeutende Einzelausstellung (gemeinsam mit István Nádler) in der Galerie Müller statt.

In seiner Serie *Streifen* (1968–69) läuft das weiße oder helle Feld aus der „Umarmung" der zuweilen unterbrochenen Farbstreifen ins Nichts. Eine noch radikalere Ausweitung des Bildfeldes bedeutete die Verwendung der Shaped canvas (der „geformten Leinwand") in seinem Werk. Seine friesartige Serie *Fényes* (*Glänzend,* 1970) zeigte er im Adolf Fényes Saal (der Nachname des ungarischen Malers bedeutet „glänzend", auf ihn verweist der Titel). Hier fanden die von der offiziellen Kulturpolitik nicht unterstützten Künstler und ihre experimentellen Bestrebungen ein Forum. Bei den 1971 im Essener Museum Folkwang gezeigten Werke verschwanden die Farben bereits vollkommen und überließen ihren Platz der Konstruktion. Das Bild überschritt seine eigenen Grenzen und wurde zum Gegenstand, zum Objekt im Raum.

Während Bak sich als Mitglied der Budapester Werkstatt gemeinsam mit János Fajó und István Nádler für die Popularisierung der geometrischen abstrakten Kunst engagierte, begann er sich um 1972 in einer Serie konzeptueller Werke mit den Zusammenhängen und Widersprüchen von bildlicher Form und sprachlichem Ausdruck zu beschäftigen. Zur Malerei kehrte er in der zweiten Hälfte der Siebziger zurück und setzte seine früheren strukturellen Experimente fort. Sein semiotisches Interesse führte ihn zur Neuentdeckung des Symbolsystems der Volkskultur. Eines der emblematischsten Werke dieser Epoche ist *Kreis-Kreuz* (1979), in dem die Symbole – fast losgelöst von ihrer Bedeutung, für sich stehend – zu geometrisch-plastischen Formen werden.

Imre Bak was one of the most committed protagonists of abstraction at a time when "non-objective" art was the target of the sharpest denunciation. As a member of the group of friends that later became known by the name "Zugló Circle," he was first drawn to the art of the École de Paris. Another important reference point for him was the artistic tradition of the Hungarian avant-garde, which was forced to the periphery in the fifties and sixties.

It was in the Galerie Müller in Stuttgart that Bak discovered for himself the art of American hard edge and new German abstraction. He also got to know certain artists personally, among them Karl Pfahler, and the meeting proved to be a turning point in his art. Bak replaced the web-like surfaces and organic character of his early paintings with precisely composed formal structures and sharply defined contours. It was in 1965, in the heartland of the Paris School that he had previously so admired, in a Parisian attic, that he was to make his first hard edge paintings. In 1968, contemporaneously with the first IPARTERV exhibition, he had his first important solo show (together with István Nádler) at Galerie Müller.

Bak's series *Stripes* (1968–69) breaks away from the embrace of colored stripes, while the white or light field runs off into nothingness. The appearance of the shaped canvas brought a still more radical expansion of the visual field to his work. The frieze-like series *Fényes* (*Splendid,* 1970) borrowed its name from the Fényes Adolf Hall in which it was shown, an exhibition space that provided a forum for experimental endeavors and those artists not supported by official cultural politics. In the works he showed at the Folkwang Museum in Essen (1971), colors had already completely disappeared and given way to structure. Painting exceeded its own borders and became an entity unto itself, a spatial object.

While a member of the Budapest Workshop with János Fajó and Nádler, Bak supported the popularization of geometric abstract art, and around 1972 he began, in a series of conceptual works, to investigate the connections and contradictions between visual form and linguistic expression. In the second half of the seventies he returned to painting, continuing the structural experimentation he'd begun in his earlier paintings. His interest in semiotics led him to rediscover the symbolic order of folk culture. One of the most emblematic works of this period is his painting *Circle-Cross* (1979), in which symbols, completely separated from their meanings, become self-sufficient geometric-plastic forms.

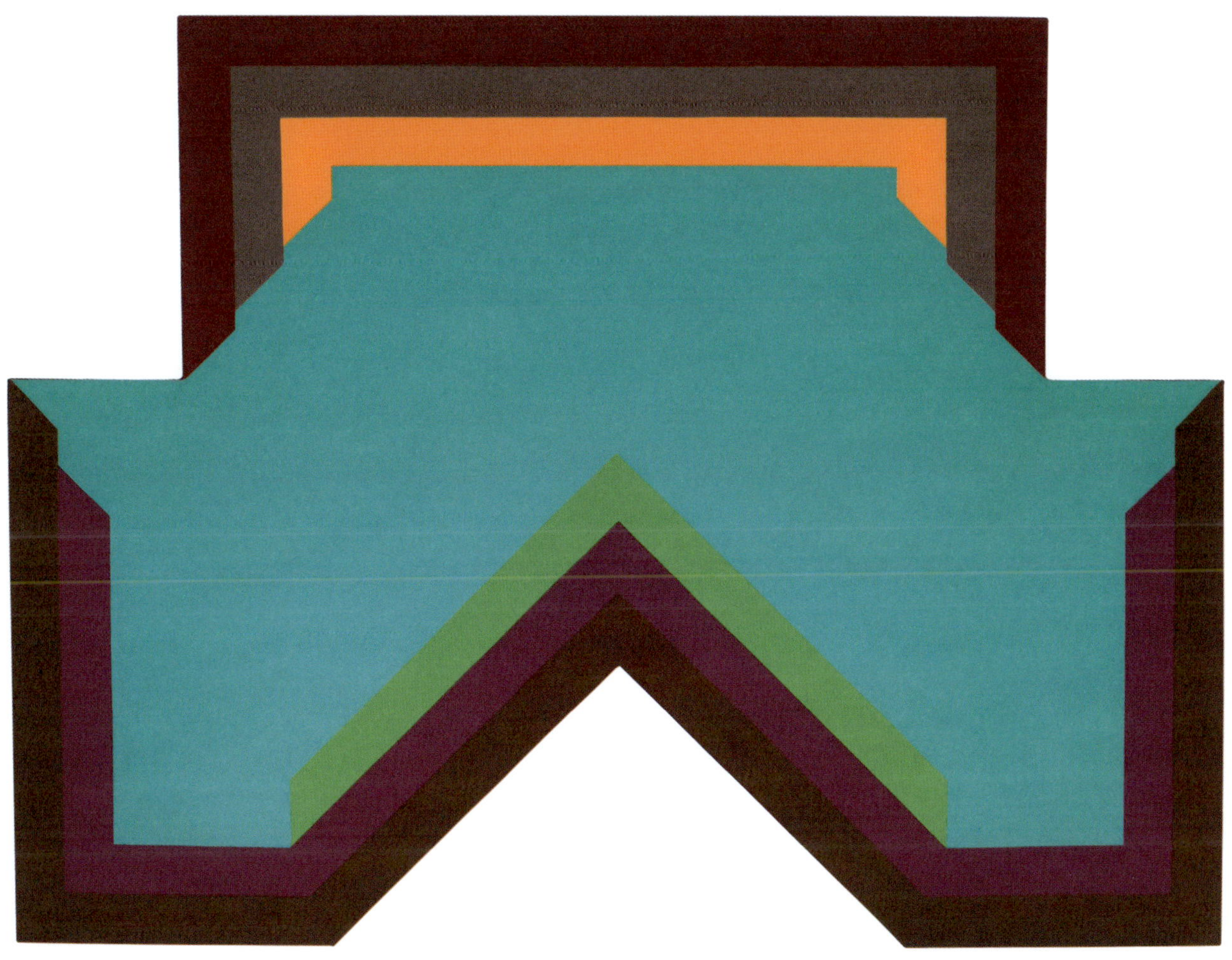

Fényes IV (Glänzend IV / Splendid IV), 1970

LANDSCAPE OBJECT

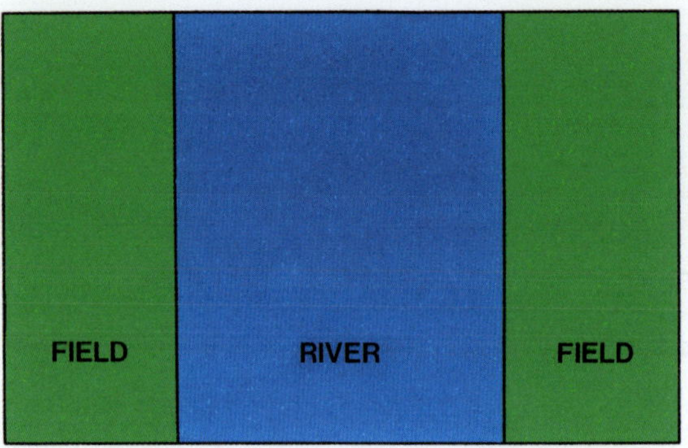

Landscape Object (Landschaftsobjekt), 1973

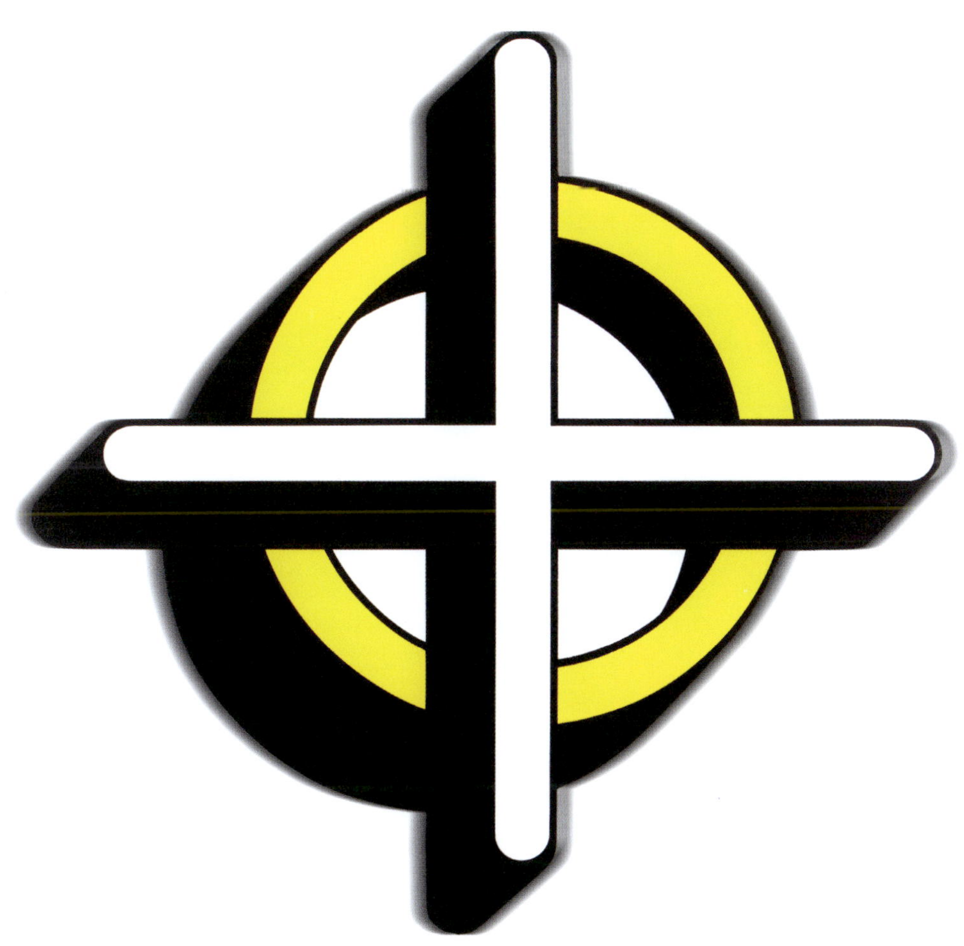

Kreis-Kreuz / Circle-Cross, 1979

Miklós ERDÉLY

Budapest, 1928 – Budapest, 1986

Miklós Erdély gehört zu den einflussreichsten Künstlern der ungarischen Neo-Avantgarde. Mit seinen theoretischen Schriften und kunstpädagogischen Tätigkeiten hat er großen Einfluss auf seine Zeitgenossen und jüngere Generationen ungarischer Künstler ausgeübt. Bis heute gilt er als wichtiger Bezugspunkt für die zeitgenössische Kunst.

Bereits seine Studien dokumentieren seine weitverzweigten Interessen: Zunächst studierte er Bildhauerei, später Architektur, auch für den Studienzweig Filmregie wurde er zugelassen (doch konnte er sein Studium dort nicht aufnehmen). Als Künstler hat er zahlreiche Gattungen bedient (und sowohl als Lyriker wie auch als Schriftsteller und Regisseur ein bedeutendes Lebenswerk hinterlassen). Ebenso interessierten ihn die neuen Ausdrucksmöglichkeiten der unterschiedlichsten Kunstrichtungen; in seinen Werken unternahm er den Versuch, wissenschaftliches Denken und Kunst miteinander zu verknüpfen, und nutzte seine Arbeiten häufig zur Veranschaulichung theoretischer, wissenschaftlicher, gesellschaftlicher und kunstphilosophischer Fragen.

1970 stellte er bei der sogenannten R-Ausstellung, der größten Ausstellung der ungarischen Neo-Avantgarde, sein Objekt *Der Schnee vom vergangenen Jahr* vor. In einer ramponierten Thermoskanne befand sich – wie Erdély behauptete – tatsächlich Schnee vom Vorjahr, den er in seinem Kühlschrank aufbewahrt hatte. Mit seiner Anspielung auf Villon („Wo ist der Schnee vom vergangenen Jahr?") baut dieses poetische Readymade jedoch auf die Assoziationskraft des Betrachters, denn der Inhalt der Thermoskanne ist nicht sichtbar, nur der Titel belegt, was sie in sich birgt. Als ebenfalls poetisches Werk gilt seine Serie *Metapher* (um 1972), die – wie der Kunsthistoriker László Beke formuliert – „auf das sehr schwer greifbare, nebulöse, geheimnisvolle und poetische Intervall abzielt, das die Spannung zwischen der metaphorischen Situation und der wortwörtlichen Deutung desselben Wortes darstellt".

Obwohl Erdély in der zweiten Hälfte der Sechziger durch Tamás Szentjóby und Gábor Altorjay ebenfalls mit Happenings und Fluxus in Berührung kam, vermied er es, laut Beke, seine Aktionen „Gattungen zuzuordnen". Bei seiner *Abendaktion* (um 1971/72) bepinselte der auf der Leiter stehende Künstler eine Glühbirne mit weißer Farbe, deren Licht im Verlauf dieser künstlerischen Aktion immer schwächer wurde.

Erdély beschäftigte sich in zahlreichen theoretischen Texten mit der Natur von Zeit. Im Möbiusband fand er jene „demonstrative Darstellung", die ihm in vielen Werken, die sich mit Zeit beschäftigten, als Ausgangspunkt diente. In der aus fünf Teilen bestehenden *Zeitreise* (um 1976) sowie in *Zeitklammer 1955–1972* (Mitte, zweite Hälfte der Siebziger) verweist er mit der Montage von eigenen Fotografien aus verschiedenen Lebensjahren auf die in sich selbst zurückkehrende Natur von Zeit.

Miklós Erdély is one of the most significant figures of the Hungarian neo-avant-garde. Through his theoretical writings and art educational activities, he exerted a major influence not only on his contemporaries, but also on the younger generations of Hungarian artists; today, he can still be regarded as an important point of reference for contemporary art.

His studies already demonstrated his interdisciplinary interests: in the beginning he studied sculpture; he followed this with architecture, and was subsequently accepted to the film-directing department (although he was not able to begin his studies). He created work in numerous artistic genres, leaving behind a significant legacy as poet, writer, and film director, and was interested in new possibilities for expression offered by various artistic fields. Erdély attempted to connect scientific thought and art through his work. He often used his art to consider the theoretical, scientific, social, and art philosophical questions that preoccupied him.

In 1970, at the so-called "R" exhibition, the largest-scale exhibition of the Hungarian neo-avant-garde in the period, he showed an object titled *Last Year's Snow*. The battered thermos flask – according to Erdély – really did contain the snow of the previous year, which he had kept in the freezer. Referring to Villon ("But where is last year's snow?"), this poetic ready-made hinged, however, on the viewer's associations, since the contents of the thermos flask were not visible, and only the title indicated what was hidden within. His *Metaphor* series (around 1972) was also a poetic work; art historian László Beke described it as "directed towards the very hard to grasp, obscure, secretive, and poetic gap that opens up between the metaphorical situation and its literal interpretation."

Although in the second half of the sixties, alongside Tamás Szentjóby and Gábor Altorjay, Erdély also came into contact with happenings and Fluxus actions, as Beke states, "he tried not to attribute to them the status of artistic genres." In the course of the *Evening Action* (around 1971–72), the artist stood on a ladder and painted a light bulb with white paint, which became darker as a result of the artist's intervention.

Erdély dealt in numerous theoretical writings with the nature of time. In the Möbius strip he found an "illustrative diagram" which was to become the starting point for numerous works examining time. Both *Time Travel* (around 1976), which was made up of five parts, and *Time Bracket 1955–1972* (mid-/second half of the seventies) are based on a montage of photographs from different periods of his own life; they point to the nature of time turning back on itself.

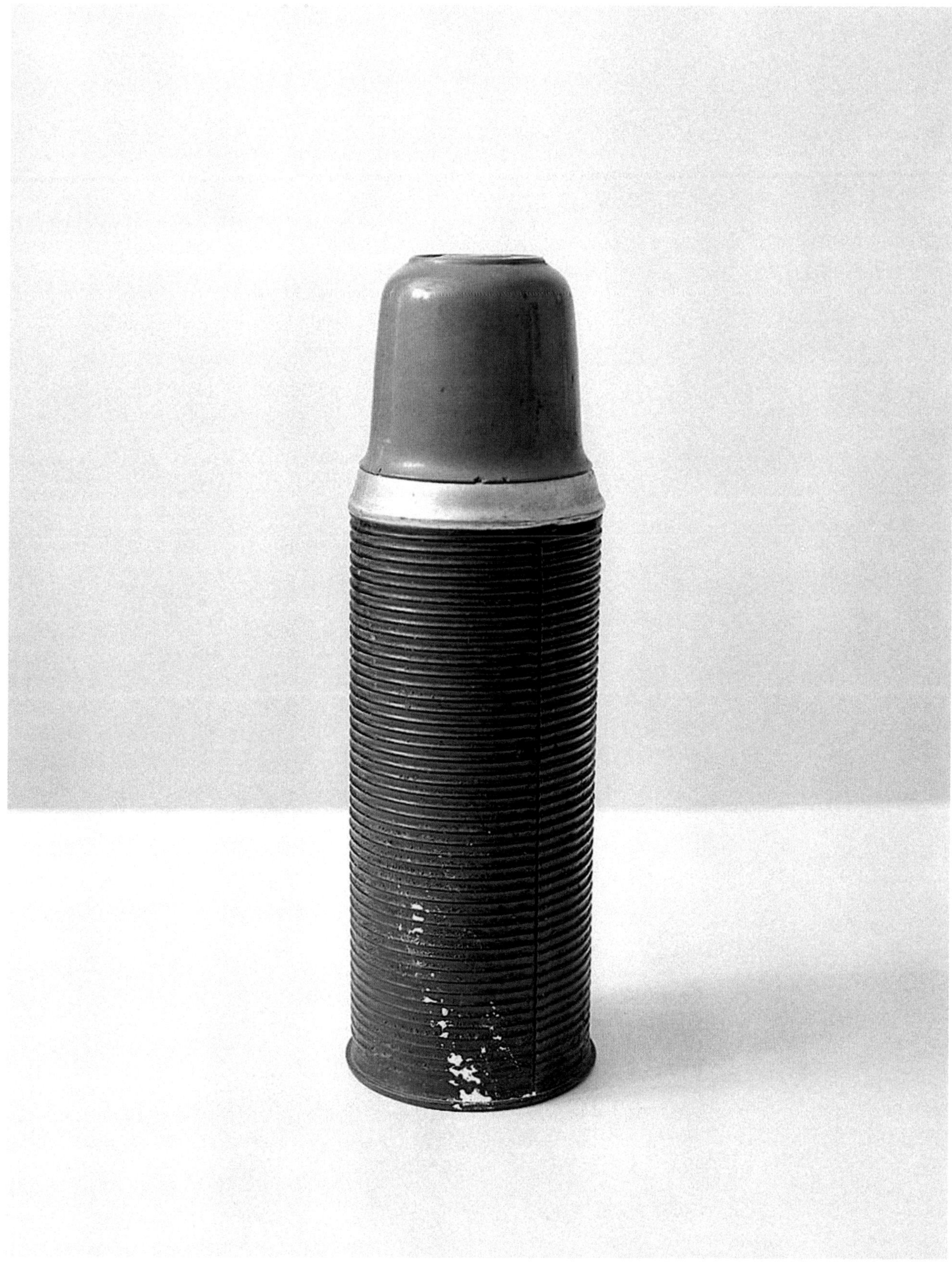

Der Schnee vom vergangenen Jahr / Last Year's Snow, 1970

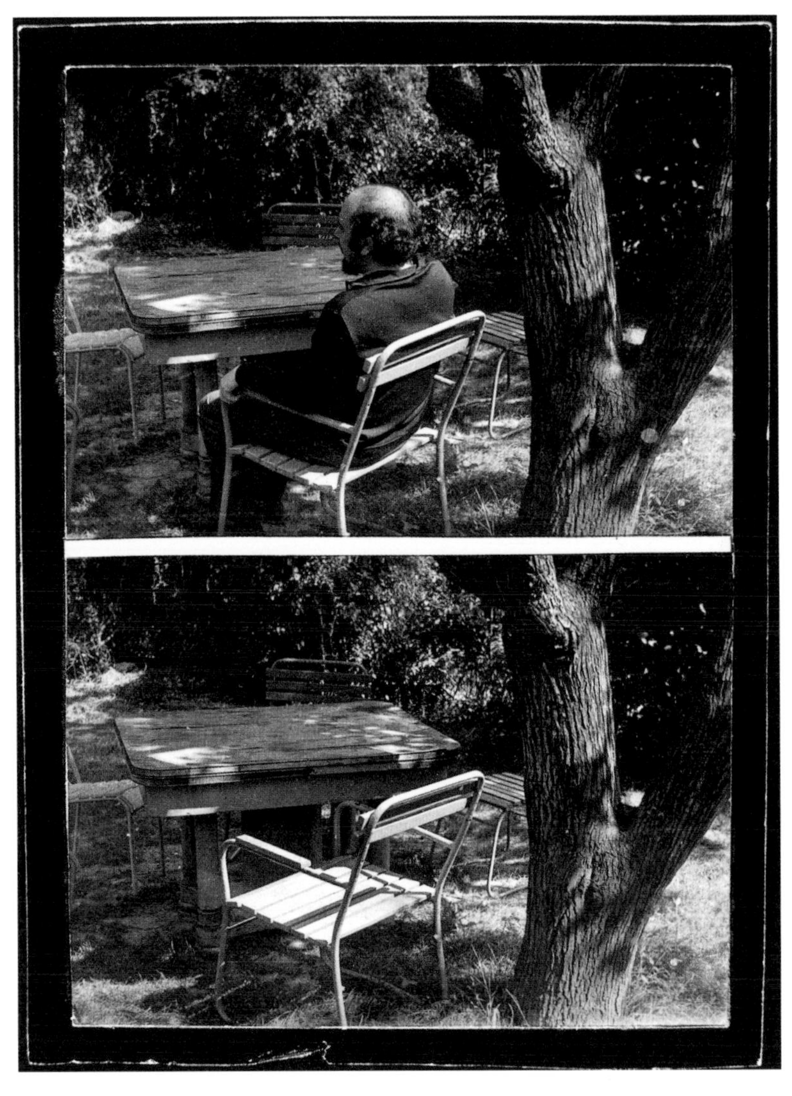

Metapher I / Metaphor I, 1972

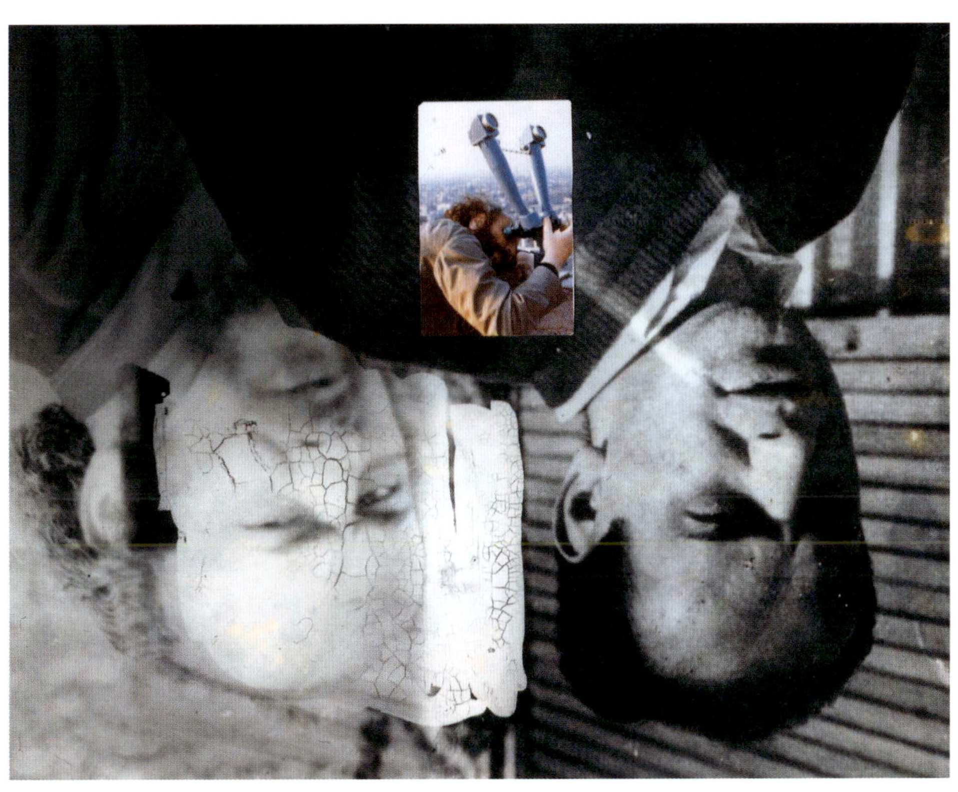

 Zeitklammer 1955–1972 / Time Bracket 1955–1972, Mitte, zweite Hälfte der Siebziger / Mid-/ second half of the Seventies

Tibor HAJAS

Budapest, 1946 – Szeged, 1980

„Tibor Hajas galt bereits vor seinem tödlichen Autounfall 1980 als mythische Gestalt der ungarischen Avantgarde." So die Worte des Kunsttheoretikers Péter György im Jahr 1989, fast zehn Jahre nach dem Tod des Künstlers. Mythenbildung, schreibt er ferner, wurde zur Grundsatzfrage in Hajas' Leben und Wirken. „Retten, konservieren, am Leben halten ... Glücklich ist der, der bereits zu Lebzeiten zum Mythos wird ...", befand er.

Hajas begann als Lyriker, und die Literatur sollte seine Karriere bis zum Ende bestimmen. Das Studium der Philologie musste er aufgrund seiner Verhaftung und einer Gefängnisstrafe von mehr als einem Jahr unterbrechen. In einem Schauprozess wurde der junge Dichter wegen seiner „systemfeindlichen" Gedichte und Einstellung verurteilt. Nach seiner Entlassung im Jahr 1967 erschienen seine ersten Gedichte, und ab Ende der Sechziger begann er sich auch mit der bildenden Kunst zu beschäftigen. Eines der herausragenden Beispiele seiner frühen, im Geist des Konzeptualismus entstandenen Arbeiten ist die Serie *Ergänzungen* (1974–76), in der er unvollständige Gegenstände mit entsprechenden Foto-Ausschnitten ergänzte. Das Werk reflektiert mit der Gleichsetzung von Gegenstand und Bild auch Hajas' fototheoretische Vorstellungen („das Foto ist ein Zitat der Wirklichkeit"). Ab Mitte der Siebziger wandte er sich dem Film als Medium zu. Seine Arbeit *Selbstmodenschau* (die er gemeinsam mit János Vető und Gábor Dobos 1976 im Béla Balázs Studio drehte) weist auf die Verletzbarkeit und Manipulierbarkeit des einfachen Menschen hin und thematisiert die eigene Verantwortung hinsichtlich der Manipulation von Künstler und Medium. Seine Videos, die er mit Udo Kier drehte, gehören zu den frühesten Experimenten ungarischer Videokunst.

Bei seinen ab Mitte der Siebziger gezeigten Performances stellte er – ähnlich wie die Künstler des Wiener Aktionismus – die Verletzbarkeit des eigenen Körpers in den Mittelpunkt. In diesen Performances, in denen er die Grenze zwischen Leben und Tod auf der Basis seiner eigenen Qualen untersucht, ist auch der Einfluss des tibetanischen Mystizismus spürbar. Ab 1978 organisierte er mit János Vető Foto-Performances. Die Fotos dieser Aktionen, die ohne Publikum, also nur für die Kamera stattfanden, ordnete er zu Tableaus an, kaschierte sie auf Leinwand und zeigte sie als Tafelbild. In *Fleischgemälde I–III* (1978) wird der nackte Körper des Künstlers in der Berührung mit Farbe und Leinwand gleichzeitig zum darstellenden Mittel und zur gemalten Ikone.

"In 1980, following a car crash, Tibor Hajas, who was already a mythical figure in the history of the Hungarian avant-garde, passed away." Art theorist Péter György wrote these words in 1989, almost ten years after Hajas's death. As he notes, the question of myth is a key aspect to Hajas's life and activities, particularly as Hajas himself believed that it "saves, conserves, keeps alive... He who during his lifetime moves into myth is fortunate, rescued..."

Hajas began as a poet, and literature continued to remain a defining factor throughout his career. His arrest and imprisonment for more than a year caused him to cut short his humanities studies: in a show trial, the young poet was condemned for his "anti-system" verses and behavior. After his release, his first poems were published in 1967. From the end of the sixties, however, he also began working in the visual arts. One of the most prominent examples of his early works made in the spirit of conceptualism was the series *Restorations* (1974–76), in which missing objects are completed with photos of details of them. The work reflects Hajas's conception of photographic theory ("the photo: quote from reality"), according to which the object and the photo made of it are identical. From the middle of the 1970s he began to use film as a medium. His *Self-Fashion Show* (shot in 1976 at the Balázs Béla Studio together with János Vető and Gábor Dobos) revealed and reflected upon the frailty and manipulability of the average person and reckoned with his own responsibility regarding the artist's and the medium's manipulations. His videos, which were shot with Udo Kier, belong to the earliest experiments of Hungarian video art.

In his performances from the mid-'70s, he placed the vulnerability of his own body at the center of attention, similarly to Viennese actionism. The influence of Tibetan mysticism can also be felt in these performances, in which the borderline between life and death is mapped out through his own torments. From 1978 on, he made photo-performances together with János Vető. Photos of these performances, which were conceived for the camera alone and with no audience present, were organized into photo-boards, mounted onto canvas, and presented as panels. In his *Flesh Paintings I–III* (1978), the artist's naked body is smeared with paint and applied to the canvas, becoming itself a vehicle for depiction and at the same time a painted icon.

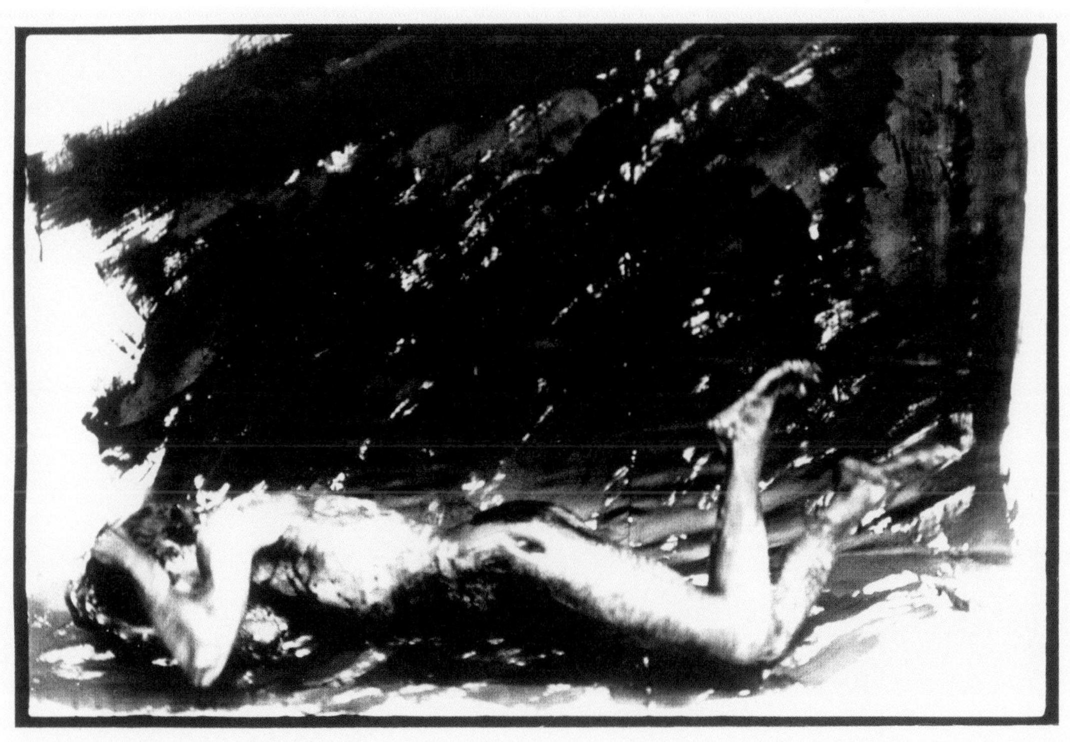

Fleischgemälde II / Flesh Painting II, 1978

Károly HALÁSZ

Paks, 1946

Károly Halász' Laufbahn begann an den verlassenen Ufern der Donau bei Paks und führte ihn später in die mediterrane Universitätsstadt Pécs. Das dortige künstlerische Umfeld inspirierte ihn sehr: als Mitglied der Pécser Werkstatt reifte er zum Künstler heran. Wie die übrigen Vertreter der Gruppe (Ferenc Ficzek, Károly Kismányoky, Sándor Pinczehelyi und Kálmán Szijártó) fühlte auch er sich zunächst von der geometrischen Abstraktion angezogen. Obwohl die Abstraktion seine künstlerische Praxis bis heute bestimmt, wandte sich Halász in der neo-avantgardistischen Atmosphäre der Siebziger gemeinsam mit anderen Mitgliedern der Gruppe ebenfalls der Konzept- und Aktionskunst sowie der Land Art, zu. Neben Land-Art-Aktionen mit der Pécser Werkstatt, führte er zur selben Zeit Licht- und Fotoexperimente durch, drehte experimentelle Filme, machte Body-Art-Aktionen und fertigte Videoarbeiten an.

Seine Museum-Serie entstand aus dem Gefühl des Mangels heraus, den ungarische und den Ländern des einstigen Ostblocks angehörende neo-avantgardistische Künstler empfanden, da die Kunst, die sie für wesentlich hielten, in den Museen und in großen, staatlichen Ausstellungen nicht gezeigt wurden. Halász wurde also selbst zum „Museumsgründer". Als sein eigenes „Archiv" verwendete er bei der Einrichtung seines *Mini-Museums* (1972) allerdings Einmachgläser, die Fragen nach der Bewahrung von Werten und damit nach der Konservierung des eigenen Werkees sowie künstlerischer Erinnerungen aufwarfen. So zum Beispiel die sein Leben verändernde documenta 5 in Kassel im Jahr 1972. Seine Einmachgläser stellte er auf unterschiedlichste Weise aus; im Garten des befreundeten Künstlers Brúnó Gellérs platzierte er sie im Rahmen einer Aktion auf einem großen Karton mit der Aufschrift „MUSEUM" (1973), aber es kam auch vor, dass die Einmachgläser an den für sie vorgesehenen Ort, auf eine Stellage (das Regal einer Speisekammer), gelangten (*Stellage-Museum*, 1972–75).

Das *Museum – Museum der Gegenwart und Zukunft I–II* (1977) ist, wie Halász sagt, „bereits das Erzeugnis schwerwiegender gesellschaftlicher Probleme und Erlebnisse". Die Kunst, genauer gesagt die Ampullen mit den Namen seiner Lieblingskünstler dienen auch als Heilmittel gegen die Hoffnungslosigkeit der Gegenwart und die Aussichtslosigkeit der Zukunft.

Károly Halász's path began on the forlorn banks of the Danube River in Paks and led him to the university city of Pécs and its Mediterranean atmosphere. The artistic scene of Pécs proved very inspiring for him: as a member of the Pécs Workshop, he became a mature artist. Similarly to the other members of the group (Ferenc Ficzek, Károly Kismányoky, Sándor Pinczehelyi, and Kálmán Szijártó), he was initially drawn towards geometric abstraction. And while abstraction has remained a defining factor of his artistic practice to this day, in the neo-avant-garde atmosphere of the seventies, Halász, together with the other members of the group, also turned to conceptual art, action art, and land art. In addition to the land art actions made collectively with the Pécs Workshop, during this time he also carried out light and photo experiments and made experimental films, body art actions, and video works.

Halász's *Museum* series was born from the feeling of lack Hungarian (and Eastern Bloc) neo-avant-garde artists experienced during the seventies due the fact that the art they considered to be relevant stood no chance of being accepted by museums or large state exhibition spaces. Halász therefore decided to become a "museum founder" in his own right. He used domestic pickling jars, however, to create his own "archive," which he called the *Mini-Museum* (1972). These jars raised questions concerning the preservation of values, including the conservation of his own works and artistic memories, for instance that of his life-changing experience of the 5th Kassel documenta in 1972. He exhibited these jars in numerous forms. Within the framework of an action, he placed them in the garden of an artist friend, Brúnó Gellér, in a paper box adorned with the word "MUSEUM" (1973), but there were also occasions when the jars found themselves in their ostensibly appropriate place, the *Stelázsi* (pantry shelves) (*Stelázsi-Museum*, 1972–75).

Museum – The Museum of Present and Future I–II (1977), as Halász puts it, "is the result of already serious social problems and experiences." Art – with transfusions named after Halász's favorite artists, to be precise – can be seen as a remedy for the current sense of hopelessness and lack of future perspectives.

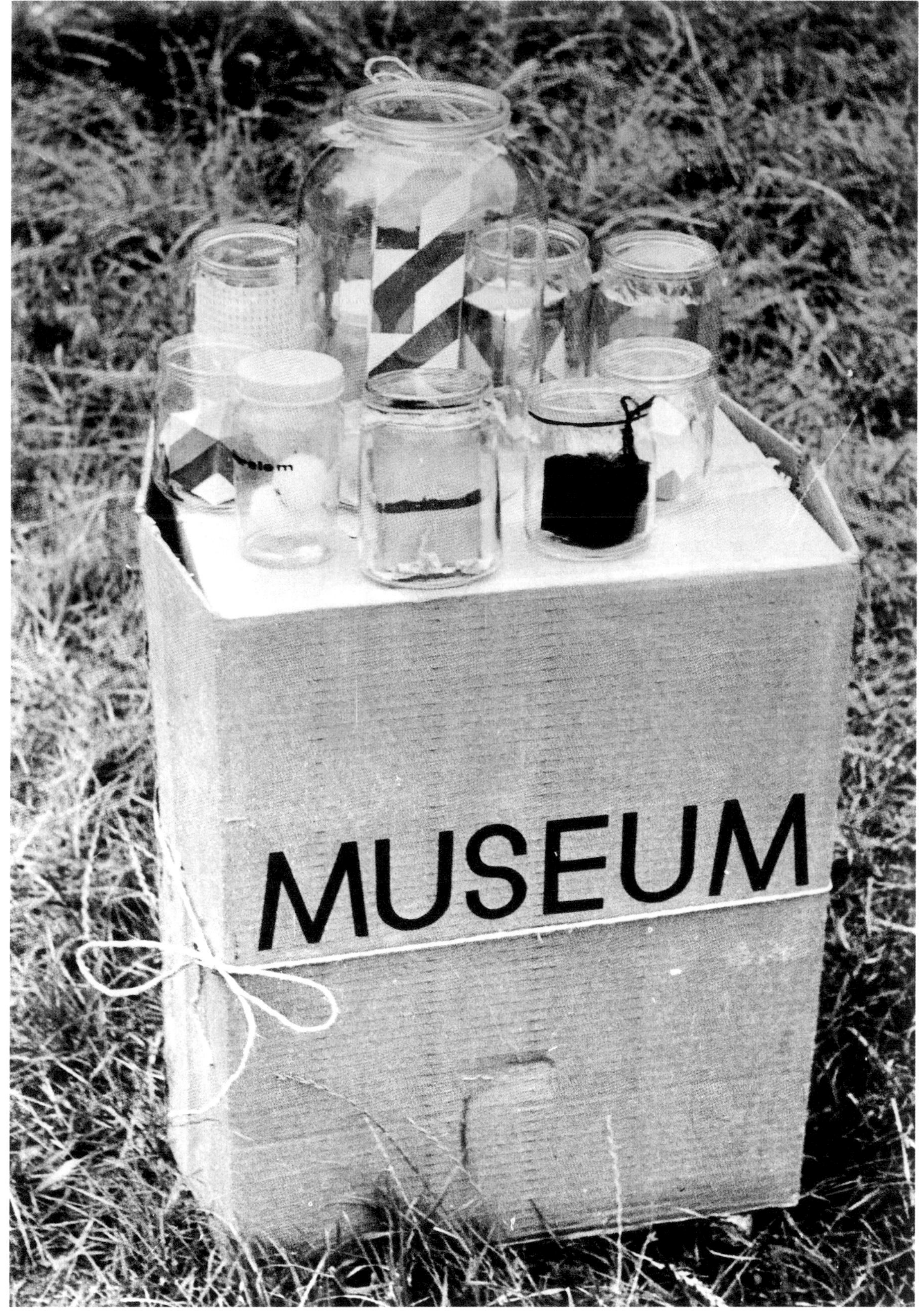

MUSEUM, **1973**

György JOVÁNOVICS

Budapest, 1939

Der Kunsthistoriker László Beke schrieb: György Jovánovics „schafft mithilfe anti-bildhauerischer Prinzipien eine klassische Bildhauerei, oder, was dasselbe bedeutet: eine Anti-Skulptur unter der Einbeziehung klassischer Prinzipien der Bildhauerei". Seine Werke brechen einerseits tatsächlich mit den herkömmlichen Regeln des Mediums, sowohl in Bezug auf Materialverwendung, perspektivische Komposition als auch hinsichtlich des ständigen Wechsels zwischen Zwei- zu Dreidimensionalität. Andererseits ist in seinen Arbeiten auch der fortlaufende Dialog mit den kunstgeschichtlichen Traditionen von großer Bedeutung.

Jovánovics studierte an der Budapester Akademie für Bildende Künste, später war er aber auch Gasthörer an der Akademie für Angewandte Kunst in Wien. Den stärksten Einfluss auf seine künstlerische Praxis hatte allerdings eine Studienreise nach Paris im Jahr 1965/66. Hier entdeckte er – unter anderem beeinflusst von Georges Segal – Gips als Material. Der Künstler, der des Modellierens überdrüssig geworden war, fand mit mechanisch angefertigten Gipsgüssen zu einer eigenen Stimme. Die aufgrund der Gusstechnik auch als „Tütenskulptur" bezeichnete, aus Teilen zusammengesetzte Plastik *Petit Polichinelle* (1966) ist das wichtigste Werk aus dieser Zeit. Bis zum Platzen volle „Tütengüsse" setzen sich zu einer Figur zusammen und erinnern in ihrer Trivialität an den Geist der Pop Art. Ebenfalls aus einzelnen Teilen fügt sich die Skulptur *Mensch* (1968) zu einem Ganzen und wurde im Rahmen der ersten IPARTERV-Ausstellung gezeigt. Auch in diesem Werk ersetzt die Technik des Gipsabdrucks den Realismus, statt der klassischen Materialien verleihen billiger Gips und ein echter Schal der im archaischen Kontrapost stehenden Figur ihre Gestalt. Das Lilienmotiv, welches das Gesicht und die Hände der Skulptur gleich einem Netz bedeckt, sowie die Figurengestaltung, anatomische Regeln außer Acht lassend, thematisieren die Frage nach der Austauschbarkeit von Draperie und menschlichem Körper.

Draperien werden im Werk des Künstlers von da an immer mehr zum zentralen Thema. So spielen sie auch in seinen Arbeiten, die er als Stipendiat des Museums Folkwang in Essen anfertigte, die Hauptrolle (*Großes Fenster*, 1971). In seinen Skulpturen und konzeptuellen Fotoarbeiten der Siebziger untersuchte Jovánovics das Verhältnis von Innen und Außen, Licht und Schatten sowie Zwei- und Dreidimensionalität. Das Relief *Vorhang zur Ekstatischen Marionette* (1979) ist ebenso ein Ergebnis dieser umfassenden Untersuchungen.

As art historian László Beke put it: György Jovánovics "brings into being classical sculpture with the help of an almost anti-sculptural principle, or, in what amounts to the same thing: he makes counter-sculpture using the principles of classical sculpture." On the one hand, his works really do break the traditional rules of the medium, both in their use of materials and in their composition for a single perspective, as well as in the constant play between the second and third dimensions. On the other hand, a continuous dialogue with art historical traditions is of crucial importance to his work.

Jovánovics began his studies at the Academy of Fine Arts in Budapest, after which he became a guest student at the Academy for Applied Arts in Vienna. It was a study trip to Paris in 1965–66, however, that brought about a significant change in his practice. Here, under the influence of George Segal and others, he discovered plaster as a material. The sculptor, who by this time had had enough of modeling, found his unique voice in mechanically produced plaster casts. In reference to the technique of pouring plaster that he used to create the piece, he called his most important work from the period *Petit Polichinelle* (1966) or "bag statue." He created the figure by joining together plastic bags filled to bursting; in its triviality, the work evokes the spirit of Pop Art. His statue *Man* (1968), which was shown in the first Iparterv exhibition, was also put together from parts. Once again, realism is replaced with the technique of plaster casting, and in place of classical materials, cheap plaster and a real scarf give form to the figure standing in an archaic contrapose. A lily motif entwines the statue's face and hands, while the figure's heaped form, which disregards anatomical rules, raises questions about the interchangeability of drapery and the human body.

From this point on, drapery appears more and more frequently as a central theme in Jovánovics's work. Drapery also played the main role in the works he showed as a grant recipient at the Folkwang Museum in Essen (*Big Window*, 1971). In his statues and conceptual photographic works from the seventies, the artist dealt with questions of outside and inside, light and shadow, the second and third dimensions. The relief *Fore-Curtain to the Ecstatic Marionette* (1979) is also the result of this profound contemplation.

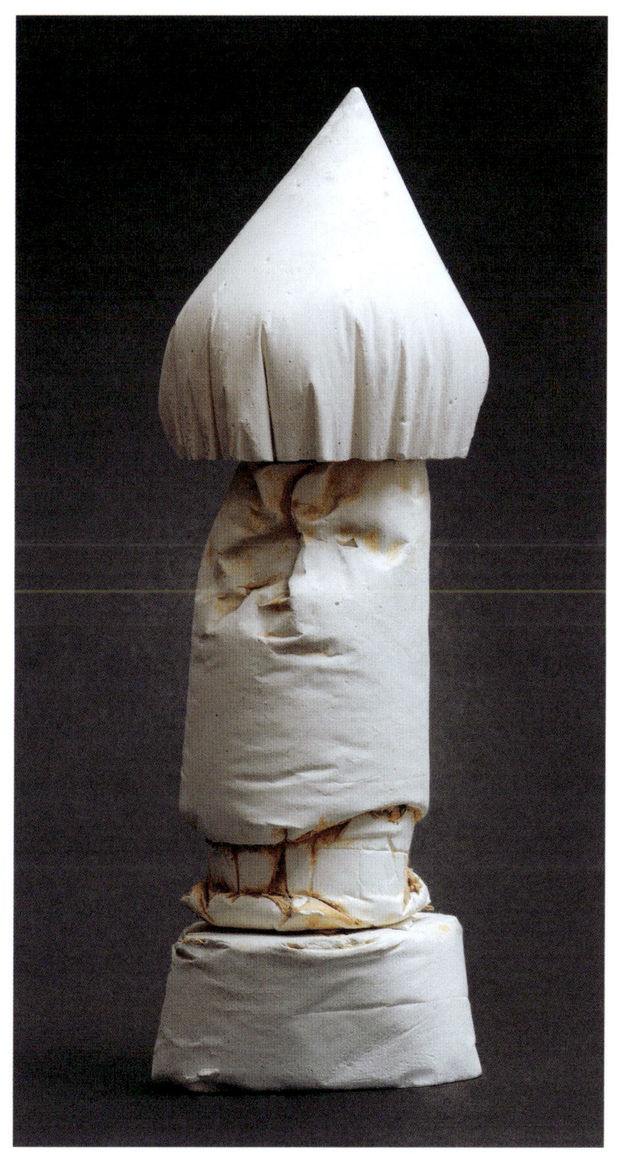

Petit Polichinelle, 1966

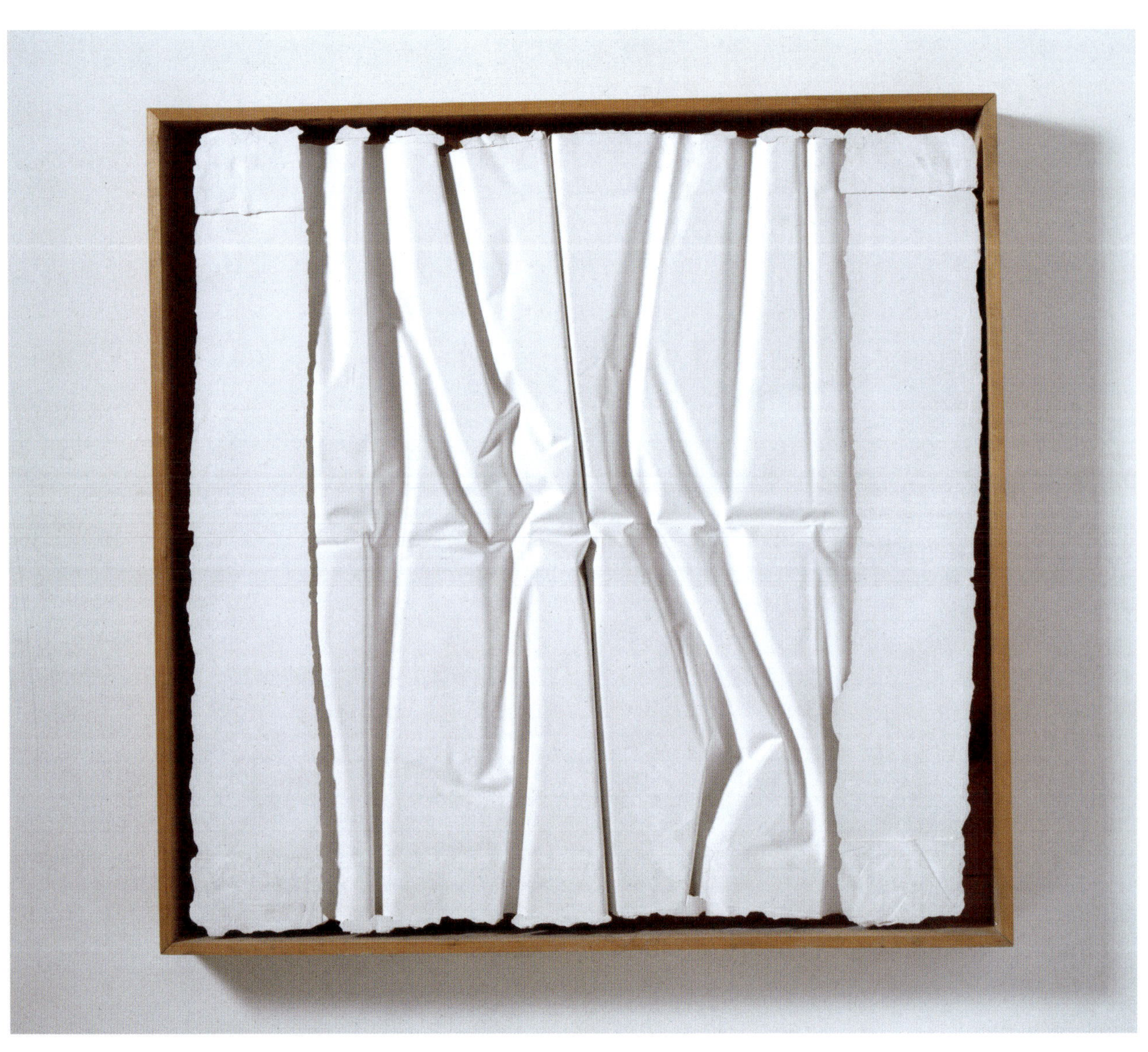

Vorhang zur EKSTATISCHEN MARIONETTE / Fore-Curtain to the ECSTATIC MARIONETTE, 1979

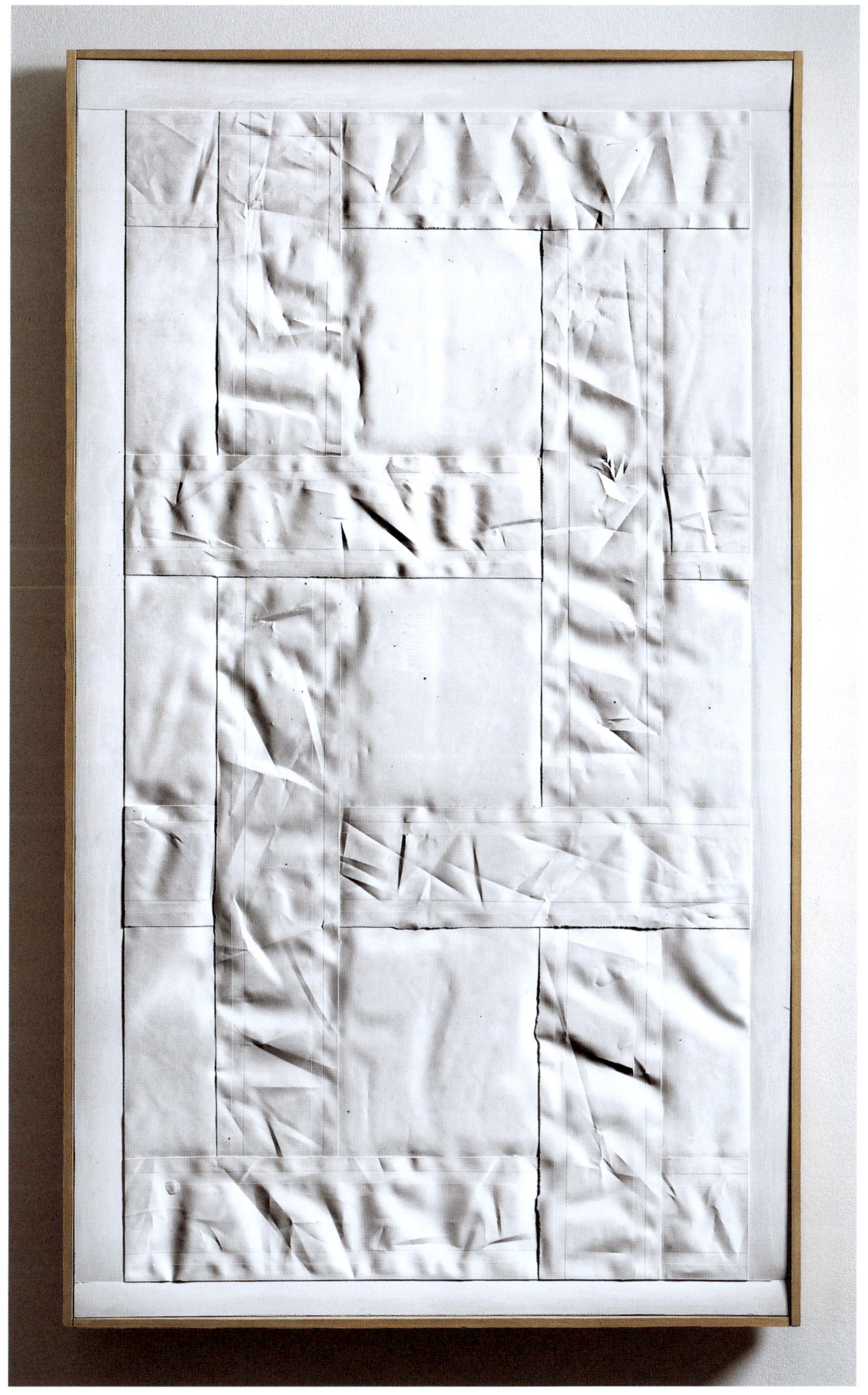

Relief K/3, 1980

Tamás KASZÁS

Dunaújváros, 1976

In der experimentellen künstlerischen Praxis von Tamás Kaszás nimmt die Theorie einen hohen Stellenwert ein. Im Zentrum seiner Kunst stehen ökologische, wirtschaftliche und gesellschaftliche Fragen, Schlüsselbegriffe wie Kollapsismus, Volksphilosophie und Permakultur spielen eine bedeutende Rolle. Kaszás verschmilzt und konfrontiert die Utopie des Modernismus mit der antikapitalistischen Globalisierungskritik, das erlernbare Wissen mit den durch Erfahrung erlangbaren Kenntnissen, die individuelle Arbeit mit dem Gemeinschaftskonzept. Die Kollektivität ist in Kaszás' Kunst ohnehin ein wichtiges Element: Unter dem Namen Ex-Artist's Collective arbeitet er mit Anikó Lóránt zusammen und in der Formation Randomroutines mit Krisztián Kristóf.

Im Mittelpunkt seiner Arbeiten steht meist ein „Anschauungsmaterial": Wandzeitungen, Transparente, Modelle baut er zu komplexen Installationen zusammen (*Pangea,* gemeinsam mit Anikó Lóránt, Istanbul Biennale, 2011; *Hütten-Turm,* Biennale of Sydney, 2014). Zur Unterstreichung der Nachhaltigkeitsidee verwendet er in seinen Arbeiten häufig Materialien des Alltags, die als Abfall der industriellen Gesellschaft scheinen (beispielsweise Aluminiumelemente, Spanplatten), aber auch natürliche Baumaterialen, die in der volkstümlichen Baukunst seit vielen Jahrhunderten verwendet werden (Reisig, Holz usw.). Der Heimwerker-Charakter seiner Werke erinnert sowohl an die Bricolage-Ästhetik der Neo-Avantgarde-Kunst als auch an die gestalterischen Lösungen der nachhaltigen Architektur.

Kaszás hat sich in den vergangenen Jahren eingehend mit der Kunst von Lajos Kassák, einer vielseitigen und herausragenden Persönlichkeit der ungarischen Avantgarde der Vorkriegszeit, beschäftigt. Kassáks Bild *Kiosk*, 1924 im Geist des utopistischen Modernismus entstanden, war der Ausgangspunkt für seine Kiosk-Bauten, deren erste Variante er in Halle im Rahmen der Ausstellung „Utopien vermeiden?" präsentierte. Im *Diorama von der Kiosk-Siedlung* (2013–14) erinnern aus Abfallmaterialien gefertigte Modell-Funde an die avantgardistische Architektur der Kiosk- und Reklamepavillons von Rodtschenko über Herbert Bayer bis zu den verschiedenen Modellkonstruktionen von Kassáks Kiosk. Kaszás' Kiosk-Variante verortet jedoch die Welt der avantgardistischen propagandistischen Reklamegebäude in ein postapokalyptisches Milieu. Seine Kiosk-Modelle sind somit eine gnadenlose Kritik am Modernismus und den Utopien.

Theory plays a prominent role in the experimental artistic praxis of Tamás Kaszás. At the center of his art stand ecological, economic, and social questions, while words such as collapsism, folk wisdom, and permaculture figure prominently in his practice. Kaszás combines and confronts modernist utopias with the anti-capitalist critique of globalization; learned knowledge with skills acquired through experience; and individual achievement with a community outlook. Collectivity is also an important element in Kaszás's art: he collaborates with Anikó Lóránt under the name "Ex-Artists' Collective" and with Krisztián Kristóf in the formation known as "Randomroutines."

Some kind of "illustrative tool" can generally be found at the center of all of Kaszás's artworks: wall newspapers, banners, and models are built up to form complex installations (*Pangaea,* with Anikó Lóránt, Istanbul Biennial, 2011; *Shanty-Tower,* Sydney Biennial, 2014). Adhering to ideas of sustainability, he often uses everyday materials in his work, some of which derive from the waste materials of industrial society (for example aluminum elements and wooden boards), others from the centuries-old natural building materials found in folk culture (sticks, wood, etc). At the same time, the DIY character of his works refers to the bricolage aesthetic of neo-avant-garde art and the formal solutions of sustainable architecture.

In recent years Kaszás has dealt particularly with the art of Lajos Kassák, the multi-talented, prominent figure of the pre-war Hungarian avant-garde. The starting point for his kiosk structures, the first version of which was shown in the context of the exhibition "Avoiding Utopias?" in Halle, Germany, was Kassák's picture *Kiosk*, made in 1924 in the spirit of utopian modernism. The model-object *Diorama of the Kiosk Village* (2013–14) was made from recycled materials and refers to specific examples of avant-garde kiosk and propaganda pavilion architecture, ranging from Rodchenko and Herbert Bayer to the various model-reconstructions of Kassák's own kiosk. Kaszás, however, places his version of the kiosk — which derives from the world of avant-garde, propagandistic, representative buildings — into a post-apocalyptic milieu. In this way his kiosk models provide a heightened critique of the faith placed in utopias and in modernism.

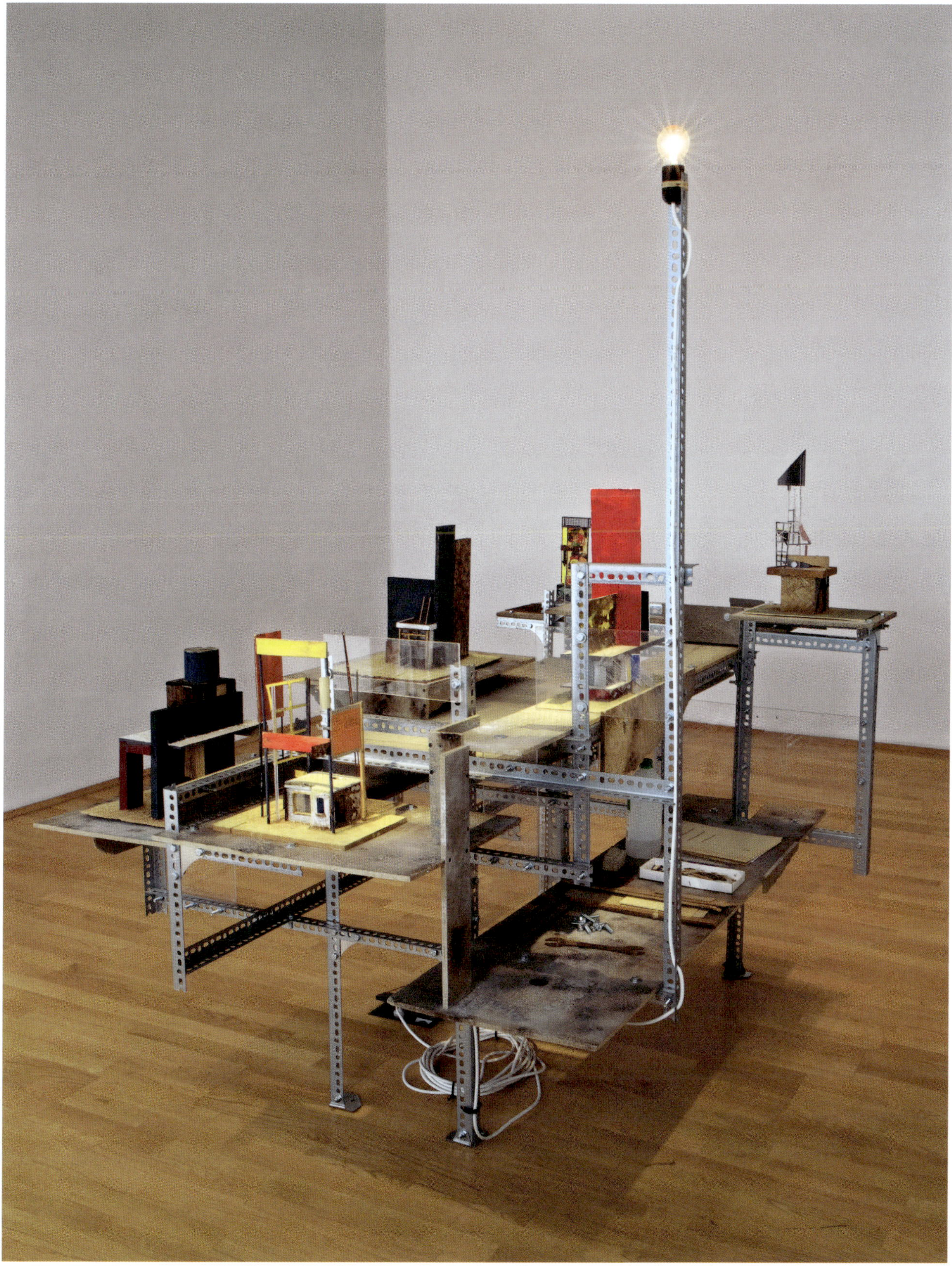

Diorama von der Kiosk-Siedlung / Diorama of the Kiosk Village, 2013–14

Ilona KESERÜ

Pécs, 1933

Péter Nádas bezeichnet Ilona Keserüs Werk aphoristisch als „organisch und konstruktivistisch. Technisch und folkloristisch. Naturwissenschaftlich und ethnografisch. Asketisch und orgiastisch. Was andere als Gegensätze erleben, erlebt sie in seiner Komplementarität. Will man ihr malerisches Temperament auf psychologischer Ebene untersuchen, dann kann man sagen, sie verlässt die ungarische malerische Tradition selbst dann nicht, wenn sie sieht, wie unfruchtbar sie ist und wie wenig Halt sie bietet." Ilona Keserü aber hatte durchaus einen Halt, denn als Kind war ihr Lehrer Ferenc Martyn, einstiges Mitglied der Pariser Abstraction Création, der sich nach seiner Heimkehr in Pécs, der Heimatstadt von Ilona Keserü, niederließ. Seine im Geist der europäischen, non-figurativen Malerei entstandenen Bilder und seine individuelle Lehrmethode bestimmen die Kunst Keserüs bis zum heutigen Tage.

Die offizielle Kunstausbildung hielt für die junge Künstlerin nicht viel Aufregendes bereit, 1962/63 bedeutete jedoch ein Stipendium in Rom eine wahre Wende. In erster Linie waren es die Zeichnungen von Cy Twombly und die Leinwände von Alfredo Burri, die befreiend auf sie wirkten, doch beeinflussten sie auch die abstrakten Gemälde von Achille Perilli, mit dem sie persönlich Bekanntschaft machte. Nach ihrer Rückkehr nach Ungarn weisen die schwungvoll-verworrenen, kalligrafischen *Gilettezeichnungen* (1963) bereits auf den Duktus ihrer Mitte der Sechziger gemalten *Nummerierten Bilder* voraus. Von den geplanten zehn Gemälden der Serie fertigte sie schließlich nur sechs an. Auf dem *Gemälde Nr. 4* (1965) werden die von der Malerin gestisch aufgetragenen Farb- und Bleistiftlinien zu den kompositorischen Hauptelementen.

1967 entdeckte Ilona Keserü auf dem Friedhof von Balatonudvar die herzförmigen Grabsteine aus dem 19. Jahrhundert, die lange Jahre zum zentralen Motiv ihrer Malerei wurden. Die Formenwelt des Bauernbarock löste sie aus ihrem ursprünglichen Kontext und betrachtete sie als rein geometrische Sprache. Ihr Bild *Annäherung II* (1969), auf dem der Grabstein als zu einem plastischen Zeichen gewordene Form erscheint, wurde bei der zweiten IPARTERV-Ausstellung gezeigt. In ihrer Kunst finden die typisch weiblichen Motive von da an eine größere Betonung. Ihre genähten Bilder, Textilapplikationen, handeln von der Rückkehr zu traditionell weiblichen Tätigkeiten, die Rolle der Frau nimmt Keserü mit diesen Bildern künstlerisch bewusst auf sich.

Péter Nádas approached the work of Ilona Keserü in an aphoristic manner: "Organic and constructivist. Technical and folk. Scientific and ethnographic. Aesthetic and orgiastic. What others conceive of as contradictory, she sees as complementary. If we were to examine the spiritual dimension of her painterly temperament, then we could say that she does not part from the traditions of Hungarian painting, even when she realizes how infertile it is and unfit to be relied upon." Ilona Keserü did, however, have somewhere to look to, since her childhood teacher was Ferenc Martyn, a former member of the Parisian group Abstraction Création, who after returning to Hungary settled in Keserü's hometown of Pécs. Both his paintings, made in the spirit of European non-figuration, and his personally tailored teaching method have exerted a decisive influence on Keserü's artistic practice to this day.

Official artistic training did not, however, offer much excitement to the young artist, for whom a scholarship to Rome in 1962–3 represented a real turning point. The drawings of Cy Twombly and the canvases of Alfredo Burri had a liberating influence on her, as did the abstract paintings of Achille Perille, whom she also met in person. The lively, fussy calligraphy of her *Gilette-Drawings* (1963) made after her return home already anticipated the gestures of her *Numbered Paintings* from the mid-sixties. Of the ten planned pieces in the series, six were completed. In her *Painting No. 4* (1965) the main compositional elements are the bold strokes of the painter's paint and pencil lines.

In 1967 she discovered the heart-shaped 19th-century gravestones in the cemetery of Balatonudvar, which were to become the central motif of her painting for many years to come. She removed the visual forms of the peasant baroque from their original context and treated them as a purely geometric language. Her painting *Approaching II* (1969), in which the gravestone appears in the form of an artistic sign, was shown at the second IPARTERV exhibition. It was from then on that characteristically feminine motifs were more strongly emphasized in her work. Her embroidery and use of textiles point to a return to traditional women's activities and the deliberate adoption of a female role in her work.

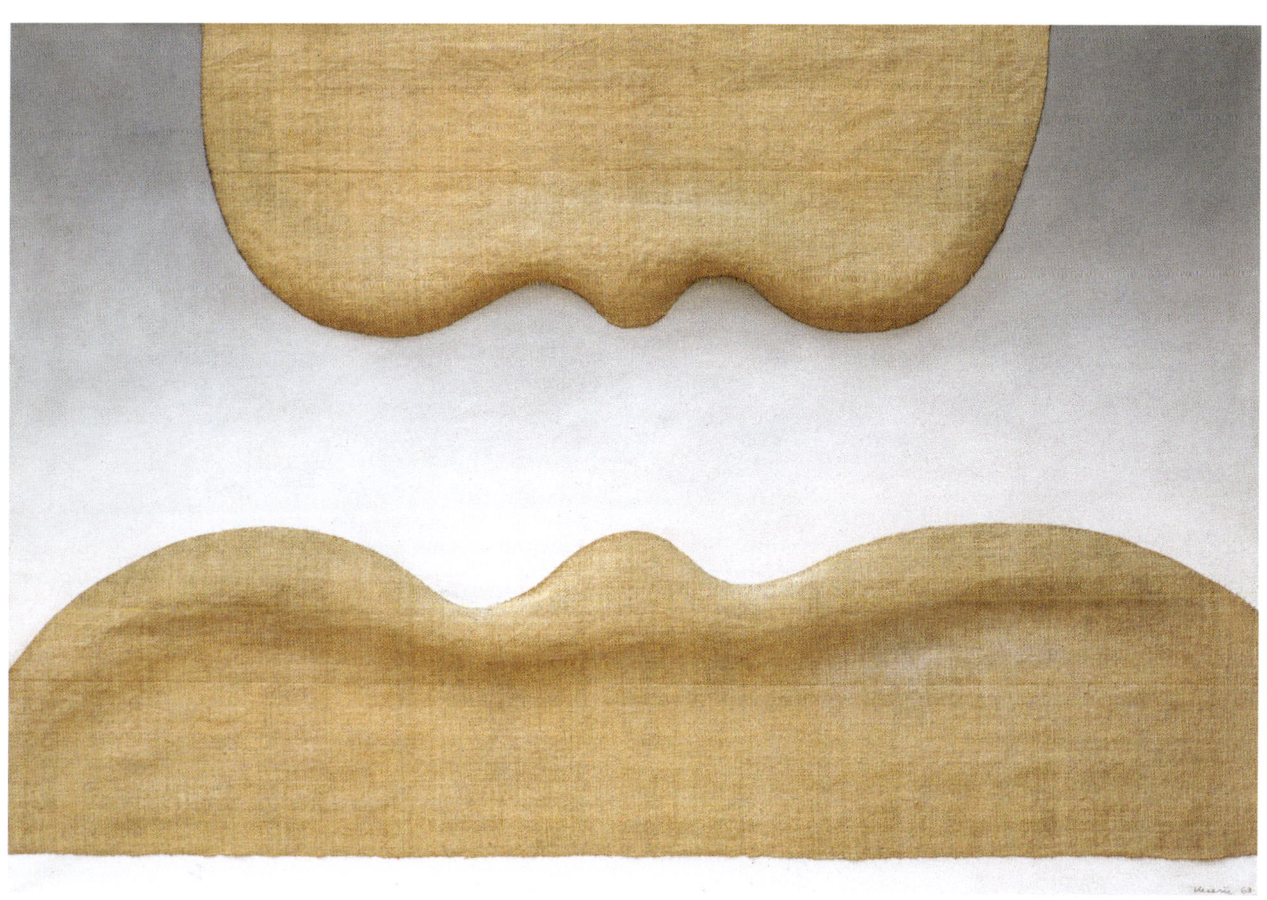

Annäherung II / Approach II, 1969

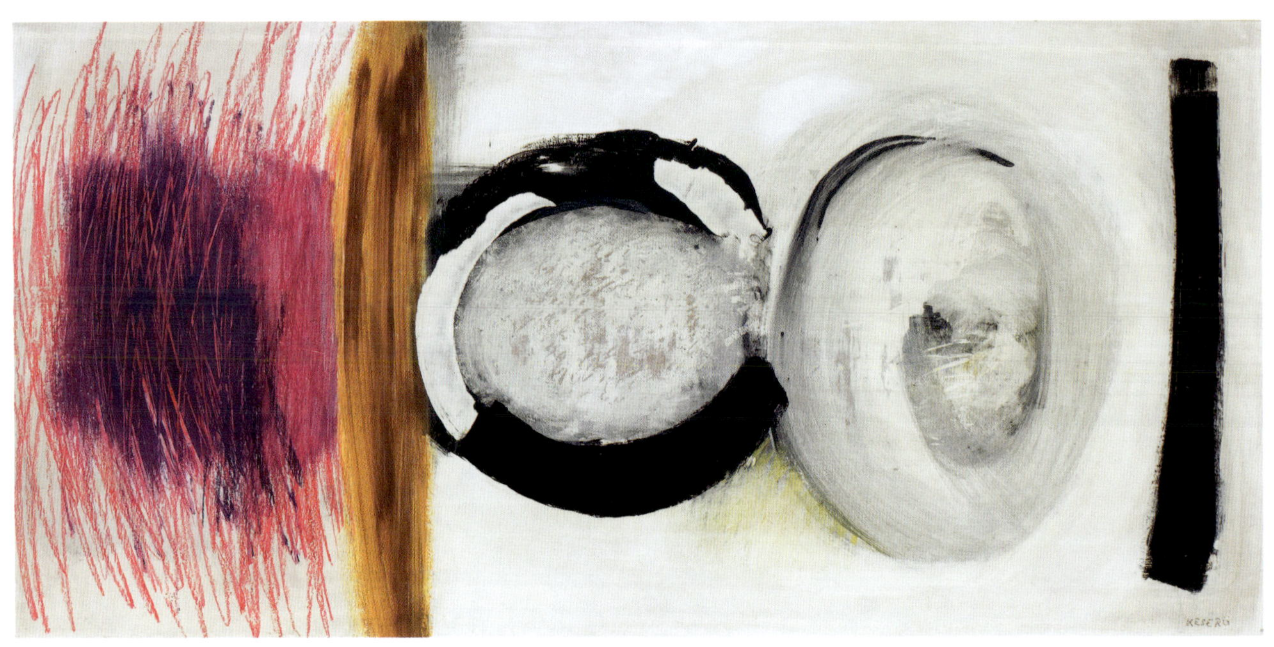

Gemälde Nr. 4 / Painting No. IV, 1965

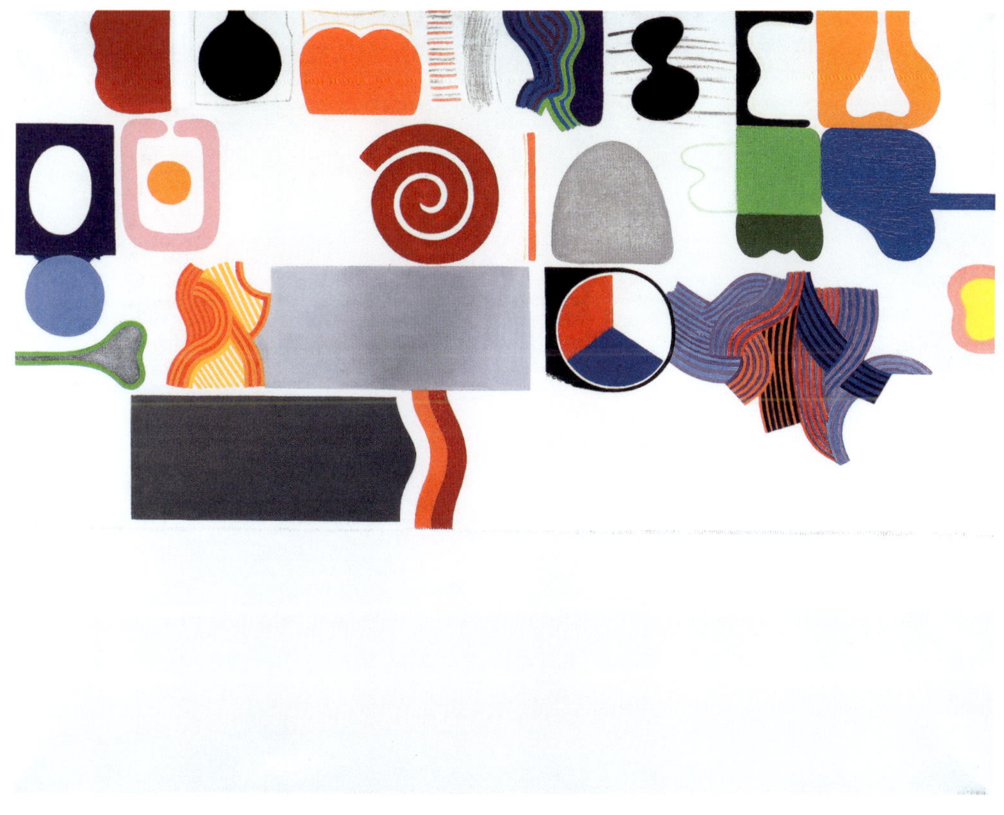

Botschaft / Message, 1968

Ádám KOKESCH

Budapest, 1973

Die Objekte und Installationen von Ádám Kokesch beziehen sich auf die Welt des Industriedesigns und auf technische Experimente. Sie erinnern an die Einrichtungsgegenstände eines Laboratoriums oder einer Produktionsstraße. Fulya Erdemci, der Kurator der 13. Istanbul Biennale, hielt fest: Kokeschs Objekte „zwingen uns dazu, die Dinge anders zu betrachten". Die scheinbar spielerischen Arbeiten des Künstlers sind nämlich komplexe gedankliche Experimente, die mindestens genauso sehr von den zeitgenössischen künstlerischen Dilemmata im Zusammenhang mit dem Schaffen eines Kunstobjekts handeln, wie von der zweifelhaften materiellen Kultur der postindustriellen Gesellschaft, das heißt unseres Alltags. Die Heimwerkerstimmung des DIY vermischt sich bei ihm mit der Sterilität wissenschaftlicher Instrumente, das Hightech mit der Tradition der Manufaktur (sein Verfahren auf Plexiglas, die sogenannte Hinterglas-Technik, entleiht er sich dabei von den deutschen Glasmalern des 18. Jahrhunderts). Die Welt der Gestaltung trifft auf eine gestaltete Welt. Kokesch schafft Scheinwelten, er spielt mit Dimensionen, generiert Datenbanken ohne Daten, erschafft Instrumente ohne Funktion.

Eine seiner neueren, unbetitelten Arbeiten (2014) scheint, frontal betrachtet und vor allem als zweidimensionale Nachbildung, entfernt mit der geometrischen Abstraktion verwandt: eine Kombination geometrischer Formen und Farben. Doch der – gleichwohl beabsichtigte – Schein trügt: Von der Seite zeigt sie sich bereits als komplexe Konstruktion, als nützlicher Gegenstand. Die Oberflächen, die wohl zuerst als dekorative Farbflecken angelegt waren, werden zu Bestandteilen einer komplizierten und überaus praktischen Einrichtung. Doch wird all dies wiederholt hinterfragt; trotz der bekannt, sogar alltäglich scheinenden Details enthüllt der Gegenstand weder seine Bestimmung noch sein Funktionsprinzip. Er bleibt ein Rätsel – wie jedes bedeutende Kunstobjekt, das sich immer wieder neu und auf die unterschiedlichste Weise mit den Dingen, die uns umgeben, verbindet.

Ádám Kokesch's objects and installations refer to the world of industrial design and technical experimentation. As if they were the paraphernalia of a laboratory or production line, Kokesch's objects "demand another way of looking at things," as Fulya Erdemci, curator of the 13th Istanbul Biennial, noted. At the same time, Kokesch's seemingly playful objects are dense intellectual experiments that have as much to say about the dilemmas of contemporary art in terms of the production of art objects as they do about post-industrial society, that is to say the questionable object culture of our times. The DIY atmosphere of tinkering is mixed in his work with the sterility of scientific instruments, while high-tech is combined with craft traditions (his method for sheets of Plexiglas is borrowed from the so-called *hinterglas*-technique of 18th-century German glass painters). The world of modeling meets the modeling of the world. Kokesch produces appearances: he plays with dimensions, models databases without data, creates instruments without function.

At first sight, and mainly as a two-dimensional reproduction, one of the newest untitled works (2014) seems to be a distant relative of geometric abstraction: a combination of geometric forms and colors. But this (probably deliberate) appearance is deceiving: viewed from the side, it looks like a complex instrument, a useful thing. The surfaces that initially seemed to be decorative spots of color turn into components of a complex and very practical device. This can all, however, be called into question again; on further examination, despite the fact that it includes details recognizable from everyday life, no organizational or functional principles can be discovered. The mystery remains, as with every significant art object that again and again reconnects, from the most disparate of perspectives, with the things in the world that surrounds us.

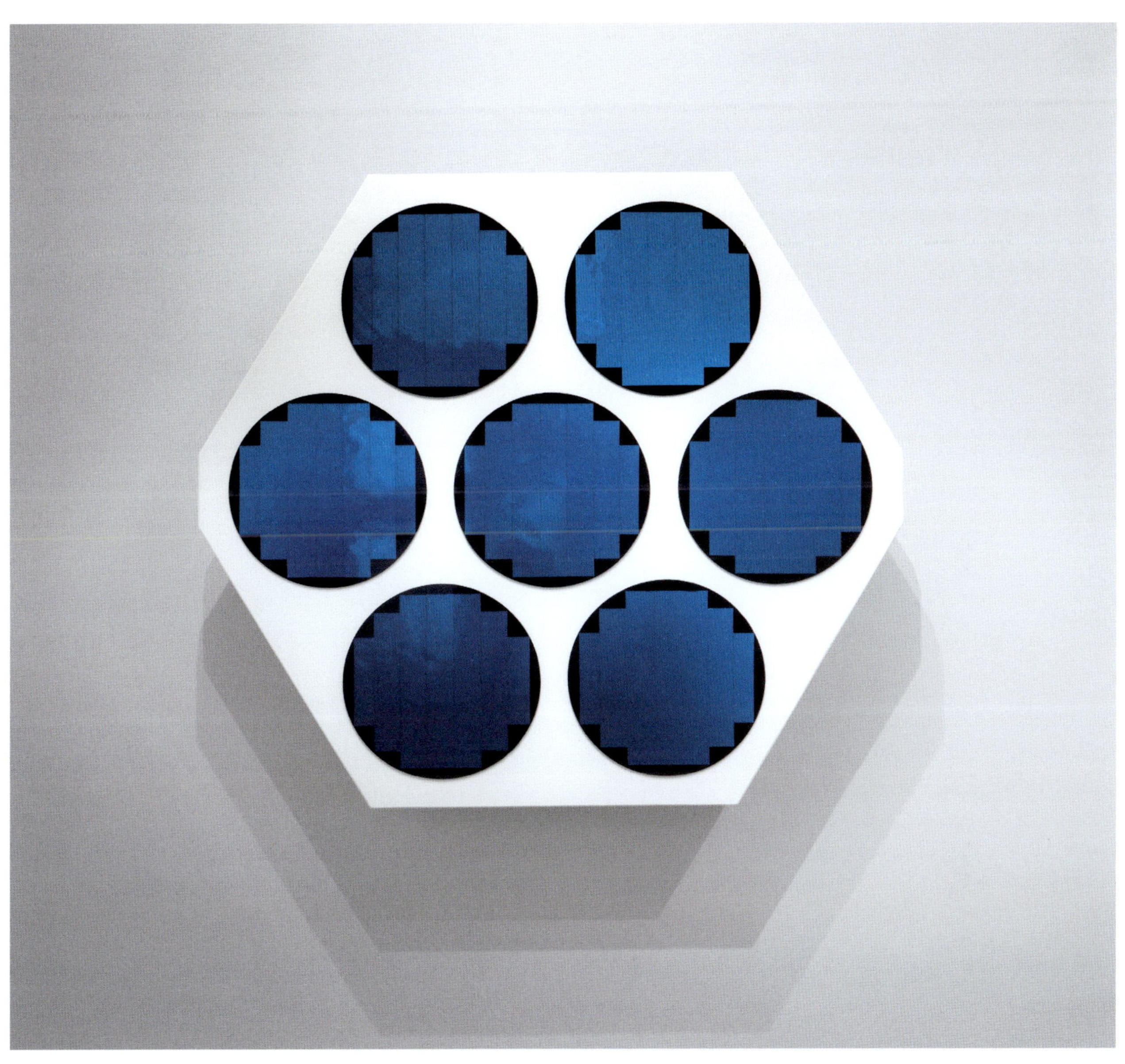

Ohne Titel / Untitled, 2013

Katalin LADIK

Novi Sad, 1942

Katalin Ladiks Karriere startete in den Sechzigerjahren in Novi Sad, einem damals von Ungarn bewohnten Gebiet Jugoslawiens, in dem sich die Avantgarde – im Gegensatz zu Ungarn – eines gewissen Forums, Freiraums, einer Rezeption erfreute. Ladik begann als Lyrikerin und war als solche Mitglied des Kreises um die avantgardistische ungarische Zeitschrift *Symposion* in der Vojvodina. Ein wesentlicher Aspekt ihrer Lyrik war von Beginn an die gesungene Vortragsweise. Beim Vortrag ihrer Gedichte verwandte sie von den Sechzigern und Siebzigern an Elemente des Happenings, der Body Art und der Performance. Ladik durchbrach mit ihrem Körper, ihrer Stimme, ihrem Geist die Grenzen zwischen den Gattungen ebenso wie die symbolische Ordnung des von Männern dominierten kulturellen Lebens. Ihre erste, auch vom Fernsehen übertragene Performance im Jahr 1970 sorgte seinerzeit für großes Aufsehen, denn sie war die erste Künstlerin in Jugoslawien, die auf der Bühne den eigenen Körper als Medium einsetzte. Ab 1973 wurde sie Mitglied der Gruppe Bosch+Bosch in Subotica, arbeitete aber auch mit zahlreichen anderen Künstlern und Künstlergruppen zusammen, wie zum Beispiel mit Miklós Erdély und Tamás Szentjóby.

Ladik ist eine wahre Intermedia-Künstlerin. Obwohl sie in erster Linie durch ihre Lautdichtung und Performances bekannt wurde, die häufig der Theatralität nicht entbehren und alte Riten wachrufen, sind die Partituren ihrer Lautdichtungen zugleich autonome visuelle Kunstobjekte. Die Vortragbarkeit dieser dadaistischen, auch die traditionelle Rolle der Frau kritisch darstellenden – beispielsweise mit Applikationen von Schnittmustern ergänzten – Collage-Gedichte ist bei Ladik tatsächlich eine zentrale Frage. Wie sie selbst einmal sagte: „Solange sie einen Inhalt haben, eine Botschaft, einen semantischen Wert, einen Umbruch, eine formale Komponierbarkeit, können sie als Partitur behandelt werden, und selbstverständlich benutze ich sie auch als solche."

Ihre Foto- und Video-Performances trug sie – meist ohne Publikum – vor der Kamera vor. Im Fall von *Poemask* (1978) dokumentierte sie den Prozess, wie die auf ihr Gesicht geblasene Farbe mittels ihrer Mimik abtropfte. In *Pseudosculptura* (1982) ist ebenfalls ihr eigener Körper das Grundmaterial. Der nackte Frauenkörper – wie bei antiken Skulpturen in feuchte Tücher gewickelt – ist der Körper der Künstlerin, was sie selbst zum lebendigen Kunstwerk macht.

Katalin Ladik's career begin in the 1960s in Novi Sad, an area of the former Yugoslavia inhabited by Hungarians, where – in contrast to Hungary – the avant-garde enjoyed a public forum, space, and reception. She began as a poet, and in her capacity as a poet became a member of the circle of the Novi Sad Hungarian avant-garde periodical *Symposion*; from the outset, an essential aspect of her verses was that they were to be sung. In the sixties and seventies Ladik began to use elements of happening, body art, and performance in her verse recitals. Playing with her body, her voice, and her mind, she pried open the borders between genres and art forms, just as she challenged the male-dominated symbolic order of cultural life. Her first performance from 1970, which was also televised, provoked a veritable storm at the time; she was the first female performer in the former Yugoslavia to use her own body as a medium on stage. In 1973 she became a member of the Bosch+Bosch group in Subotica, although she also worked with numerous other artists and artists' groups, for instance Miklós Erdély and Tamás Szentjóby.

Ladik was a true intermedia artist: while she first became known for her sound poetry renditions and her inevitably theatrical performances that often referred to ancient rituals, the sheet music for her sound poetry pieces are at the same time autonomous visual artworks. For Ladik, a central question is the performability of these Dadaist collage-verses, which critically highlight traditional women's roles (for example through the addition of clothes patterns). As she herself has said: "While it has content, a message, semantic value, pagination, formal composition, it can also be handled as sheet music, and naturally I use it like that."

Ladik made her photographic and video performances in front of the camera, for the most part without an audience. In the case of *Poemask* (1978), she documented the process by which quick-drying paint was blown onto her face and dripped off, following the movement of her face. For her *Pseudosculptura* (1982), which was performed on the Croatian island of Hvar, she again used her own body as the basic material. The naked woman's body wrapped in wet sheets, a familiar motif of antique sculpture, is the artist's own; in this way, she herself becomes a living artwork.

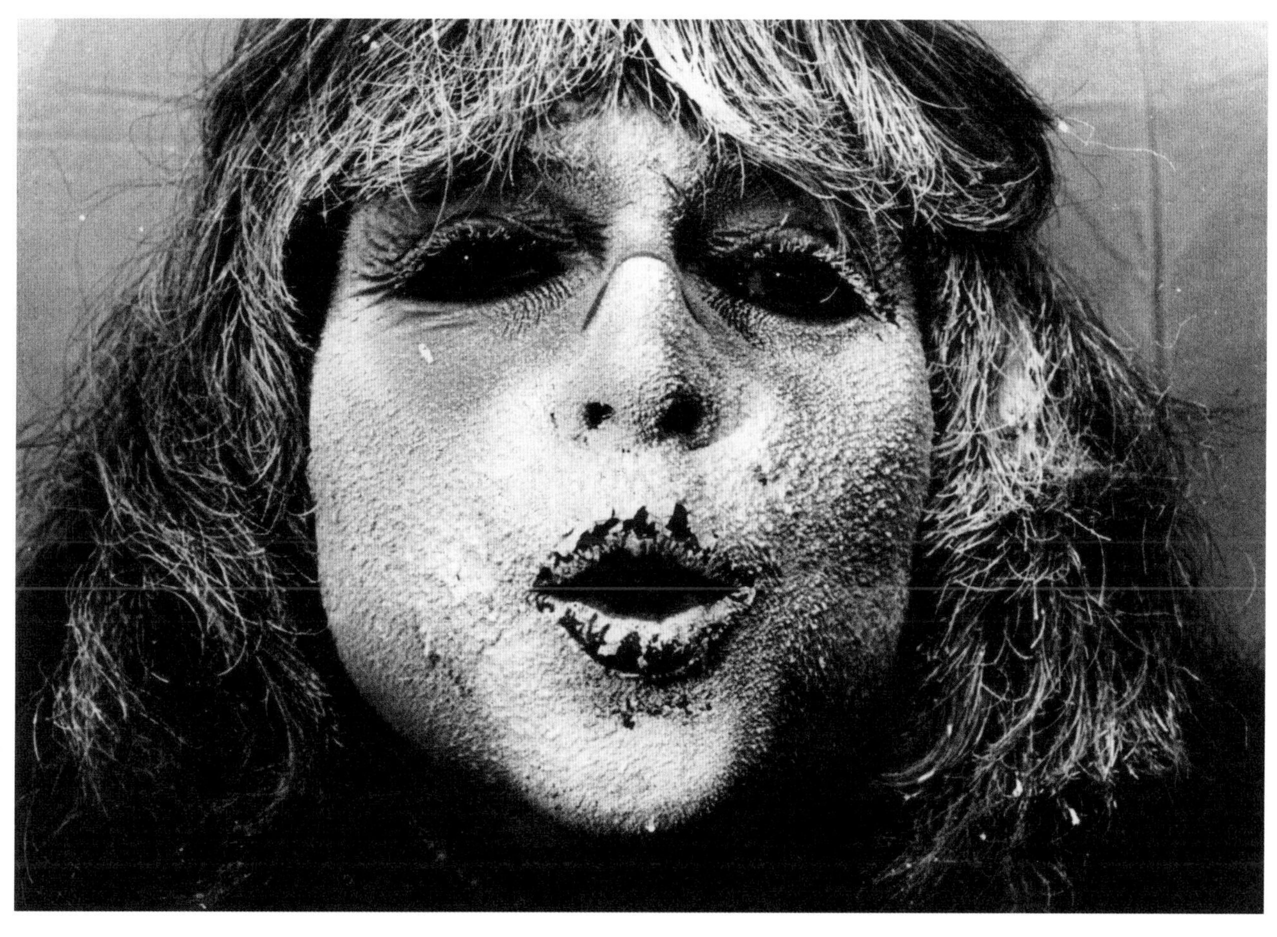

Poemask II, 1982

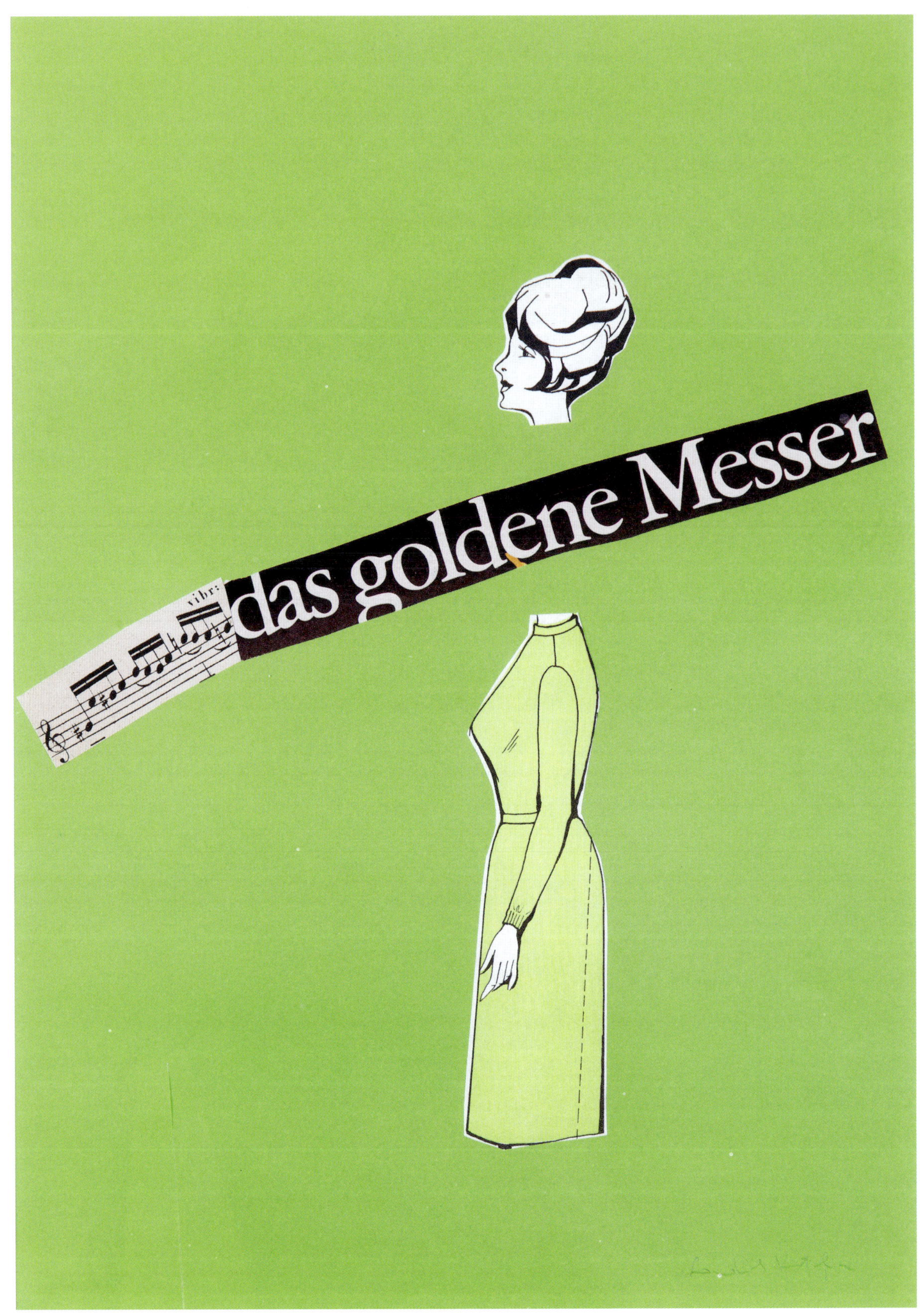

<u>Das Lied von dem goldenen Messer</u>, 1979

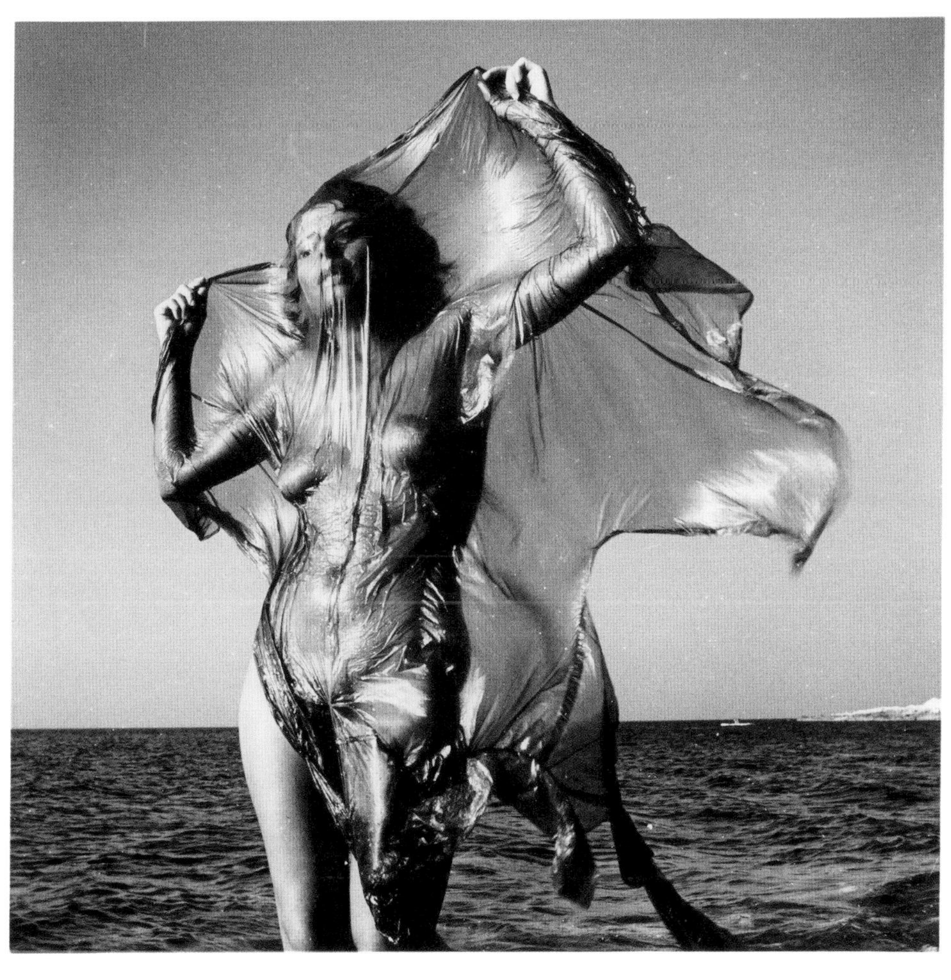

Pseudosculptura II, 1982

László LAKNER

Budapest, 1936

László Lakner war in Ungarn lange Zeit fast ausschließlich dafür bekannt, die Pop Art in Ungarn heimisch gemacht zu haben, und galt als einer der wichtigsten Teilnehmer der IPARTERV-Ausstellungen. Im Ausland hat er sich seinen Ruf (nach seiner Emigration nach Berlin 1974) mit sensiblen, expressiven Gemälden erworben, in denen der Schrift und der Literatur (den handschriftlichen Zeilen Marcel Duchamps, Paul Celans und anderer) eine besondere Rolle zukommt (*Isa pur,* 1982, Museum Ludwig, Köln).

In dem beeindruckend vielfältigen Lebenswerk Lakners stellte der Übergang von den Sechzigern zu den Siebzigern einen besonders spannenden Wendepunkt dar. Die zu dieser Zeit entstandenen konzeptuellen Fotoarbeiten rückten allerdings erst in den vergangenen Jahren in den Mittelpunkt des Interesses. Eine wichtige Wende in seinem Frühwerk bedeutete eine Reise nach Venedig im Jahr 1964. Der junge Maler zeigte sich hier maßgeblich von Rauschenberg beeindruckt. In seinem Œuvre trifft die amerikanische Pop Art auf einzigartige Weise auf die großen Meister, vor allem Rembrandt. Bei den damals entstandenen Gemälden scheute Lakner keine politischen Stellungnahmen, und so wurde *Gehorsam* (1966) zu einem emblematischen Werk jener Zeit. Bereits Ende der Fünfziger beschäftigte ihn die Fotografie als künstlerisches Mittel. Ab Ende der Sechziger malte er immens vergrößerte Gesichtsausschnitte und bereitete zeitgleich zu diesen Gemälden seine ersten konzeptuellen Fotoarbeiten vor. Daneben arbeitete er in zahlreichen anderen Gattungen, von Objekten und Aktionen über Klangarbeiten bis hin zu experimentellen Filmen.

Während er seine großformatigen, hyperrealistischen Gemälde anfertigte (*Selbstbildnis mit Selbstauslöser,* 1970, Uffizien, Florenz; *Fahrausweis von Béla Bartók,* 1974, Ludwig Forum Aachen), stellte er in seinen konzeptuellen Fotoarbeiten Fragen zur Kunstproduktion, zur Rolle des Künstlers und zur Ontologie der Kunst. Auch hier durchaus nicht frei von politischen Anspielungen. Die beiden ausgestellten Werke – *Neuer Verband* und *Leaded-Art* (beide 1971) – zeigen den Künstler als Gefangenen einer zentral gesteuerten Kulturpolitik. Nicht nur seine Hände sind gebunden, vielmehr wird er als eifriger Arbeiter der sozialistischen Kultur, als gezäumtes Tier gezeigt, das von der Macht an der Nase herumgeführt wird.

While in Hungary, László Lakner was for long exclusively known as an adapter of Pop Art and one of the most significant artists of the IPARTERV exhibitions. Following his emigration to Berlin in 1974, he won high-level international recognition and was acclaimed for his exceptionally sensitive expressive paintings, in which writing and literature (the handwritten lines of Marcel Duchamp, Paul Celan and others) played a prominent role (*Isa pur,* 1982, Ludwig Museum, Cologne).

In Lakner's stunningly multifarious career, the turn of the seventies was an especially exciting moment, although the conceptual photographic works he created at the time have only begun to attract attention in recent years. A significant turning point in his work of this early period occurred on a trip to Venice in 1964, where Rauschenberg had a deep impact on the young painter. Lakner's work brought American Pop Art together with the great masters, especially Rembrandt, in a singular manner. In his paintings of the time, Lakner was not one to shy away from taking a political stand; his *Obediently* (1966) went on to become one of the emblematic works of the period. He'd already been using the photograph as a medium since the late fifties. From the late sixties onwards, he painted massively enlarged facial details, and alongside these paintings created his first conceptual photo works, as well as works in a variety of other artistic media ranging from objects and actions to voice works and experimental films.

While he made large-format and conceptually-minded hyperrealist paintings (*Self-portrait with Autotimer,* 1970, Uffizi; *Béla Bartók's Travel Pass,* 1974, Ludwig Forum, Aachen), in his conceptual photographic works (among others) he examined questions of artistic production, the role of the artist, and the ontology of art. It should be added that he never eschewed political overtones. The two works in the exhibition, *New Bandage* and *Leaded-Art* (both 1971), show the artist as a prisoner of centrally directed cultural politics, who not only has his hands bound, but is led by the nose by power, like an animal in a bridle or a diligent worker for socialist culture.

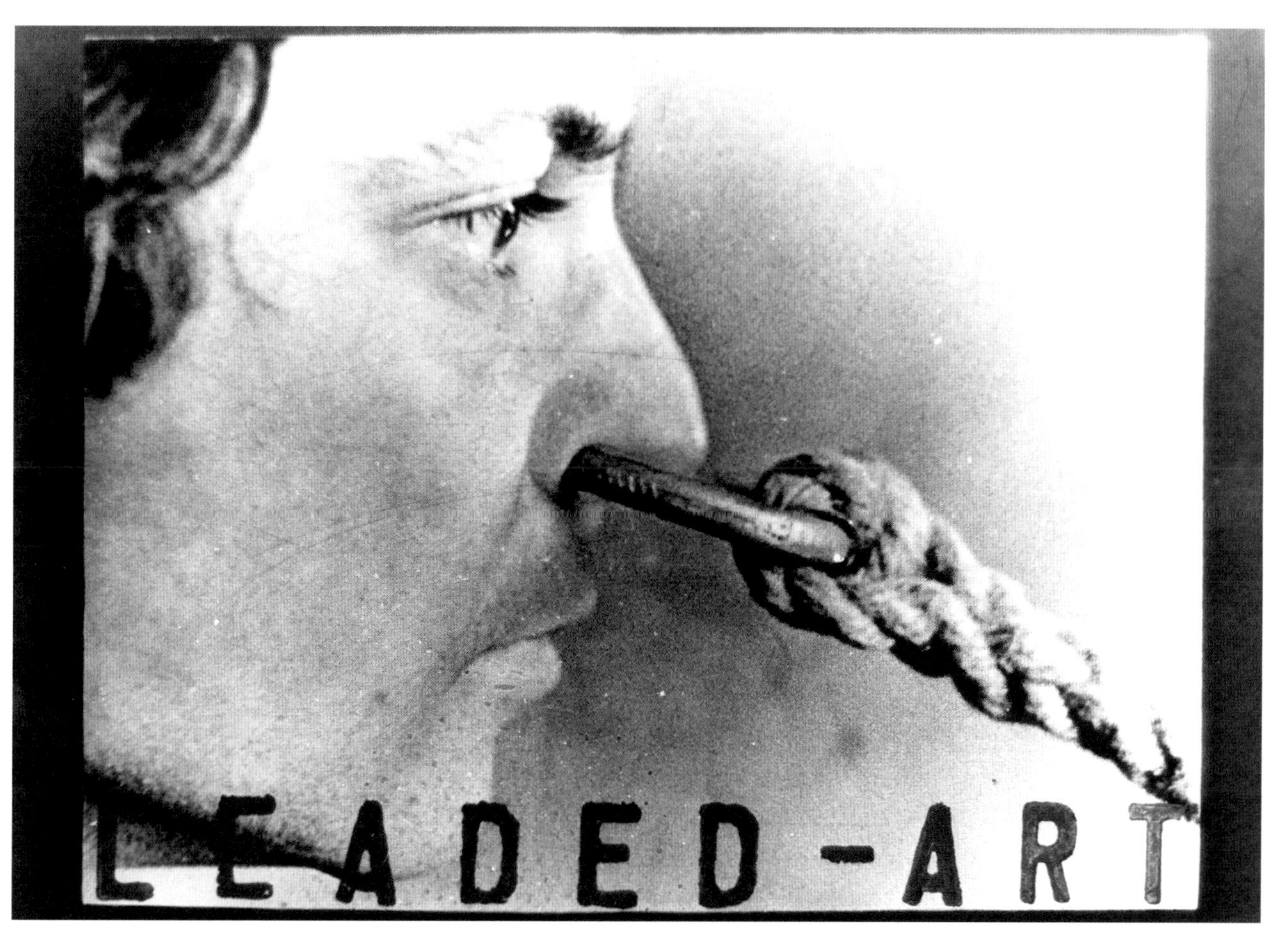

Leaded-Art, 1971

LITTLE WARSAW

(András Gálik, Budapest 1970; Bálint Havas, Budapest 1971)

Eines der berühmtesten Werke des seit 1999 aktiven Künstlerduos Little Warsaw ist das 2003 anlässlich der Biennale in Venedig präsentierte Projekt *Der Körper von Nofretete*: Sie ergänzten die berühmte Kalksteinbüste der Nofretete um einen Bronzekörper, was zu zahllosen Interpretationen führte. Unter anderem wurden Fragen nach der zeitgenössischen künstlerischen Verwendung jahrhundertealter, ikonischer Kunst, nach den Möglichkeiten eines Dialoges zwischen den Kulturen und nach den Eigentumsverhältnissen unseres künstlerischen Erbes gestellt. Little Warsaw beschäftigt sich in Filmen, Installationen und vielen anderen Medien mit historischer Erinnerung, indem sie persönliche Erlebnisse stets mit gesellschaftlichen Erfahrungen kollidieren lassen. Vergessene öffentliche Denkmäler werden so aus ihrer Umgebung herausgehoben, Archivaufnahmen in ein neues Narrativ eingefügt. Dabei gehen sie auch der Frage nach der Rolle des Kunstobjekts und der gesellschaftlichen Situation des Künstlers nach.

Der aggressive, männliche Heroismus auf Kriegsdenkmälern war das Thema der als Environment angelegten Skulpturenmontage *Kampf um die innere Wahrheit* (2011, Galerie für Zeitgenössische Kunst Leipzig). Aus Kleinplastiken verschiedener öffentlicher Sammlungen bauten sie eine imaginäre Schlachtenszene zusammen und stellten so die ursprüngliche Bedeutung der Skulpturen, die aus verschiedenen Zeiten und Regionen stammten und somit unterschiedliche Bedeutungen hatten, in einen neuen Kontext. Das Werk *Kämpfer* (2014) hingegen ist ein eigenständiges Werk beziehungsweise die Neuinterpretation einer Holzskulptur aus der ersten Hälfte der Zwanzigerjahre. Little Warsaw hat die ursprüngliche Skulptur nicht nur ihres Kontextes beraubt, ihre Bedeutung verändert, sondern sie sowohl im praktischen wie auch im übertragenen Sinne verbildlicht. Sie haben den dreidimensionalen Körper auf eine transparente, ebene Glasoberfläche übertragen, sodass nur noch die Illusion von Räumlichkeit übrigblieb. Hierfür experimentierten sie mit zahlreichen fotografischen Verfahren, bis sie schließlich diese außergewöhnlich zarte, an die Glasnegative des 19. Jahrhunderts erinnernde fotografische Glasoberfläche erhielten, die uns mit ihrer Fragilität und Transparenz unsere geliebten Vorstellungen von Heldenhaftigkeit in Erinnerung ruft.

One of the best-known works of the artist duo working since 1999 under the name of "Little Warsaw" is the project *The Body of Nefertiti*, presented at the Venice Biennale in 2003, in which they made a bronze body to complete the famous limestone bust of Nefertiti. The act opened up an extremely rich field of associations, including the question concerning the use of the centuries-old iconic art object in contemporary art and the possibilities it offers for intercultural communication, while at the same time teasing out property relations of the artistic heritage of the past. Through films, installations, and a wide variety of media, Little Warsaw addresses historical memory and confronts personal encounters with social experience. They take public monuments that have been condemned to amnesia and liberate them from their environment, using archival footage to situate them in a new narrative. At the same time, they examine questions concerning the role of the artwork and the artist's social situation.

The aggressive, macho heroism of war memorials was the theme of the large-scale environmental sculptural montage *The Battle of Inner Truth* (2011) they showed at the Museum of Contemporary Art, Leipzig, where they arranged small sculptures belonging to various public collections to form a battle scene, overriding the original meanings of the statues derived from their geographical locations and periods. On the other hand, the work *Fighter* (2014) is their own creation, a reinterpretation of a wooden sculpture originating from the first half of the twenties. Not only did Little Warsaw extract the original sculpture from its context and change its meaning, but they also transformed it into an image in both the literal and figurative sense of the word. The artists transposed the three-dimensional body onto a translucent, flat glass surface, such that only the illusion of its spatiality remains. They experimented with numerous photographic techniques until they managed to realize this exceptionally delicate photographic glass surface, which is reminiscent of the glass negatives of the nineteenth century, and which in its fragility and transparency calls to mind our cherished images of heroism.

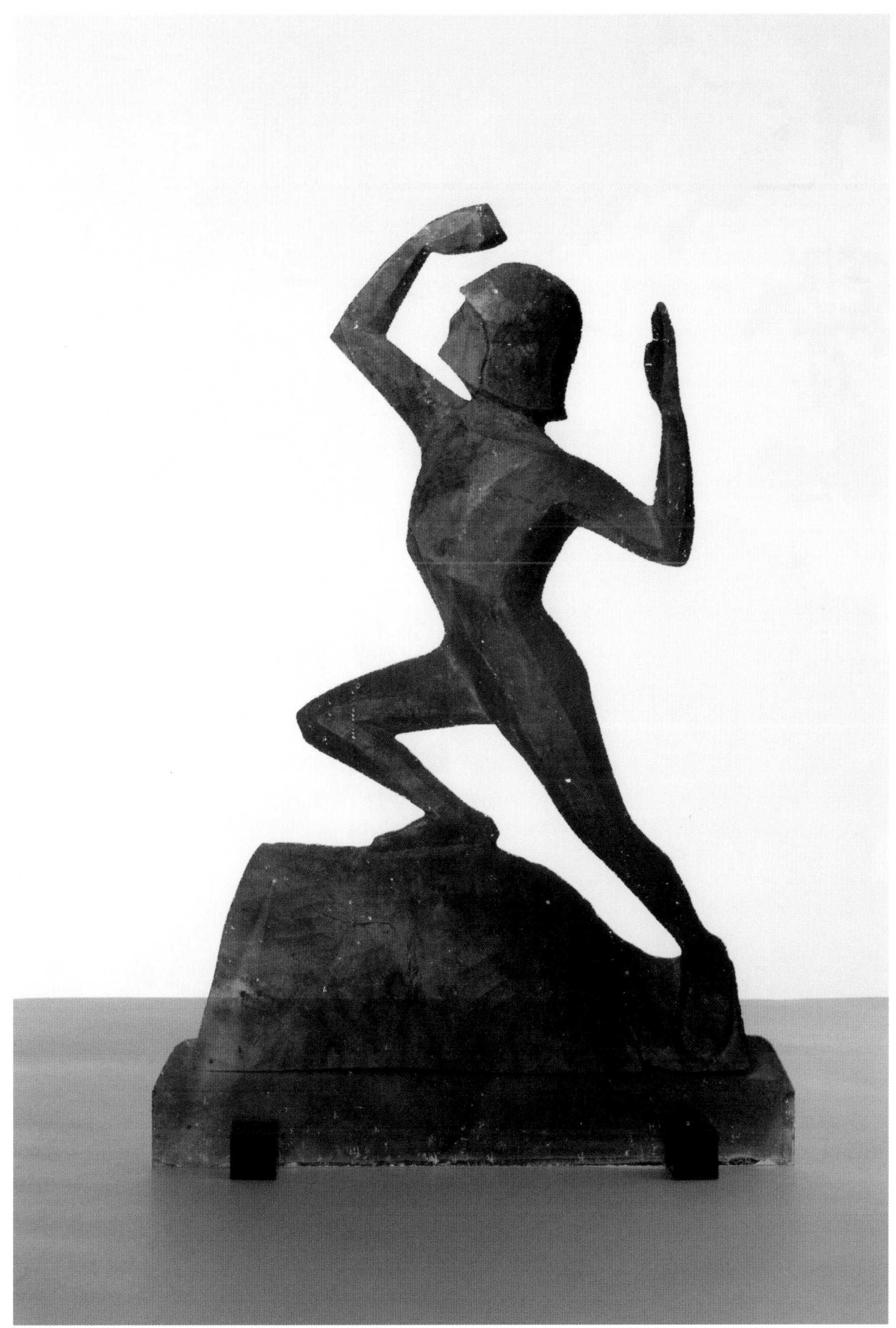

Kämpfer / Fighter, 2014

Dóra MAURER

Budapest, 1937

„Wenn man wie ich in den sechziger und siebziger Jahren nach Ungarn reiste und die Künstler fragte, wer denn im Augenblick besonders interessant sei, wurde immer wieder Dóra Maurer genannt. So kam auch ich auf ihre Spur", schrieb Dieter Honisch, ehemaliger Direktor der Neuen Nationalgalerie Berlin. Dieses „Interesse" an Dóra Maurer besteht bis heute, sowohl in Ungarn als auch im Ausland. Aufgrund ihrer vielschichtigen pädagogischen und kuratorischen Tätigkeiten übt sie nicht nur auf ihre Zeitgenossen, sondern auch auf jüngere Künstlern großen Einfluss aus.

Anfang der Sechziger begründete Maurer, beeinflusst vom Informel, ihre Karriere mit Kupferstichen. Eine bedeutende Wende stellten ihr Wien-Stipendium im Jahr 1967 und das damit beginnende „Doppelleben" dar, da sie sich abwechselnd in Wien und Budapest aufhielt. In den frühen Siebzigern fertigte sie bereits konzeptuelle Arbeiten an. In dieser Zeit konzentrierte sie sich auf eine Reihe von Werken mit mathematischen Zahlenreihen, auf Aktionen in der freien Natur und auf serielle Arbeiten. Sie fertigte *Schautafeln* (1972) an, magische Quadrate aus unterschiedlichen Materialien, baute aus minimalen Bewegungen Sequenzen und untersuchte das komplexe Relationssystem geometrischer Grundformen (wie Quadrate und Rechtecke). Die Bewegung, der Ortswechsel sind in Maurers Kunst als Hauptaspekte durchweg präsent, sowohl auf ihren Fotos als auch in ihren experimentellen Filmen. In der Serie *Displacements* (*Verschiebungen, 1972–75)* verändern sich die Farbeindrücke und-relationen bzw. die zu sehenden Muster aufgrund von Verschiebungen. Ihre Fotoserie *Sieben Drehungen* (1977–78) behandelt ebenfalls Bewegungen, die mittels Formverschiebungen stattfinden.

Ende der Siebziger beschäftigte sie sich mit „verborgenen Strukturen". In ihrer gleichnamigen Frottage-Serie (1977) bleiben die durch das Falten des Papiers entstehenden geometrischen Formen verborgen, nur ihr Abdruck ist sichtbar. Aus derselben Zeit – Ende der Siebziger, Anfang der Achtziger – stammen Arbeiten, in denen sie Licht chemische und optisch auswertet. In der Fotogramm-Serie *Schleusen* (1980–81) erweitern sich die Lichtexperimente Maurers, für die sie Staub und Flüssigkeit verwendet, bereits zu einer Art Strukturanalyse. Ab den Achtzigern färbte sie ihre Bilder ein und ließ sie in den Raum hinausgreifen. Auf ihren geformten Leinwänden untersucht sie jedoch weiterhin dieselben mathematischen Prinzipien und Gesetzmäßigkeiten wie in ihren früheren Arbeiten.

"Visiting Hungary in the sixties and seventies, and asking artists who in their opinion was really interesting at that time, one heard over and over again the name Dóra Maurer. That's also how I first came across her," remembered Dieter Honisch, former director of the Neue Nationalgalerie Berlin. The "interest" aroused by Maurer remains evident to this day, both in Hungary and abroad, and not just among her contemporaries, but also for a younger generation of artists for whom her multi-faceted art educational and curatorial activities are equally influential.

At the beginning of the sixties, reflecting the influence of Informel, Maurer started her career with etchings. A scholarship to Vienna in 1967 represented a turning point in her work and also the beginning of her "double life": from this point on, she was to divide her time between Vienna and Budapest. At the beginning of the 1970s she was already making conceptual works. During this period she directed her attention to making a series of works with rows of numbers; to environmental actions; and to serial works. She made *Quantity Boards* (1972), magical squares consisting of various materials, as well as sequences built from minimal movements, and examined the complex relational system of basic geometrical forms, such as squares and rectangles. Movement and place-changing is present as a key consideration throughout her work, both in her photos and experimental films. In the series *Displacements* (1972–75), transformations in color relations accompany the changes in screen patterns that arise when offset forms are displaced from one another. Movements that take place between forms also appear in her photo series *Seven Turns* (1977–78).

At the end of the '70s, Maurer addressed the question of "Hidden Structures." In her series of frottage works bearing the same title (1977), geometrical forms created through folding paper remain hidden; only their impressions remain visible. Belonging to the same period — the late '70s to the early '80s — are works that used light as a chemical and optical medium. The experiments in her photogram series *Sluices* (1980–81), made with dust and liquids, represent a kind of expansion into structural analysis.

From the beginning of the eighties, Maurer's paintings are colored in and extend into space. In a manner similar to her earlier work, she continued to examine mathematical principles and seriality on her shaped canvases.

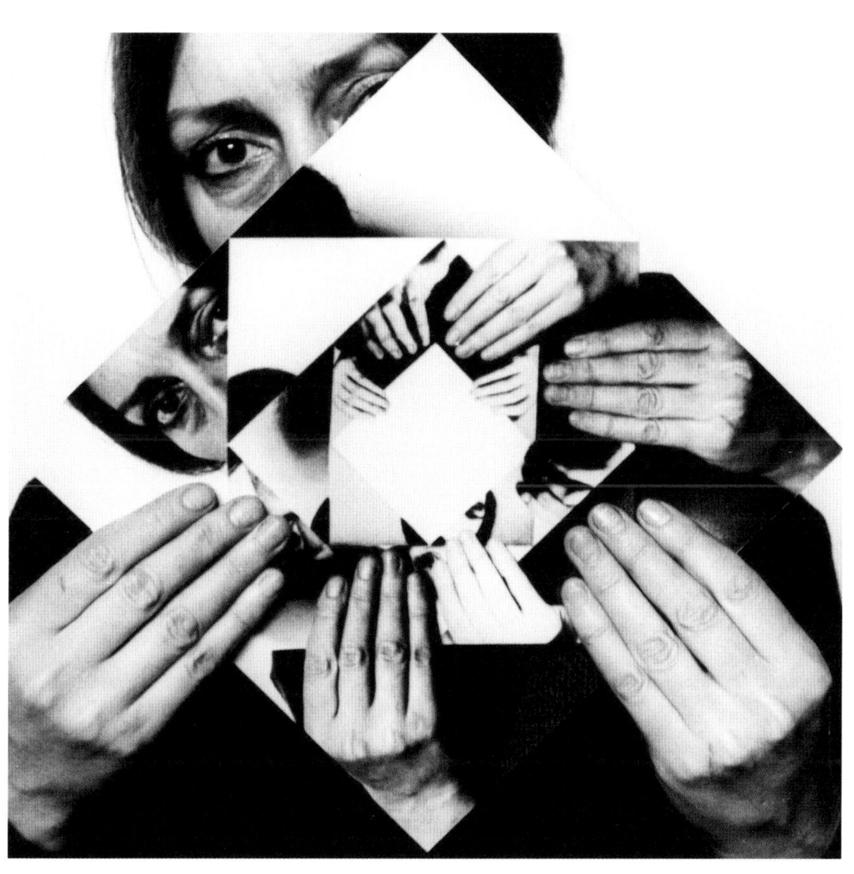

Sieben Drehungen V /Seven Twists V, 1977–78

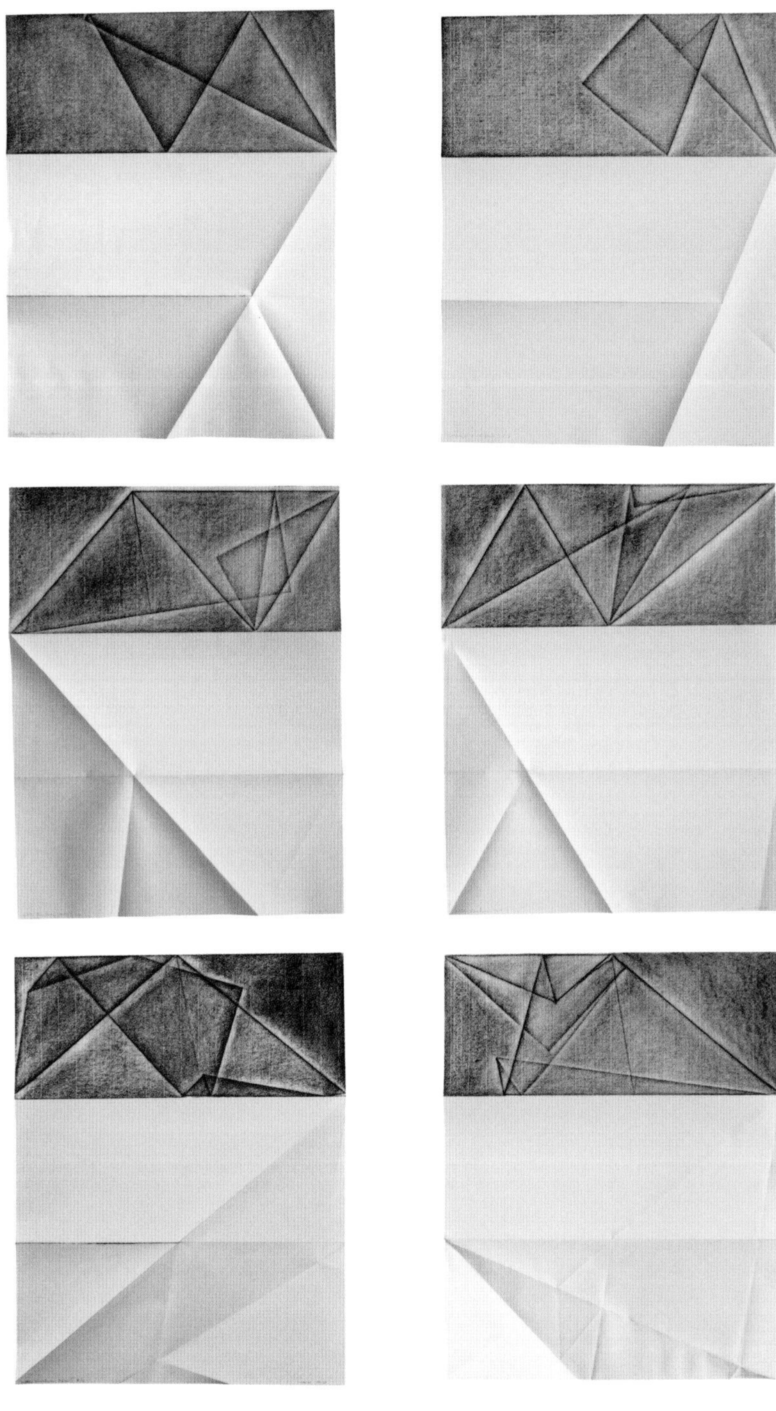

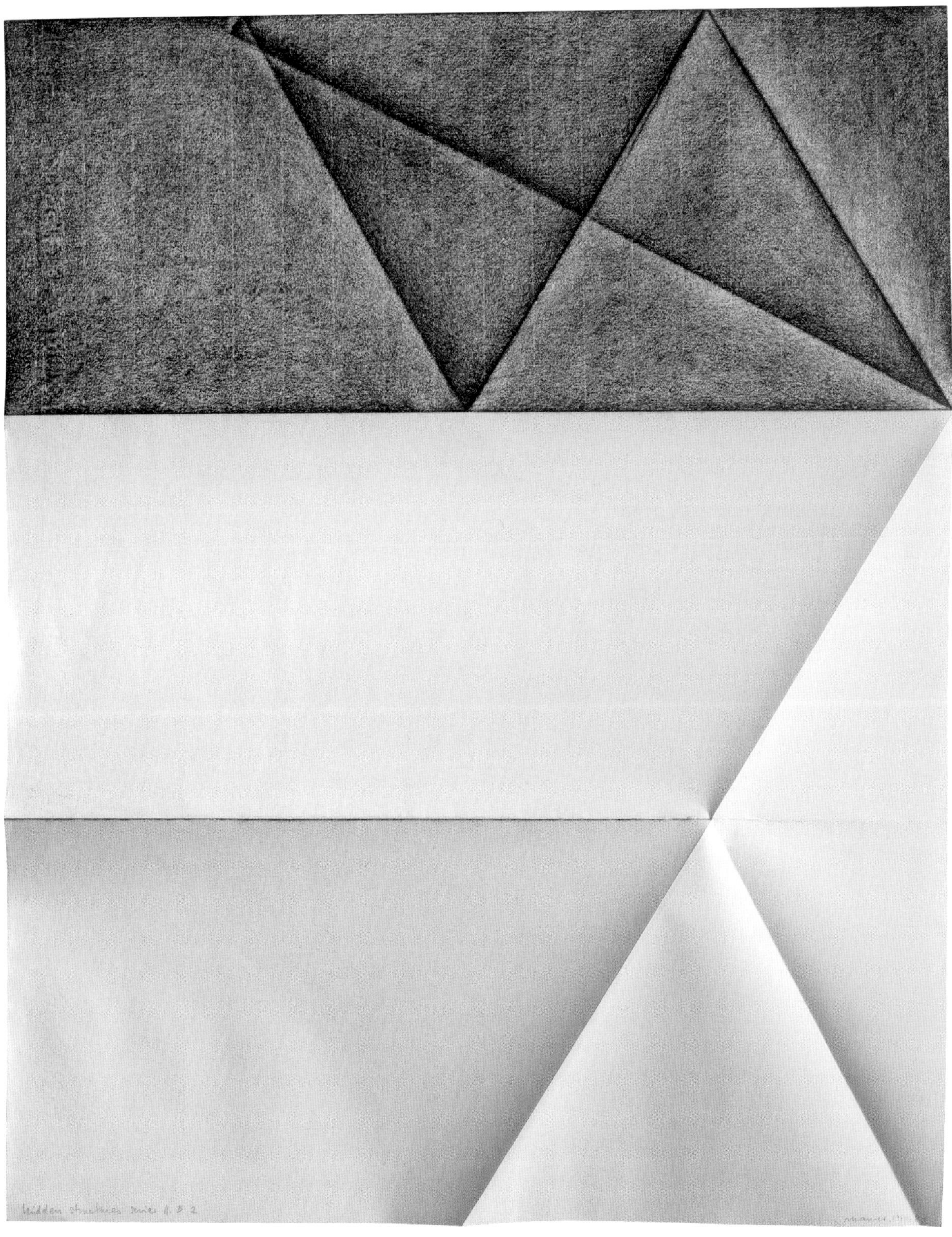

Verborgene Strukturen I–VI / Hidden Structures I–VI, 1977

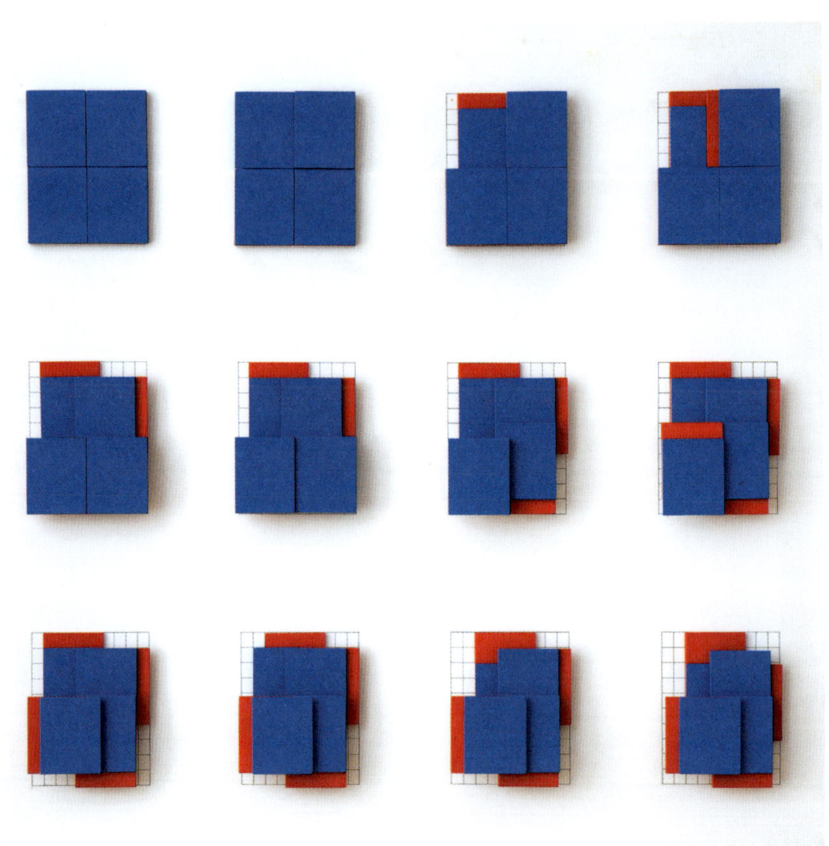

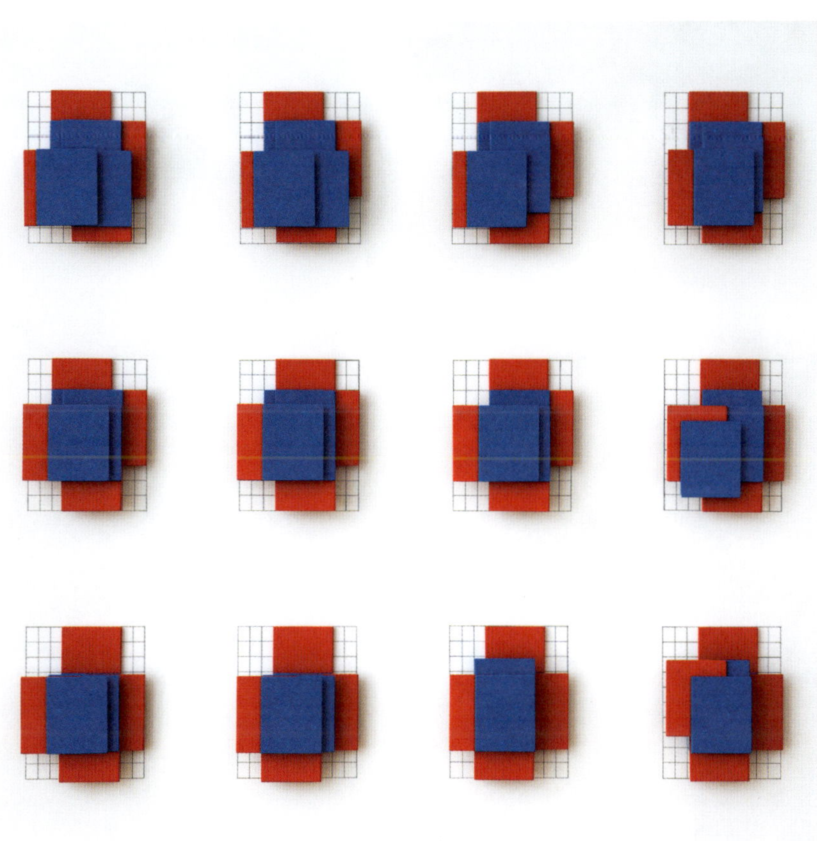

Displacements I–II (Verschiebungen I–II), 1974–75

István NÁDLER

Visegrád, 1938

István Nádlers Laufbahn als Maler gründet im geistigen Umfeld des „Zuglóer Kreises". Dieser lockere Freundeskreis, der zum Selbststudium anregte, sah seine hauptsächliche Aufgabe darin, die ungarische und internationale Kunst der Avantgarde kennenzulernen. Das intellektuelle Klima des Ateliers bestimmt die Kunst Nádlers bis zum heutigen Tage. In seinen frühen Bildern ist der Einfluss von Pierre Soulages und Alfred Manessier zu spüren, zugleich zeigt sich auch sein Interesse an der kunstgeschichtlichen Tradition (*Nike,* 1963). Nádler wandte sich jedoch relativ schnell dem amerikanischen Hard Edge zu. Auf den Leinwänden erschienen, in scharfen Konturen und reiner Farbe, durch Bartók inspirierte volkstümliche Motive. Mit diesen Bildern nahm er 1968 und 1969 an den IPARTERV-Ausstellungen (*Blütenmotiv Nr. 2,* 1968) teil. Neben den ungarischen und mitteleuropäischen Motiven beschäftigte Nádler auch die widersprüchliche Schönheit von Großstädten und Industrielandschaften. Seine Schwarz-Weiß-Kontraste und dynamischen Bildstrukturen zeigen die Welt in einer modernen, industriellen Ästhetik. Gemeinsam mit Imre Bak und János Fajó gründete er Anfang der Siebziger die Budapester Werkstatt. Dieser sowohl als Künstlergruppe wie auch als Verlag wirkenden Werkstatt schloss sich unter anderen auch Ilona Keserü an. Die Traditionen der klassischen Avantgarde fortführend, setzte er sich dafür ein, moderne Kunst populär und für alle zugänglich zu machen.

Seine Studienreisen ins Ausland (Vence, Paris, Stuttgart usw.) wirkten sich ebenfalls stark auf seine Kunst aus. Die gemeinsame Ausstellung mit Imre Bak in der Stuttgarter Galerie Müller 1968 führte zu einer Freundschaft mit Dieter Honisch sowie anderen internationalen Bekanntschaften. 1970 reiste er auf Einladung der Stiftung Károlyi erneut nach Vence. Seine zu dieser Zeit entstandenen Gemälde sind ironische Betrachtungen der technischen Zivilisation (*Säulen,* 1970). 1971/72 war er zusammen mit Imre Bak Stipendiat am Museum Folkwang in Essen. Hier verarbeitete er in seinen großformatigen Gemäldekompositionen das neue Erleben einer großindustriellen Umwelt (*Westfalen,* 1972). In den Achtzigern kehrte er zu der lyrischeren, gelösteren Malerei seines Frühwerks zurück. Dennoch bleibt in Nádlers Arbeiten eine gewisse Dualität präsent: Unabhängig von seinen geometrischen oder dynamischen Interessen – die malerisch-lyrischen Elemente dominieren.

The painting career of István Nádler began in the intellectual community of the Zugló Circle. This loose circle of friends functioned as a kind of autodidactic group; its main task was to acquaint itself with the art of the Hungarian and international avant-garde. The influence of this intellectual workshop on Nádler's art has continued to the present day. His early paintings bear the influence of Soulages and Manessier, while an interest in art historical tradition can also be seen (*Nike,* 1963). Not long afterward, however, Nádler turned to American hard edge. Influenced by Bartók, folk motifs appeared on canvases marked by sharp contours and unmixed colors, and in 1968 and 1969, he showed these new paintings in the IPARTERV exhibitions (*Petal Motif No. 2,* 1968). Along with Hungarian and Central European motifs, Nádler also explored the contradictory beauty of the industrial landscape of the metropolis. Black and white color contrasts and a dynamic pictorial structure refer to the world of modern industrial aesthetics. In the early seventies Nádler formed the artistic group "Budapest Workshop" together with Imre Bak and János Fajó. The workshop, which functioned both as artists' group and publisher, was joined by Ilona Keserü, among others. Building on the traditions of the classical avant-garde, they sought to make modern art popular and understandable for everyone.

Study trips abroad (Vence, Paris, Stuttgart, etc.) also had a major influence on Nádler's artistic practice. In 1968, he and Imre Bak held a joint exhibition at the Galerie Müller in Stuttgart, which also marked the beginning of their friendship with Dieter Honisch and other international acquaintances. In 1970 he traveled to Vence again at the invitation of the Károlyi Foundation. Ironic surveys of the objects of technological civilization appear in the paintings he made at the time (*Pillars,* 1970). In 1971–2 he received a grant from the Museum Folkwang in Essen together with Imre Bak. The large-format compositions he painted here addressed his experience with the new environment of heavy industry (*Westfalia,* 1972). In the eighties he returned to the more lyrical and relaxed painterly approach of his early years. Since then, however, a duality has been present in Nádler's work: whether it's a matter of geometrical forms or dynamic gestures, painterly-lyrical surfaces dominate.

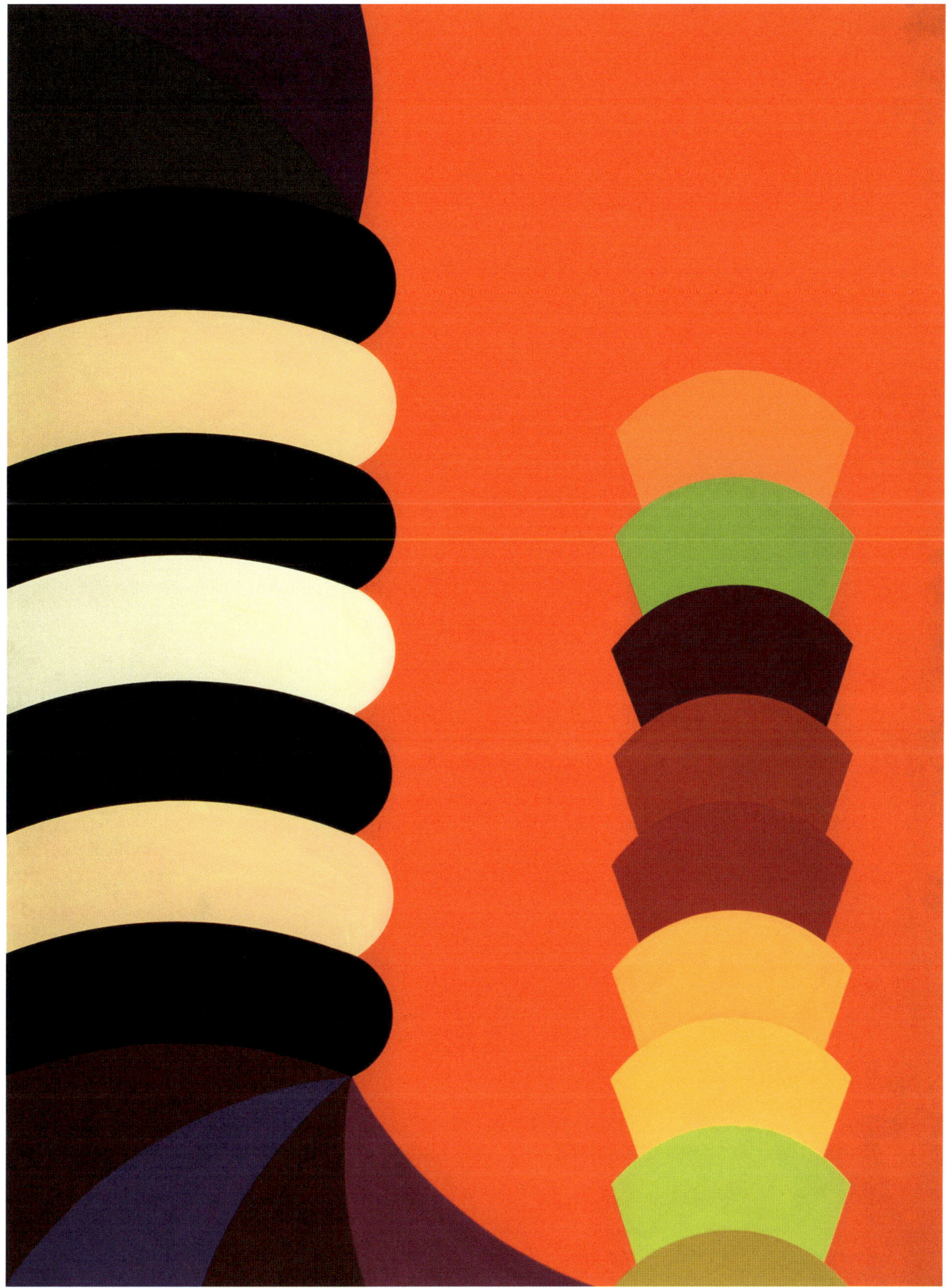

Säulen / Pillars, 1970

Géza PERNECZKY

Keszthely, 1936

Der seit 1970 in Köln lebende Géza Perneczky ist vor allem für seine charakteristischen kunstgeschichtlichen und -kritischen Texte bekannt. Jedoch war er bereits seit der ersten Hälfte der Sechzigerjahre auch als Künstler aktiv. Perneczky konnte als Mitarbeiter eines der größten ungarischen Kunstverlage und später als Kritiker bedeutender Tages- und Wochenzeitungen im Vergleich zu seinen Zeitgenossen relativ oft nach Westeuropa reisen und sich unmittelbar über die neuesten Kunsttrends informieren. Seine erste Ausstellung wurde entsprechend im Ausland gezeigt: Die Galerie Orez in Den Haag präsentierte seine von Paul Klee und Jean Dubuffet beeinflusste frühe Monotypie-Serie. Bei einer Studienreise im Jahr 1969 hatte er die Gelegenheit, sich Harald Szeemanns legendäre Ausstellung in Bern, *When Attitudes Become Form* anzusehen, woraufhin er das Publikationsreihe *Five Books* mit eigenen Fotoarbeiten und Collagen in 50/100 Kopien herausbrachte. Nach seiner Emigration arbeitete er als Kunstlehrer an einem Gymnasium und wurde freier Mitarbeiter der Deutschen Welle, später des Deutschlandfunks. 1973 schloss er sich der internationalen Mail-Art-Bewegung an und wurde einer ihrer wichtigsten Theoretiker. Seine Mail Art-Sammlung stiftete er 2009 der Staatsgalerie Stuttgart.

1971 begann er mit seiner konzeptuellen Fotoserie *Concepts like commentary*, die mit dem Kunstbegriff als solchem spielt. Mit Tischtennisbällen, die die Aufschrift „Art" tragen, führte er verschiedene „Mini-Aktionen" durch – Fotos, die diese Handlung dokumentierten, behandeln ästhetische Fragen wie die Praxis des „Spiegelns" oder die Verknüpfung von Bildlichkeit und Textualität. Die Serie *Art Bubble* (1972) ist ebenfalls eine satirische Kritik an der radikalen Ausweitung des Kunstbegriffes: die sich in den Seifenblasen spiegelnde Aufschrift „Art" verschwindet mit dem Platzen der Blasen.

Géza Perneczky, who has lived in Cologne since 1970, is best known for the individual style of his art historical writings and art criticism, although he was also, in fact, active as an artist in the first half of the 1960s. As an employee of one of the largest Hungarian art book publishers, and later as a critic of major daily and weekly papers, Perneczky – in contrast with his contemporaries – was able to travel relatively frequently to Western Europe and inform himself of the latest artistic trends in person. His first exhibition was also organized abroad: his early monotype series, which reflected the influence of Klee and Dubuffet, was shown in Galerie Orez in The Hague. A research trip in 1969 also afforded him an opportunity to see Harald Szeemann's legendary exhibition in Bern, "When Attitudes Become Form," under the influence of which he produced the publication series *Five Books* (in editions of 50-100) that brought together his photo works and collages. After emigrating, he worked as a high school drawing teacher and was also a correspondent for Deutsche Welle and Deutschlandfunk radio. In 1973 he got involved with the international Mail Art movement, becoming one of its important theoreticians. His own Mail Art collection was donated to the Stuttgart Staatsgalerie in 2009.

In 1971 Perneczky started a conceptual photography series titled *Concepts like commentary*, which played with the notion of art as such. He carried out various "mini-actions" with ping-pong balls labeled "art," photographically documented actions that framed aesthetic questions such as "mirroring" or the connection between visuality and textuality. His satirical critique of the radical extension of the art concept also appears in the series titled *Art Bubble* (1972): the word "art" is reflected on soapsuds and disappears as the bubbles burst.

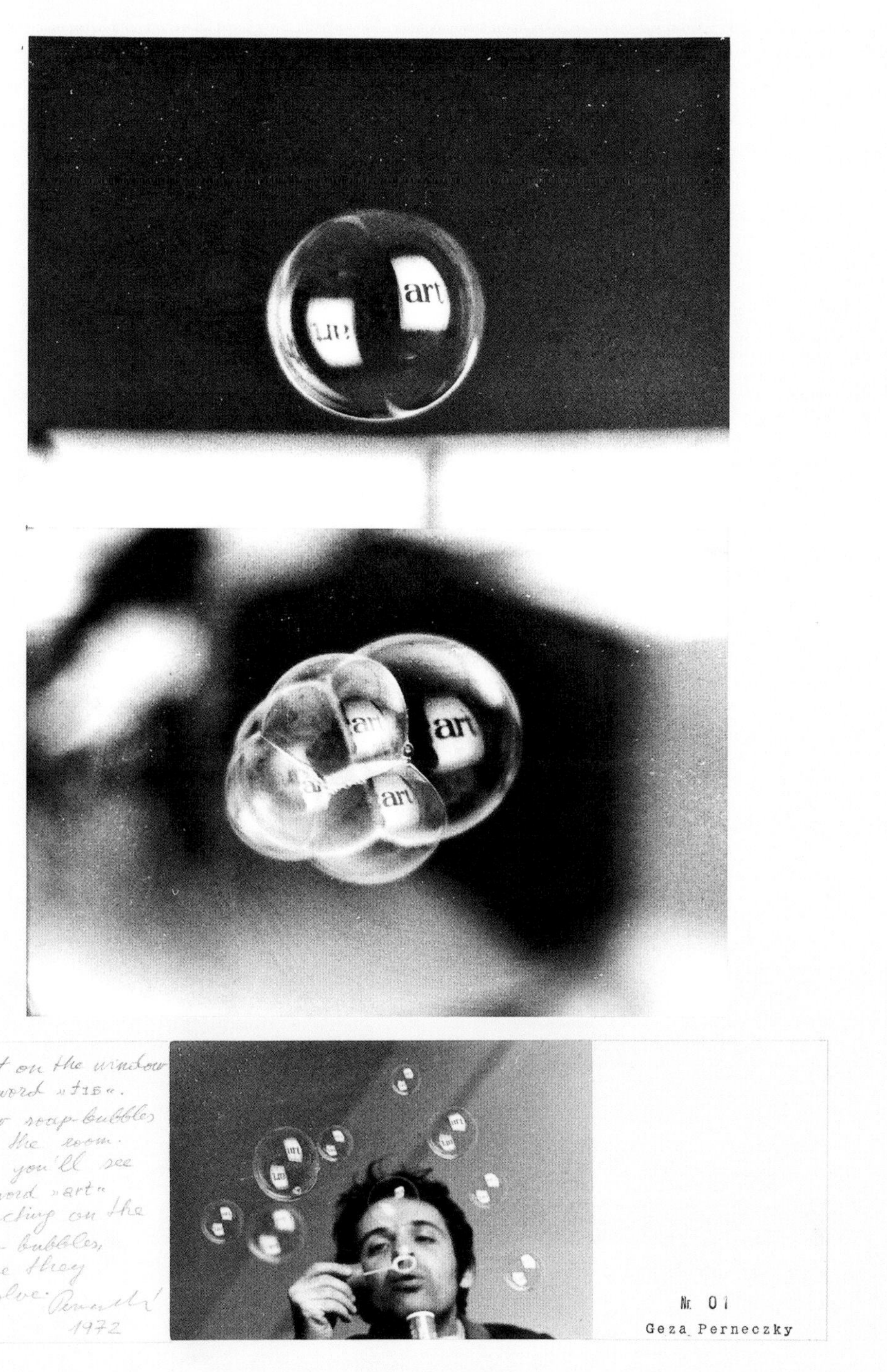

Art Bubble, 1972

SOCIÉTÉ RÉALISTE

(Ferenc Gróf, Pécs, 1972; Jean-Baptiste Naudy, Paris, 1982)

Das französisch-ungarische Künstlerkollektiv mit Sitz in Paris wurde 2004 von Ferenc Gróf und Jean-Baptiste Naudy gegründet. In ihren Ausstellungen, Publikationen und theoretischen Arbeiten reflektieren sie die visuelle Sprache von politischem Design, experimenteller Wirtschaftslehre und Sozialtechnik. Ihre Visualisierungen von Grafiken, Indizes und Infografiken machen auf soziale Probleme und geschichtliche Kataklysmen aufmerksam und beleuchten kritisch die Ungerechtigkeit des Gesellschaftssystems. Mit ihren Landkarten, Diagrammen, Emailschildern, Skulpturen und Installationen erwecken sie kulturgeschichtliche Kuriositäten zum Leben und setzen diese in ein weiter gefasstes Interpretationsfeld. Durch die Kontextwechsel und das Aufzeigen neuer Narrative schaffen sie komplexe „politische Raritätensammlungen“, wie etwa bei ihrer Ausstellung *Empire, State, Building,* die unter anderem von der Galerie nationale du Jeu de Paume in Paris gezeigt wurde (2011).

Die Plastik *March of Victory* (2014), die den Auftakt ihrer experimentellen, monumentalen Skulpturen-Reihe mit dem Titel *Mesomemorial* bildet, reflektiert den mit politischen Symbolen überfrachteten Budapester Szabadság tér (Freiheitsplatz). Das obeliskartige sowjetische Ehrenmal in der Mitte des Platzes und die vor einigen Jahren daneben aufgestellte, etwa lebensgroße realistische Skulptur von Ronald Reagan werden in ihrer Aluminiumstatue auf einen Nenner gebracht. Als mahnendes Bindeglied vereint sie symbolisch die beiden Großmächte des Kalten Krieges und bildet somit die Summe zweier Denkmäler.

The Paris-based French-Hungarian artists' collective Société Réaliste was founded in 2004 by Ferenc Gróf and Jean-Baptiste Naudy. In their exhibitions, publications, and theoretical work, they reflect on political design, experimental economic theory, and the visual language of social engineering. Often using the to-the-point visual language of graphs, signs, and infographics, they depict social problems and historical cataclysms and formulate their criticism of the unfair nature of the social system. Curiosities of cultural history are brought to life and placed in wider interpretive fields through their maps, diagrams, aluminum boards, sculptures, and installations. With changes in context and the highlighting of new narratives, they bring into being complex "collections of political rarities," for example in their exhibition "Empire, State, Building," which was shown at the Jeu de Paume in Paris, as well as in other venues.

The statue *March of Victory* (2014), the first in a series of experimental monumental sculptures titled *Mesomorial*, reflects on the symbolically charged space of Budapest's Freedom Square. Their aluminum statue is the common denominator between the obelisk-style Soviet memorial in the center of the square and the slightly larger-than-life-sized realistic statue of Ronald Reagan, which was erected nearby a few years ago. This joint memorial statue came about as an averaging out of the form of the two monuments, as a result of which the two great superpowers of the Cold War are unified as one.

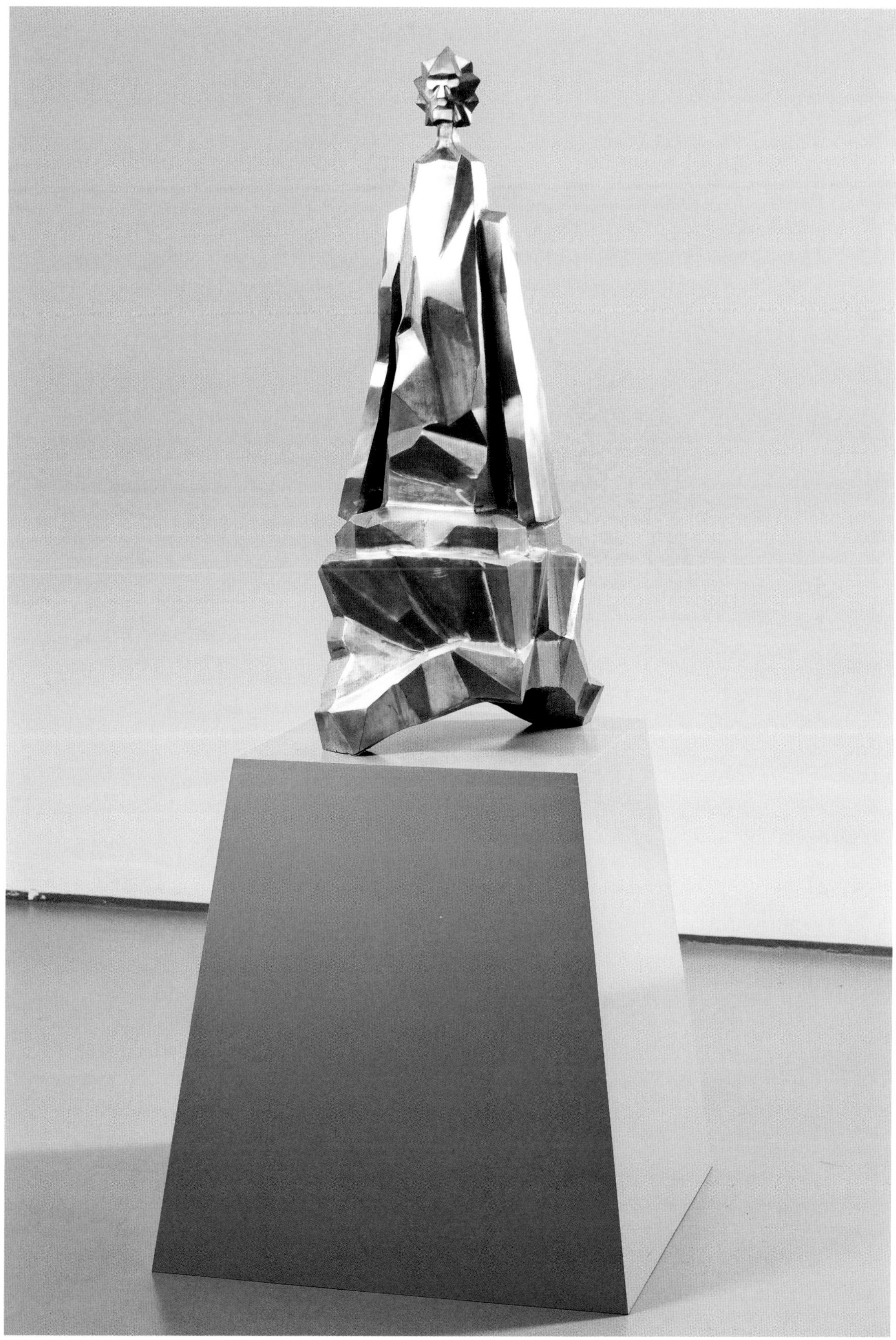

Mesomemorial: March of Victory, 2014

Dezső SZABÓ

Keszthely, 1967

Dezső Szabó untersucht in seinen Fotografien die gegenständliche, physische Wirklichkeit von Bildern und damit die Möglichkeiten, wie Fotos als Medium künstlerisch verwendet werden können. Zentrales Element seiner Kunst ist die Kritik an der Überproduktion von Bildern.

Szabó studierte an der Budapester Akademie für Bildende Künste bei Zsigmond Károlyi, der seine Studenten unter anderem anleitete, mittels einer konsequenten monochromen Malerei bildnerischen Darstellungsweisen kritisch zu begegnen. In seinen frühen, analytisch-monochromen Bildern versuchte Szabó, die Retinalität zu überwinden. Die künstlerische Einbeziehung der Fotografie war einen weiteren Schritt auf diesem Weg. Mit Darstellungen des leeren Himmels oder reglosen Wasserspiegels in seinen ersten Fotografien übertrug er die Lehren der monochromen Malerei auf ein anderes Medium.

Das Hinterfragen von Bildinhalten wurde zum Ordnungsprinzip jener simulierten Fotoserien, die er auf der Basis seiner selbstgebastelten Modelle anfertigte. Seine frühen Serien beschäftigen sich, angefangen mit den *Feldübungen* (1998), mit der Beziehung von visueller Darstellung und Wirklichkeit. Szabós Kunst kritisiert den dokumentierenden Charakter von Fotos und das Bilderdumping der vermittelnden Medien. Seine illusionistischen, dokumentartigen, typisch körnigen Fotografien erinnern an Standbilder von Dokumentarfilmen oder Fernsehberichten. Sie zeigen Naturkatastrophen und Autounfälle, die Bilder erzeugt Szabó jedoch selbst, indem er Modelle konstruiert, die eine mediatisierte Wirklichkeit spiegeln.

In der Arbeit *Turbo & Still* (Fotos und ein 16-mm-Film, 2009) wird eine (ebenfalls als Modell nachgebaute) Windturbine zum charakteristischen Landschaftselement der modernen industriellen Gesellschaft – im Rahmen einer künstlerischen Auseinandersetzung ein starkes Bild. In seinen neuesten Arbeiten verwendet er Nebelmaschinen, pyrotechnische Erzeugnisse, Wasserstromgeneratoren sowie ein großes Spektrum an Gerätschaften, um drastische Naturphänomene und physikalische Effekte nachzustellen. Die Bilder der Serie *Electric Field* (2012) machte er mithilfe eines eigens zu diesem Zweck gebauten Tesla-Transformators. Die elektrischen Entladungen des Gerätes sind Miniaturausgaben von Blitzen bei Sommergewittern. Szabó setzt seine Analyse über den Funktionsmechanismus fotografischer Bilder in diesen Fotografien fort.

Dezső Szabó's photographs investigate the objective, physical reality of the image and the possibilities it offers for using photography as an artistic medium. A central element of his art is his critical position towards the over-production of images.

Szabó was a student of Zsigmond Károlyi at the Academy of Fine Arts, who (among other things) taught his students to critique the pictorial image through his systematic program of monochromatic painting. Szabó's early analytical monochrome canvases can be viewed as just such an attempt to eradicate retinality. The artistic use of photography represents a further step along this path. In his first photographs of the empty sky or a motionless reflection on water, the artist transposed the lessons of monochromatic painting into another medium.

The questioning of spectacle became the organizing principle for photo series made with simulation technology and based on models the artist produced. His early series, beginning with *Field Trip* in 1998, investigated the connection between the depicted spectacle and reality. In Szabó's art, the critique is directed against the documentary character of the photographic image and visual dumping of transmission media. His illusionary, document-like, characteristically grainy photos resemble stills from documentary films and TV reports. Natural catastrophes and car accidents are featured in them; the depicted spectacle, however, was brought into being by the artist himself, using a model to construct a mediatizable reality.

In the work *Turbo & Still* (photos and a 16-mm film, 2009), a wind turbine, also built in model form, appears as the characteristic landscape element of modern industrial society. It is also, from the point of view of artistic analysis, an exciting form. In his most recent work Szabó uses fog machines, pyrotechnics, wave machines, and a broad range of other special equipment to create spectacles of extreme natural and physical phenomena. The images from his series *Electric Field* (2012) are brought into being using a specially built Tesla transformer. The electrical sparks of the instrument are miniature copies of the lightning that strikes during summer storms. In these photos, Szabó continues his research into the working mechanisms of photographic images.

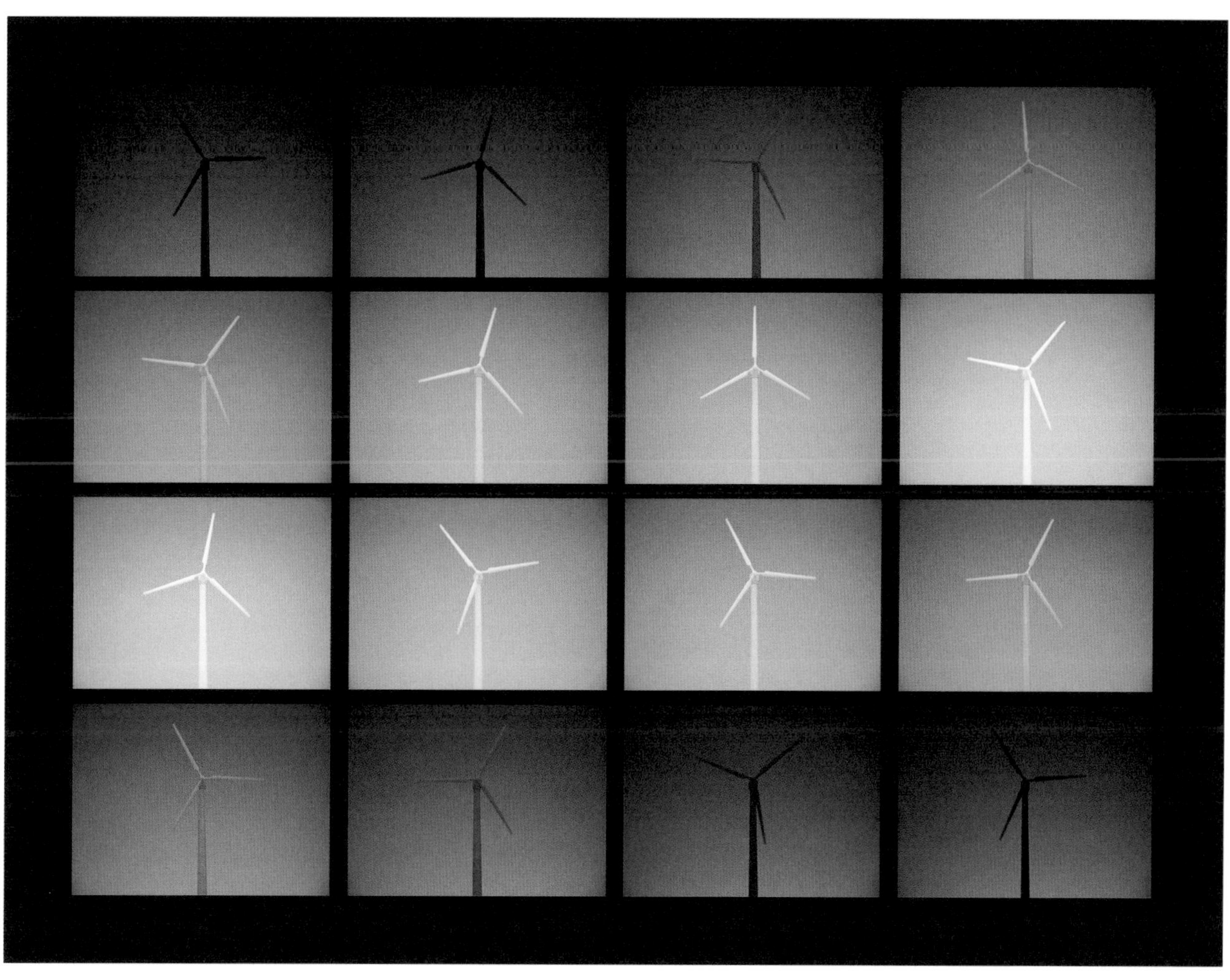

TURBO & STILL / TURBO STILLS, 2009

Péter SZALAY

Pécs, 1981

Péter Szalay, der jüngste Teilnehmer dieser Ausstellung, gilt mit seinen aus gefundenen Gegenständen gefertigten ironischen Objekten, Mobiles und Installationen als einer der vielversprechendsten Vertreter der jüngeren Generation des ungarischen Konzeptualismus. Er nutzt zahlreiche Ausdrucksformen, von kinetischen Skulpturen über Ölgemälde bis hin zu Kunststoffnippes mit Porzellaneffekt und animierten Gipsbildern, doch sein besonderer Humor, seine unerwarteten Assoziationen, seine experimentelle Neigung sowie seine kritische Art weisen auf einen sehr konsequenten individuellen Lebensweg hin.

Szalay ist ein vielstimmiger Künstler: Seine Werke beinhalten politische Gags, abstrakte bildhauerische Probleme, die Visualisierung wissenschaftlicher Thesen sowie zeitgenössische kunsthistorische Reflexionen. Gemein ist allen Werken, dass sie von gefundenen und recht kunstfremden Gegenständen ausgehen (Seife, Expander, Löwenzahn, Schuhkarton, Zimmerpflanze, mechanisches Uhrwerk, Fernsehantenne, aus Spitze gefertigtes Basketballnetz), die der Künstler mit einer nahezu kindlichen Neugierde entdeckt und sich aneignet. Eine seiner komplexesten Arbeiten, *Restwert* (2014), hat er aus dem Bauschutt einer gerade renovierten Galerie gebaut. Szalay präsentierte den Schutt, die Putzstücke in Schaukästen, setzte mit einer mechanischen Konstruktion die Schutthaufen in Bewegung und erweckte sie quasi zum Leben. So hauchte er dem toten Material in mehrfachem Sinne Leben ein und erhob den Bauschutt im musealen Kontext zu einem Kunstobjekt, das es zu bewahren gilt.

Die beiden in „Bookmarks" ausgestellten Arbeiten sind ebenfalls aus gefundenen Gegenständen entstanden. Das Uhrwerk aus *Statische Zeit* (2011) dreht sich um die eigene Achse, während es auf seinen Zeigern steht, und die im Wasser rostende Eisenrose aus *Gute Absicht* (2014) verweist auf Vergänglichkeit und Verfall.

The youngest artist in the exhibition, Péter Szalay's ironic objects built from found objects, mobiles, and installations make him one of the most promising representatives of the younger generation of Hungarian conceptualism. From kinetic statues and oil paintings to faux-porcelain plastic knick-knacks and animated plaster pictures, he works in countless mediums, while his individual sense of humor, unexpected associations, experimental tendencies, and critical attitude bring to fore a systematically constructed, singular life path.

Szalay is a polyphonic artist: his works encompass numerous themes, ranging from political gags to problems of abstract sculpture, from the visuality of academic categories to contemporary art historical reflections. What almost all his works have in common is that they take as their starting point found objects that are rather far from the usual art context (soap, a chest expander, a child's daisy chain, a shoe box, a house plant, mechanical time piece, television antenna, a basketball net made of lace), which the artist discovers with almost childlike curiosity and appropriates for his own purposes. One of his most complex works, *Residual Value* (2014), is built from the debris of a recently renovated gallery space. Szalay arranges the rubble and pieces of plaster into a display, using mechanical structures to transform the bags of rubble into moving, living things, breathing life into materials that have died several times over and elevating the construction rubbish to precious art objects in a museum situation.

Two works exhibited here are also constructed from found objects. The time-keeping mechanism in *Static Time* (2011) turns around on its own axis, while its clock hands remain motionless. The rusting iron rose submerged in water in *Good Intent* (2014) draws attention to the inevitable fading and decay of objects.

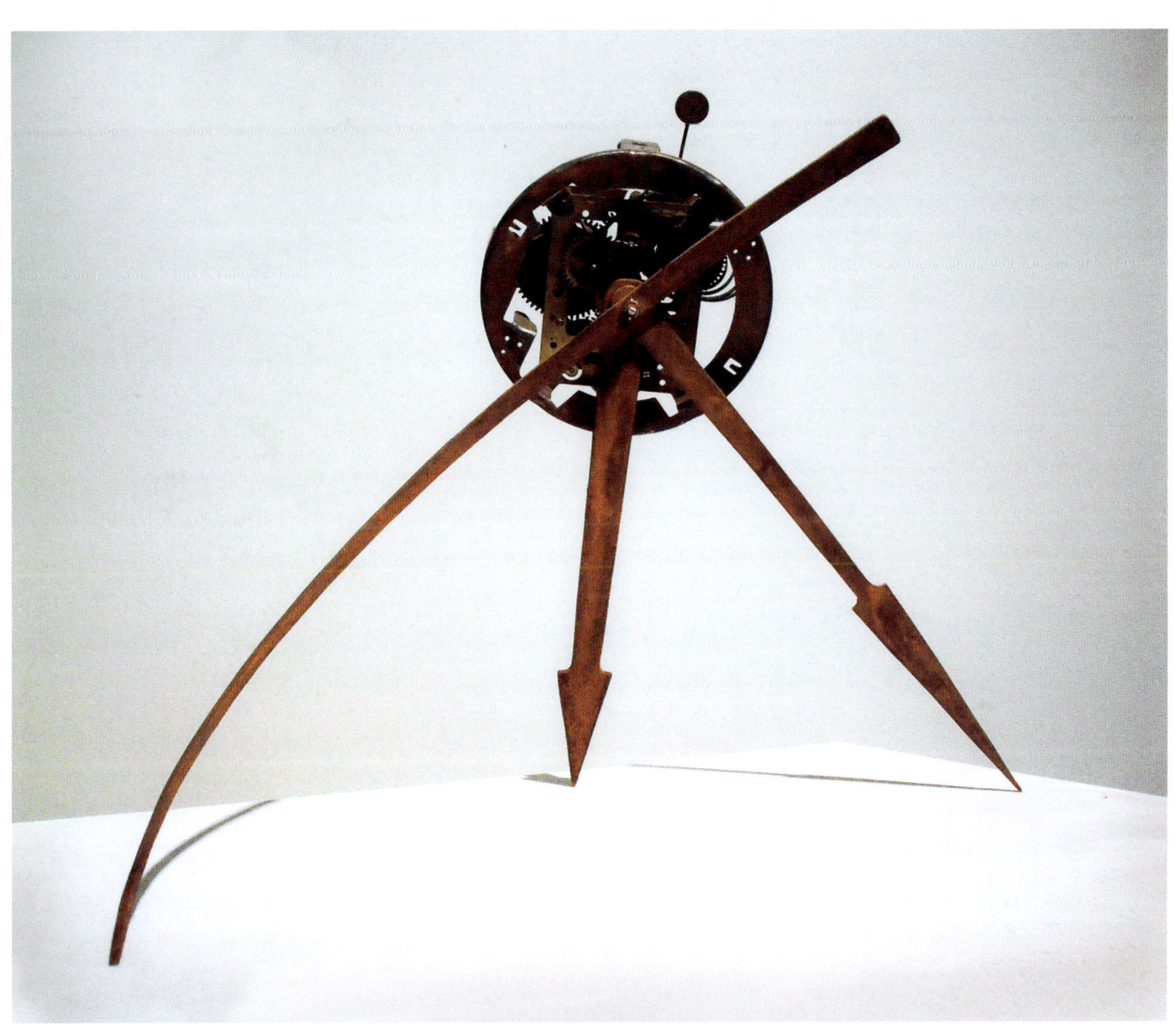

Statische Zeit / Static Time, 2011

Tamás SZENTJÓBY

Fót, 1944

Die ab Mitte der Sechzigerjahre zu beobachtenden Erscheinungsformen des ungarischen Aktionismus – Happening, Fluxus – gehen in erster Linie auf Tamás Szentjóby (auch St. Auby, St. Aubsky, T. Taub, usw., heute: St. Turba) zurück. Szentjóby begann als eines der vielversprechendsten Talente der neuen Dichtergeneration, dessen lyrische Praxis sich bereits früh von der Sprache und Struktur der traditionellen Dichtung distanzierte und einen wichtigen Teil des Paradigmenwechsels des Modernismus beziehungsweise der Avantgarde darstellte. Vor dem ersten Happening (*Das Mittagessen. In Memoriam Batu Khan,* 25. Juni 1966), das er mit Gábor Altorjay organisierte, entstanden Szentjóbys erste Bildgedichte, die unter der Berücksichtigung der plastischen Dimension des Textes die Charakteristika eines intermedialen Denkens aufwiesen. Der Begriff Intermedia – das dialektische Verhältnis zwischen den Medien – ist für seine Bildgedichte, Objekte, Aktionen, aber auch für seinen 1973–75 entstandenen Film *Zentaur* bestimmend. *Die biochemische Wirkung auf das Vaterunser* (1983) mit den dazu gehörenden neun Bildgedichten stellt eine repräsentative Werkgruppe in der avantgardistischen Lyrik von Tamás Szentjóby dar, deren wichtiges Merkmal die Ersetzbarkeit beziehungsweise Austauschbarkeit von Medien ist, wie auch in seinem Werk *Schöne Dunkelheit – Audio-taktylisches Bildgedicht für Blinde* aus dem Jahr 1970 zu sehen. Ein anderes Beispiel, ein im Augenblick der ersten Mondlandung entstandenes Aktionsobjekt (1969), vergegenständlicht die poetischen Dimensionen dieses wichtigen Ereignisses der Raumfahrt mittels einer unkonventionellen Auffassung von Fotografie.

Szentjóby blieb nicht nur als Dichter durchweg in der Illegalität (seine Gedichte wurden einzig von avantgardistischen Zeitschriften in Jugoslawien publiziert), sondern entwickelte bewusst als Oppositioneller ein parallel zur Kultur und Realität des Sozialismus verlaufendes, abgekoppeltes Programm: *Parallelkurs/Lehrbahn* (ab 1968) – den theoretischen Hintergrund lieferte die esoterische Philosophie des ebenfalls oppositionell aktiven Béla Hamvas – zielte auf eine parallele Wirklichkeit ab, die entgegen einer korrupten Wirklichkeit ins Leben gerufen werden sollte. *Emblem – Parallelkurs/Lehrbahn* (1968) kombiniert (als Vergegenständlichung dieses Programms) die Duchampsche Tradition des Readymade mit dem Element Schwefel als chemisch-alchimistische Komponente. Schwefel – als beißende, unangenehme und gefährliche Substanz – ist ein wichtiger Bestandteil seines vielleicht explizitesten politischen Werkes, *Tschechoslowakisches Radio 1968* (1969), das sowohl mit den Ereignissen der Prager Intervention als auch der (neuen linken) Wende Szentjóbys infolge der 68er in Verbindung zu bringen ist.

After emerging in the mid-sixties, Hungarian Actionism (happening, Fluxus) is primarily associated with Tamás Szentjóby (also St. Auby, St. Aubsky, T. Taub etc., today: St. Turba). As one of the most promising figures of the new poetry, Szentjóby's poetic praxis soon moved away from the language and structure of traditional poetry writing to play an important role in the modernist/avant-garde paradigm shift. Even before the first happening (*The Lunch. In memoriam Batu Khan,* June 25, 1966) was organized, he had created visual poems that took into account the plasticity of text and bore characteristics of intermedial thinking. The notion of intermedia – the dialectic relationship between media – fundamentally defines his visual poems, objects, actions, and even the film *Centaur,* which was made between 1973 and 1975. With the nine visual poems accompanying it, *The influence of biochemistry on Our Father* (1983) is a representative body of work within Szentjóby's avant-garde poetry, one of the important characteristics of which is the substitutability or interchangeability of media, as can be seen in his *Beautiful Darkness – Audio-tactilist visual poem for the blind* from 1970. Another example is the action-object he made at the moment of the first moon landing, which objectifies the poetic dimensions of an important space-age event through an unconventional approach to photography (1969).

Not only did Szentjóby remain illegal as a poet (his poems were only published in Yugoslavian avant-garde magazines), but as a conscious oppositionist, he also constructed a program parallel to, and therefore entirely outside, the culture and reality of socialism. This was the *Parallel Course / Study Track* program (from 1968), the theoretical background of which lay in the esoteric philosophy of the similarly oppositionist Béla Hamvas, which aimed for a parallel reality as opposed to the prevalent corrupt reality. As a materialized version of this program, the *Emblem – Parallel Course / Study Track* (1968) combined the Duchampian tradition with the chemical/alchemical component embodied by sulphur. A pungent, unpleasant, and dangerous material, sulphur is an important element of Szentjóby's perhaps most explicitly political work, *Czechoslovak Radio 1968* (1969), which is related both to the events of the intervention in Prague and the artist's turn towards the New Left in the wake of 1968.

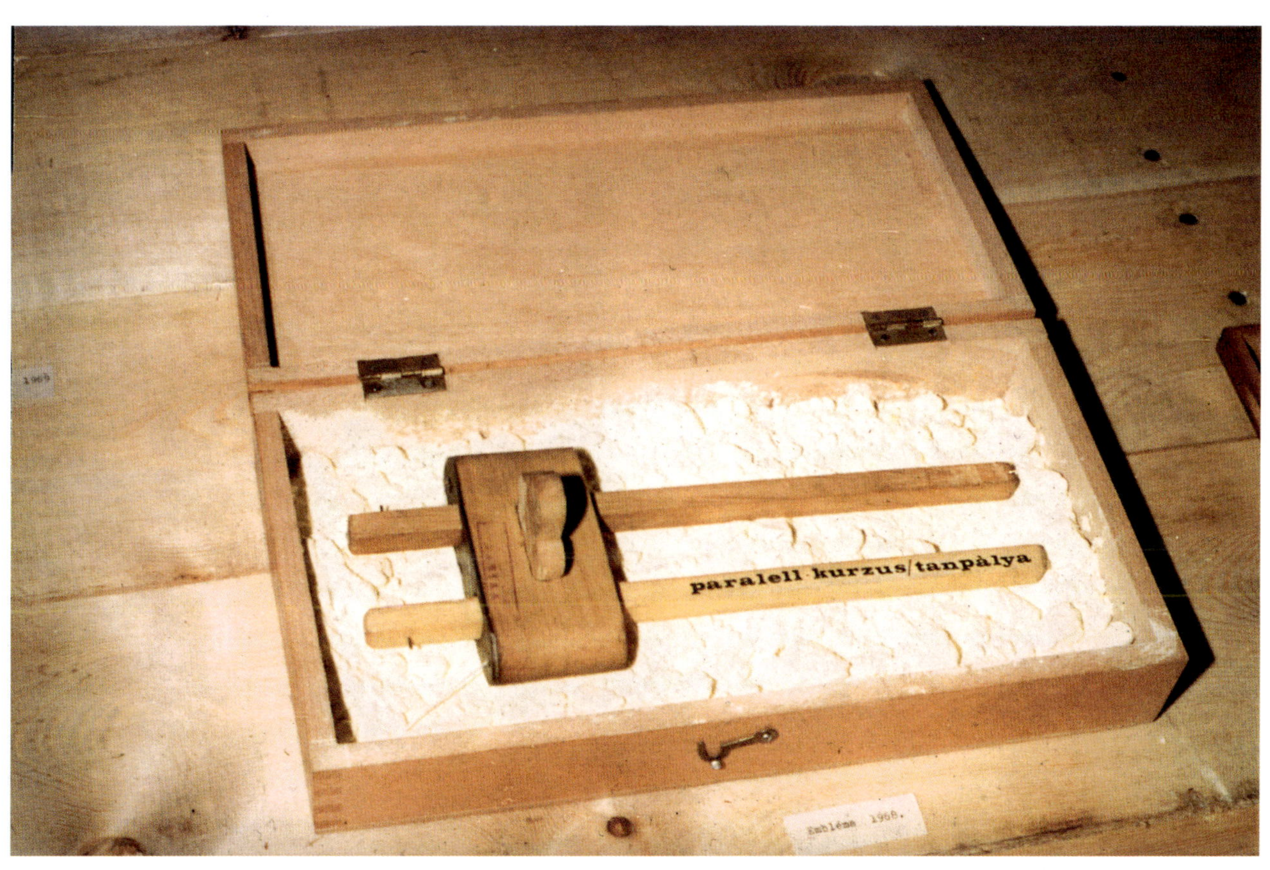

Emblem – Parallelkurs / Lehrbahn // Emblem – Parallel Course / Study Track, 1968

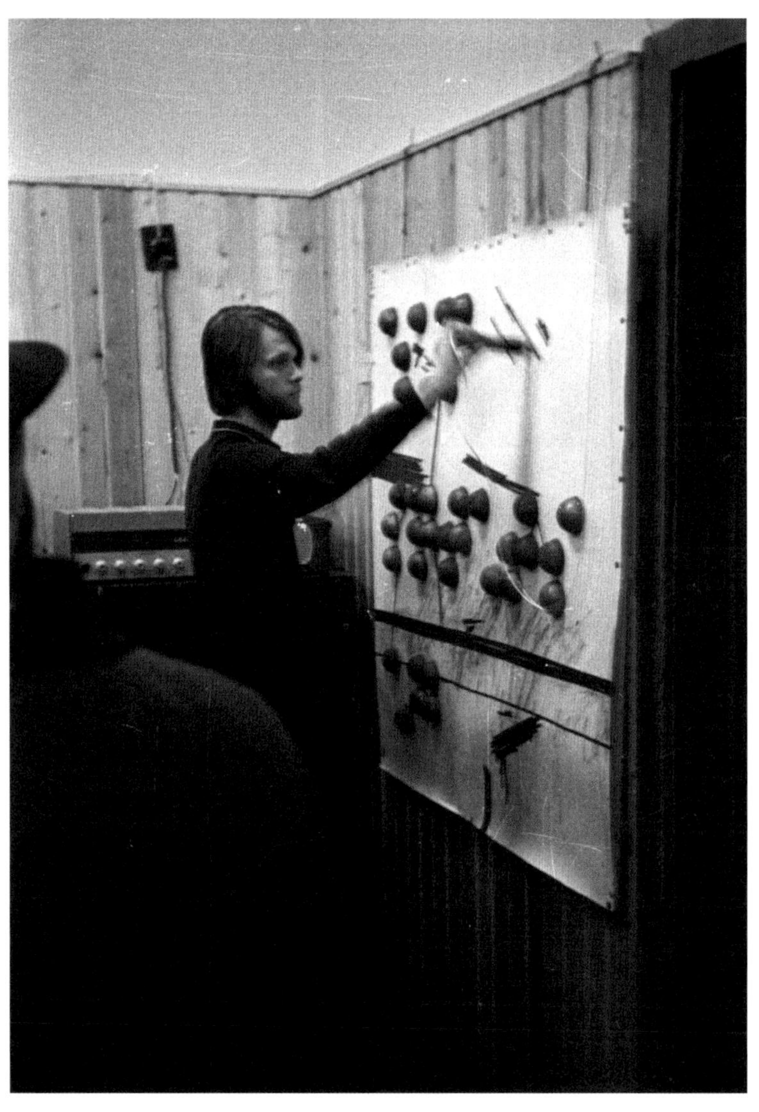

Schöne Dunkelheit – Audio-taktylisches Bildgedicht für Blinde /
Beautiful Darkness – Audio-tactilist visual poem for the blind, 1970

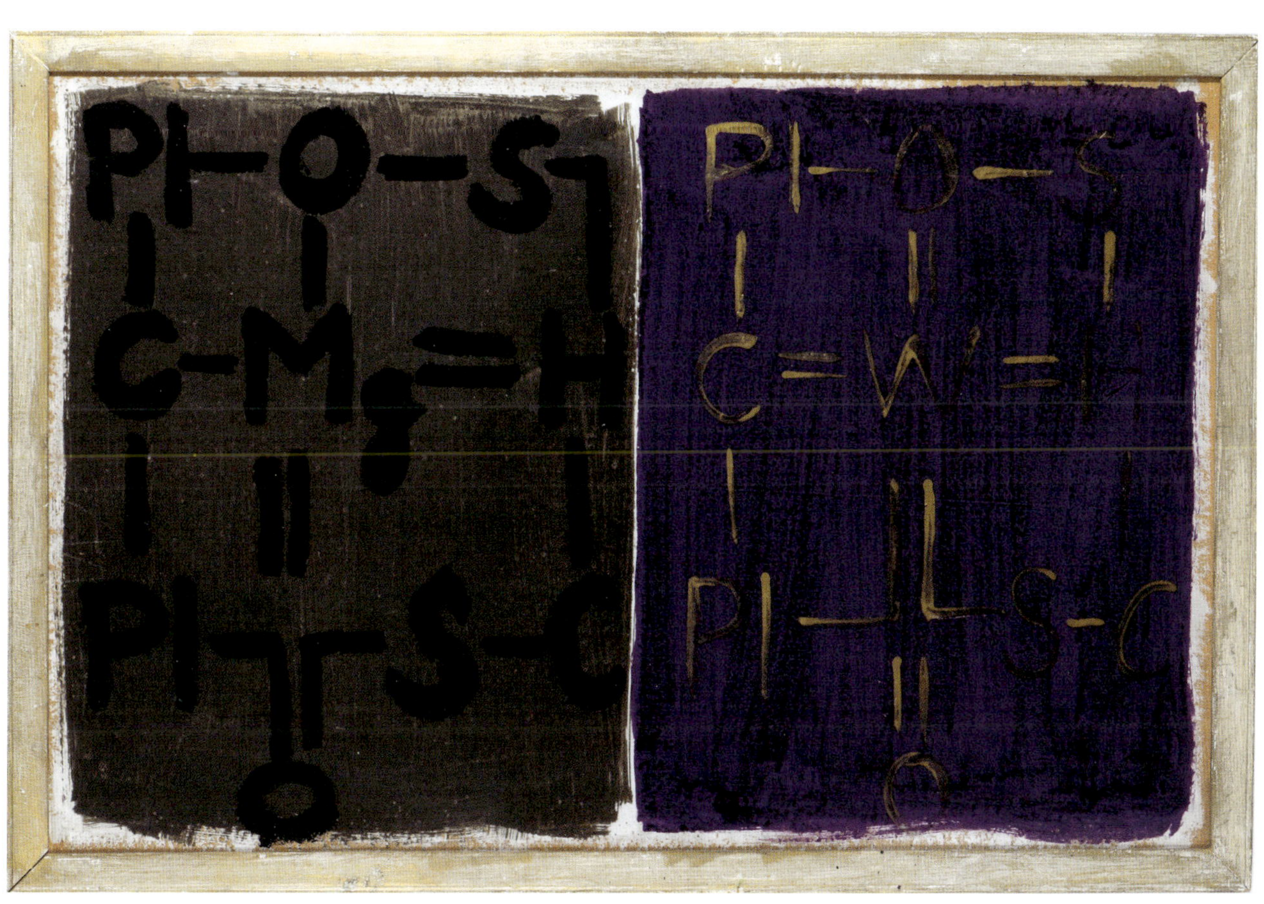

 Die biochemische Wirkung auf das Vaterunser / The influence of biochemistry on Our Father, 1983

Endre TÓT

Sümeg, 1937

Pierre Restany schrieb: „Endre Tót: der Yves Klein der Mail Art, ein postalisches Monochrom." Die recht enigmatische Aussage des französischen Theoretikers bringt das Werk des Künstlers jedoch auf den Punkt. Tót begann als Maler, und der ständige Dialog mit der Malerei blieb auch dann in seiner Kunst präsent, als er 1970/71 radikal mit diesem Medium brach.

Seine künstlerische Laufbahn begann Anfang der Sechzigerjahre. Nach dem Studium an der Hochschule für Angewandte Kunst malte er kalligrafische, dem Informel nahestehende Gemälde, bis ihn Ende der Sechziger die Pop Art stark beeinflusste. Seine mit minimalistischen, geometrischen Oberflächen kombinierten, collage-artigen Bilder wurden in den legendären IPARTERV-Ausstellungen (1968–69) gezeigt. Doch wie so viele seiner Generation empfand auch Tót den Rahmen der traditionellen Kunstgattungen und -arten als zu eng. Er hatte „die Malerei satt", und in seiner Kunst tauchten neue Elemente und Medien auf: Telegramme, Postkarten, Briefmarken, Stempel, Filme, Plakate, Graffiti, Transparente, Aktionen, Kunstbücher usw. Von da an widmete er sich ganz der Untersuchung dreier Schlüsselbegriffe: *Nothing/Zero*, *Rain* und *Gladness*. Sein erstes Kunstbuch, eine Auseinandersetzung mit dem Thema der gefühlten Leerstelle, war *Meine ungemalten Bilder* – leere Rahmen beziehungsweise die reinen Maßangaben der Werke ersetzten tatsächliche Gemälde.

Wie für so viele osteuropäische Künstler bedeutete auch für Tót die Mail Art zu jener Zeit die einzige Möglichkeit, einen Anschluss an die internationale Kunst zu finden. Mit seinen *Zero*-Werken nahm er 1971 in der Sektion „Envois" an der Pariser Biennale wie auch an der ebenfalls von Jean-Marc Poinsot veranstalteten ersten Mail-Art-Ausstellung 1972 teil. Mit seinen postalischen Sendungen kam er so auch unter anderen mit Ken Friedman und Ben Vautier in Kontakt, mit denen er seitdem befreundet ist.

In dieser Zeit fertigte er das erste Stück seiner Serie *TÓTalJOYs* an (ab 1973), einen auf einen Karton im A5-Format gedruckten Text – „Ich freue mich, diesen Text gedruckt haben zu können." Seine Aktionen trug er damals in Ungarn noch vor der Kamera vor, seine erste gefilmte *TÓTalJOY*-Demonstration zeigte er in Genf. Nach seiner Emigration (1978 verließ er Ungarn endgültig, seit 1980 lebt er in Köln) veranstaltete er zahlreiche Joy- beziehungsweise Zero-Demonstrationen überall auf der Welt.

In the words of Pierre Restany: "Endre Tót: the Yves Klein of Mail Art, a postal monochrome." The French theorist's rather enigmatic sentence does actually give a precise and solid description of Tót's career. He began as a painter, and a constant dialogue with the tradition of painting is still present in his art, even after – in 1970-71 – he broke radically with this medium.

His artistic career began in the early years of the sixties. After graduating from the University of Applied Arts, he made lyrical, calligraphic paintings that were closely related to Informel, while at the end of the sixties Pop Art also had a serious influence on his practice: he participated in the legendary IPARTERV exhibitions (1968-69) with minimalist, geometrical surfaces combined on collage-like pictures. In common with many in his generation, Tót also found the traditional genres and artistic frameworks to be too narrow. He was "fed up" with painting, and new media appeared in his work (telegrams, postcards, postal stamps, rubber stamps, film, posters, graffiti, banners, actions, artist books, etc). From this point onwards he devoted his work to the investigation of three key concepts, *Nothing/Zero*, *Rain*, and *Gladness*. In one of his earliest artist books, *My Painted Canvases* (1971), empty spaces and the bare details (dimensions) of the works stand in place of reproductions of actual paintings, reflecting on the problem of absence.

As in the case of so many Eastern European artists, Mail Art represented in this period the only means for Tót to connect with the international art scene. He took part with his works *Zero* in the special "Envois" section of the 1971 Paris Biennial, as well as in the first Mail Art exhibition of 1972, both of which were curated by Jean-Marc Poinsot. At the same time, sending things through the post brought him into contact with Ken Friedman and Ben Vautier amongst others, resulting in a lasting friendship.

At that time he also created the first part of his series *TÓTalJOYS* (since 1973), consisting of the following text printed on an A5 piece of cardboard: "I'm glad that I was able to print this text." In Hungary he carried out the first of his actions in front of a camera, while the first *TÓTalJOYS* demonstration to be recorded on film was held in Geneva, and after emigrating (in 1978 he left Hungary for good and has lived in Cologne since 1980), the artist has held numerous *Joy* and *Zero* demonstrations all around the world.

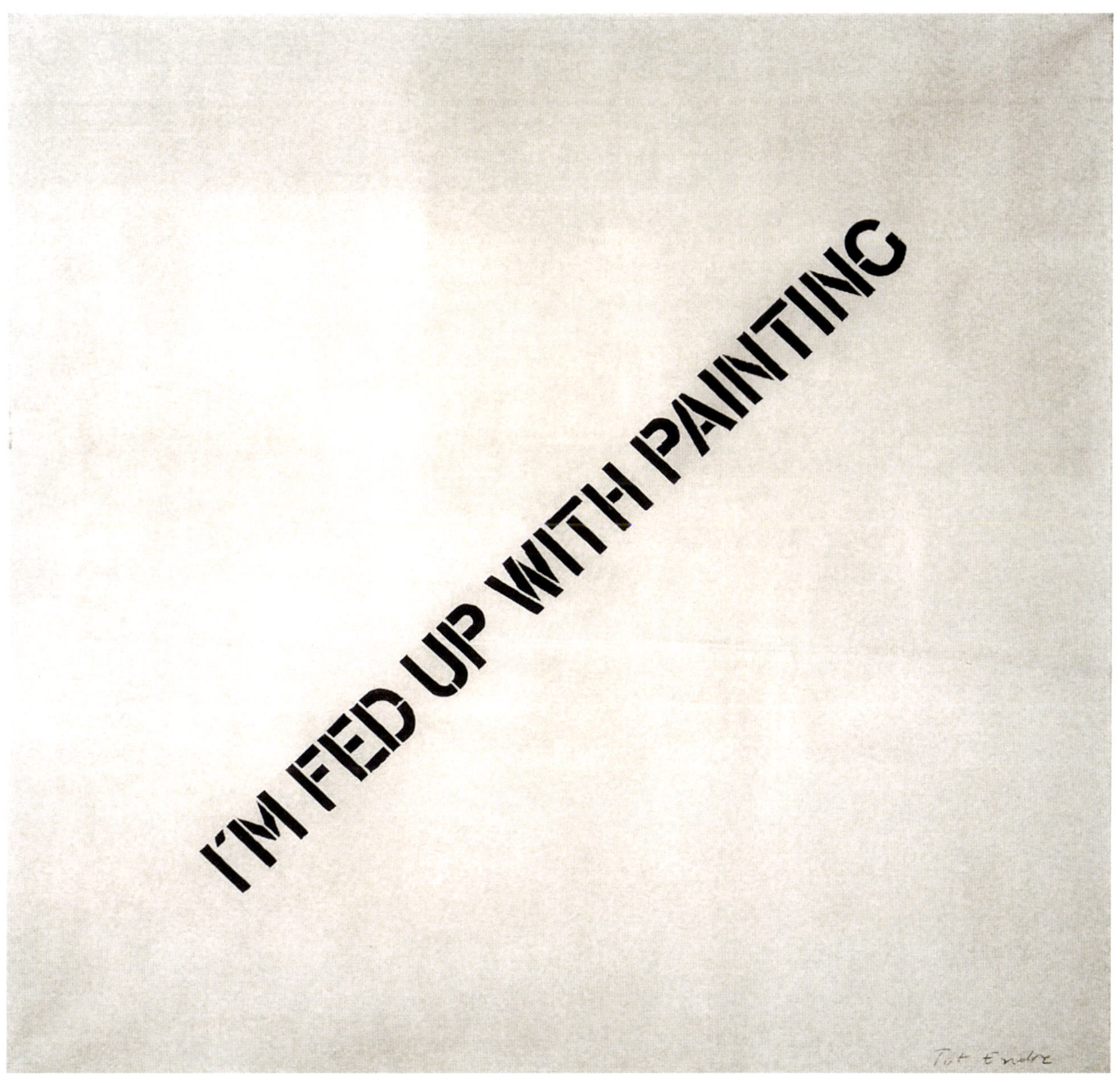

I'm fed up with painting, 1972

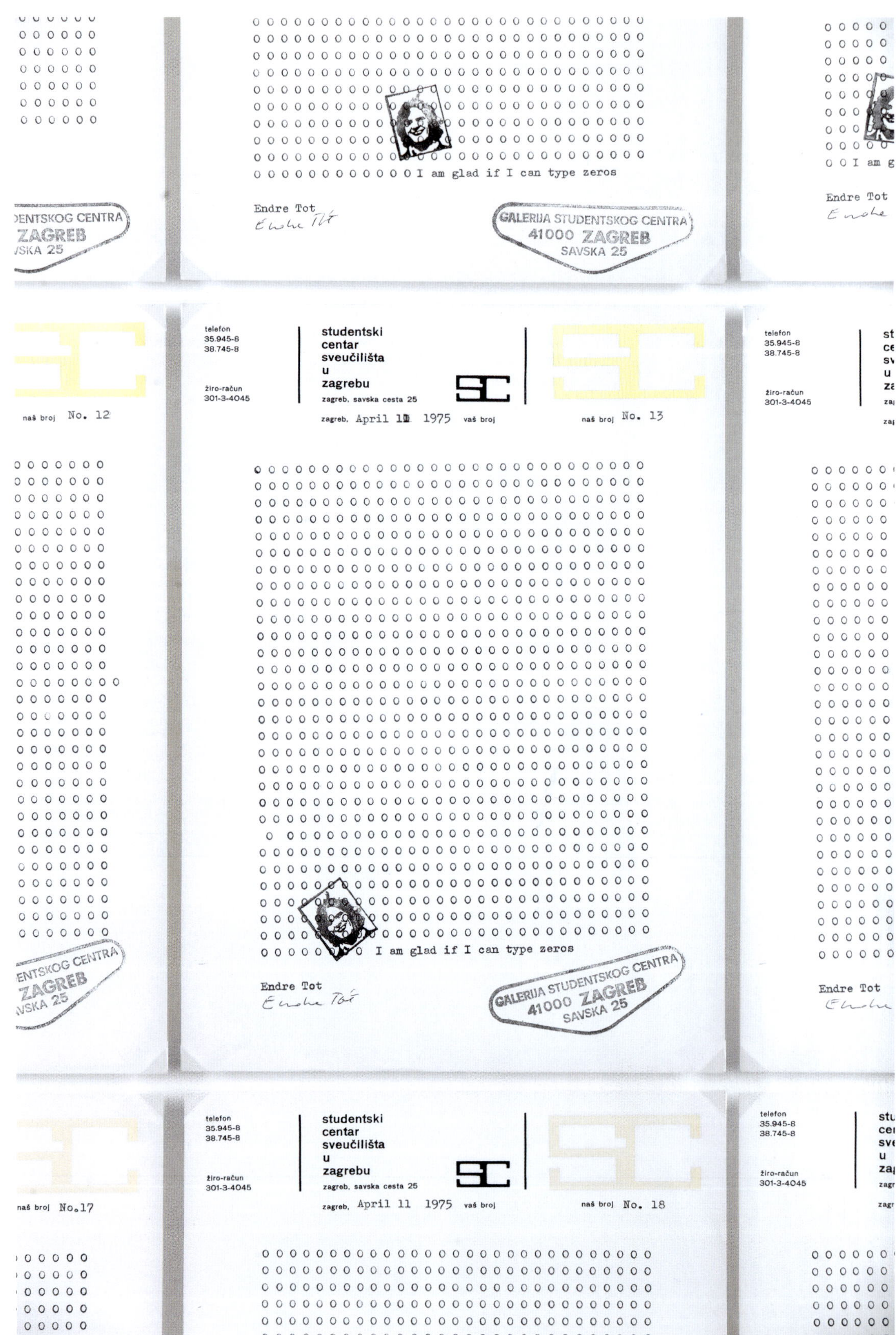

<u>I am glad if I can type zeros</u>, 1975

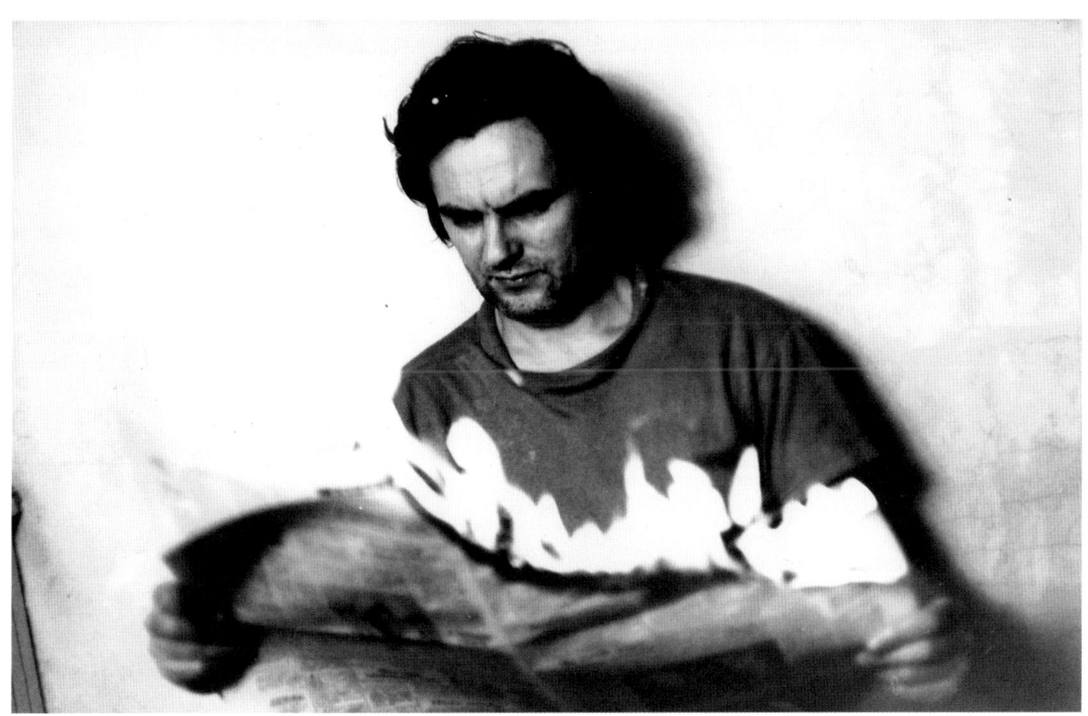

I am glad if I can read a burning newspaper, 1973-76

Gyula VÁRNAI

Kazincbarcika, 1956

Gyula Várnai hat die zeitgenössische ungarische Kunst insofern geprägt, als dass er von Anfang an außerhalb des institutionellen Rahmens Position bezogen hatte. Er besuchte keine offizielle künstlerische Einrichtung, sondern studierte Mathematik und Physik und arbeitete später als Drucker. Die Liebe zur Musik bestimmt seine Kunst jedoch bis zum heutigen Tage. Seine künstlerischen Techniken eignete er sich an seinem Wohnort, in Dunaújváros, an einer freien Schule an. Doch ging er auch seinen eigenen Weg, als er Assemblagen aus Schrott, den er sich aus dem Eisenwerk Dunaújváros beschaffte, zu bauen begann, was auf eine Ausweitung seiner Interesse verweist. Das Material seiner Werke kann alles sein, Türen, Fenster, diverse Möbelstücke, es umfasst alltägliche Gegenstände wie Harmonien, Waschbecken, Schultafeln, Tonbandgeräte, Lautsprecher, Rasierspiegel und Taschenlampen. Die Loslösung der gefundenen Gegenstände aus ihrem Kontext, das Zusammenwirken von gegenständlicher „Armut“ und konzeptueller Klarheit bestimmen die Arbeiten. Sie handeln von Berührbarkeit, von den körperlichen und geistigen Grenzen der (physischen) Wahrnehmung und den spielerischen Möglichkeiten, wissenschaftliches und philosophisches Denken mit der Sprache der bildenden Kunst auszudrücken. Die von der Neo-Avantgarde übernommene Bircolage-Ästhetik geht bei ihm mit einer beispiellosen Demut gegenüber dem Material einher: Indem er die ursprüngliche Funktion der gefundenen Gebrauchsgegenstände bewahrt, erfahren sie eine neue Verwendung in seinen standortspezifischen Installationen.

In seiner aus Tonbändern und Lautsprechern angefertigten „phonometrografischen“ Installation mit dem Titel *Philophonie* (1999) – einer Hommage auf Erik Satie – werden die ewig währenden, unerschütterlichen Regeln der mathematischen Addition hinterfragt. In seinem mobilen Objekt *Raum und Zeit* (2012) hingegen hält er unsere Wahrnehmung von Raum und Zeit in ständiger Bewegung und schafft mittels stetiger Wechsel des Betrachterstandpunkts eine optische Illusion.

Gyula Várnai has become one of the defining figures of Hungarian contemporary art by occupying a non-institutional position from the very beginning. He did not graduate from an official art school, having studied mathematics and physics instead, after which he worked as a printer, while his love of music has remained a defining influence on his art to this day. Várnai acquired his artistic techniques by attending evening classes in his hometown of Dunaújváros, but even then he followed an individual path, building assemblages of objects from bits and pieces salvaged from the Dunaújváros Ironworks, which reflected a widening of his interests. Anything could end up as material for his work: doors, windows, various pieces of furniture – in fact, the everyday objects that crop up in his works range from a harmonica, bathroom basin, school black board, and audio tape and speakers to a shaving mirror and torch. His works are defined by the way in which they change the context of the found elements, the “poorness” of the objects, as well as an accompanying conceptual clarity. Várnai's works speak about the tangibility of objects, the borders of physical and intellectual sensing, and the playful possibilities of connecting philosophical thinking with the language of art. The bricolage aesthetic inherited from the neo-avant-garde coincides with an unheard-of humility towards the material: keeping their original function, the found objects are reused and frequently incorporated into site-specific installations.

Made from audio tape and loud speakers as a tribute to Erik Satie, Várnai's “phonometrographic” installation *Philophonia* (1999) overwrites what are assumed to be the eternal and unwavering rules of mathematical addition, while his mobile object *Space and Time* (2012) keeps our sense of space and time in constant motion, creating an optical illusion through a continuous change of viewpoint.

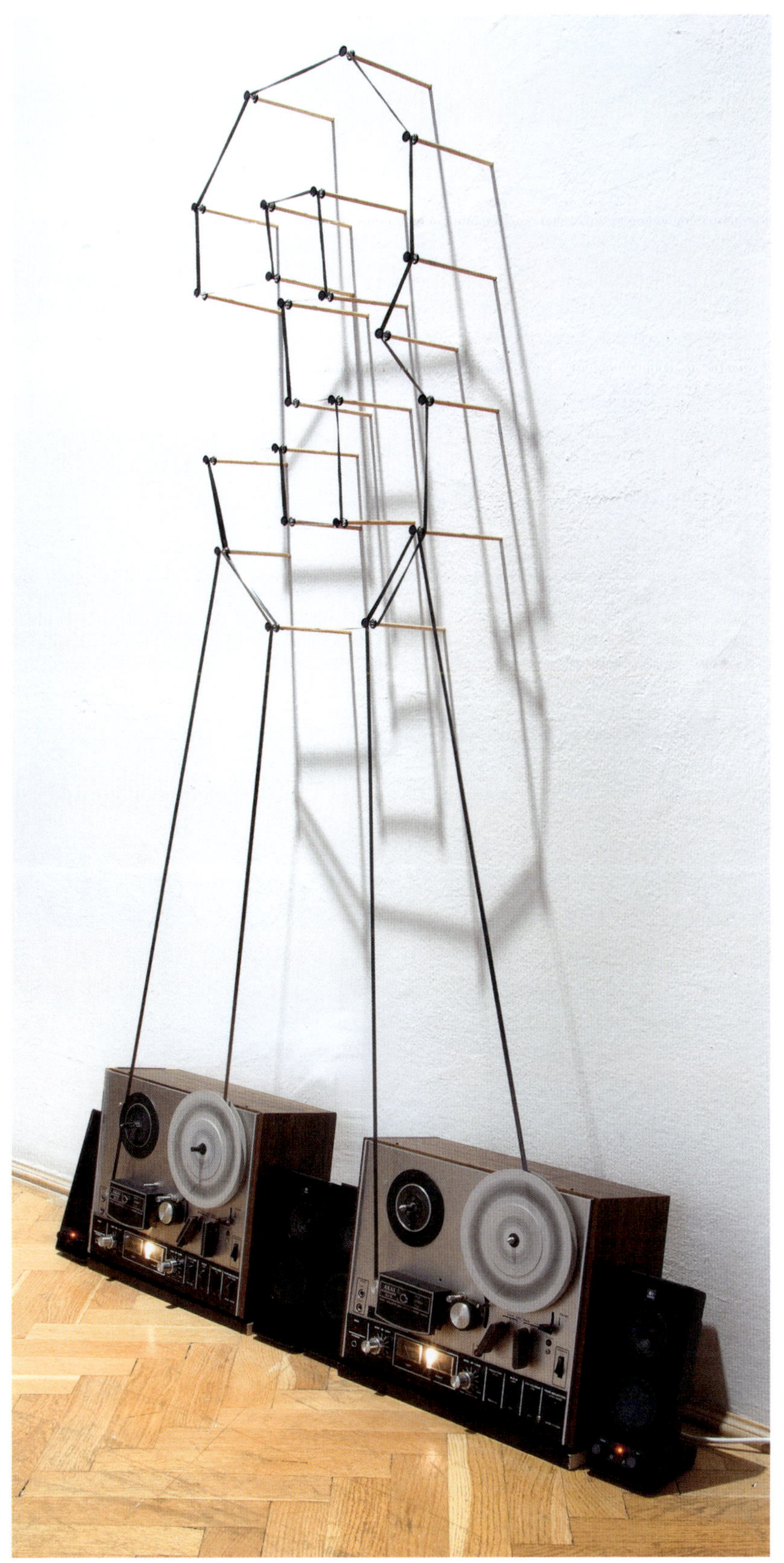

Philophonie / Philophony, 1999

Gábor Erdélyi, András Gálik (Little Warsaw), Bálint Havas (Little Warsaw), Dezső Szabó

Die gegenständliche Welt, 2014
[Zsigmond Károlyi: *ETALON*, 1992. Öl auf Leinwand, 80 × 60 cm]

„Vier Künstler wollen sich das Gemälde eines fünften Künstlers beschaffen. Sie entscheiden, es gemeinsam zu kaufen. Mithilfe eines Rechtsanwalts schließen sie einen Vertrag zur Aufteilung des gemeinsamen Kunstobjekts ab. Wie aber kann die geometrische Struktur des Gemäldes in die Sprache juristischer Normen übersetzt werden? Und was ist das, was die vier Künstler von nun an besitzen?"

Beim Besuch des Budapester Art Market beschlossen Little Warsaw (András Gálik und Bálint Havas) und zwei weitere Künstler (Dezső Szabó und der Maler Gábor Erdélyi), das dort ausgestellte Gemälde *Etalon* von Zsigmond Károlyi zu kaufen. Károlyi war ihr Lehrer an der Akademie der Bildenden Künste Budapest und seine konzeptuelle Malerei, seine intellektuelle Sensibilität, seine internationale Ausrichtung sowie seine spezielle Weltsicht haben seine Schüler stark beeinflusst. Ausgangspunkt ihres gemeinsamen Projekts war aber doch in erster Linie das Bild, das abstrakte Gemälde Károlyis. *Die gegenständliche Welt* (2014) ist nämlich – auf das Buch *Die gegenstandslose Welt* von Malewitsch aus dem Jahr 1927 verweisend – nichts anderes als eine Antwort auf die Frage, wie ein „gegenstandsloses" Gemälde vergegenständlicht werden kann.

Das Werk bot quasi selbst die Möglichkeit zur Aufteilung, denn das die Position des Bildes und seine (schiefe) Installationsweise bestimmende schwarze Rechteck schneidet vier gleiche Teile aus dem weißen Hintergrund aus. Diese Geometrie, die Relation von Teilen und Ganzem, findet sich insofern im Vertrag wieder, der den gemeinschaftlichen Besitz des Gemäldes regelt, und zwar, dass das Bild vierteljährlich seinen Besitzer wechselt. Das Schriftstück hält ebenfalls fest, dass über eine eventuelle Leihgabe des Werkes oder dessen Restaurierung nur gemeinsam entschieden werden kann.

Obwohl es sich um das gemeinsame Werk von vier Künstlern handelt, ist sowohl die künstlerische Aneignung als auch die Hinterfragung des Warencharakters eines Kunstobjekts am stärksten in der künstlerischen Praxis von Little Warsaw präsent. Mittels *Die gegenständliche Welt* wird nicht nur die Hochachtung gegenüber dem Meister als Geste erfahrbar, sondern auch das Nachdenken über das Wesen von Kunst, die Mechanismen des Kunstmarkts sowie die Besitzbarkeit von Kunstgegenständen.

The World as Objectness, 2014
[Károlyi Zsigmond: *ETALON*, 1992. Oil on canvas, 80 × 60 cm]

"Four artists would like to acquire a fifth artist's painting. They decide to buy it together. With the help of a lawyer, they draw up a contract about how to share the jointly owned art object. But how should the painting's geometrical structure be translated into the language of legal norms? And what is it that the four artists will actually possess?"

While visiting the Budapest Art Market, Little Warsaw (András Gálik and Bálint Havas), together with two other artists, Dezső Szabó and the painter Gábor Erdélyi, decided to collectively buy the painting *Etalon* by Zsigmond Károlyi, which was exhibited there. Károlyi had been their teacher at the Academy of Fine Arts, and his conceptual painting, intellectual sensitivity, international orientation, and individual worldview had had a decisive influence on his students. To begin with, however, the painting itself, Károlyi's abstract painting, formed the starting point for the joint project. In a reference to Malevich's volume *The World as Objectlessness* from 1927, the significance of *The World as Objectness* is nothing other than an examination of how one might objectify an "objectless" painting.

The work itself presented the possibility for division in the sense that the position of the painting and its sloped installation are defined by the way four identical parts of a black rectangle are cut off from a white base. These geometrical characteristics, the relation between the part and the whole, are transferred into the contract drawn up to regulate the joint ownership of the painting, which determines the way in which possession of the picture rotates between the four artists four times a year. The document also records how the eventual lending and restoration of the work is only to be decided together.

While what's at stake here is an act of collective creation, both the artistic use of appropriation and the questioning of the commercial character of the artwork are chiefly present in the artistic practice of Little Warsaw. In *The World as Objectness*, not only can we detect a gesture of respect towards the artists' former master, but also a profound reflection on essential questions concerning the mechanisms of the art market and the ownership of artworks.

Die gegenständliche Welt / The World as Objectness, 2014 [Zsigmond Károlyi: ETALON, 1992]

WERKLISTE / LIST OF WORKS

[Nach den ursprünglichen Titeln der Werke / Following the original titles of the works]

Gábor ALTORJAY

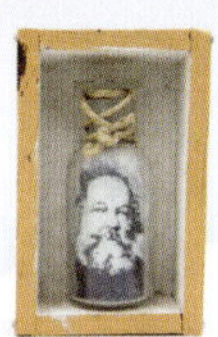

Anti-Apotheke Bakunin / Anti-Pharmacy Bakunin, 1968
Objekt / Object; 14 × 9 × 5 cm
Photo: Csaba Aknay

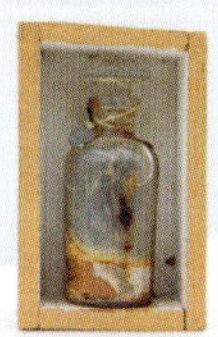

Vostell in Milch / Vostell in Milk, 1968
Objekt / Object; 14 × 9 × 5 cm
Photo: Csaba Aknay

5-Tage-Rennen / 5-Day Race, 1968
Einladungskarte (Offsetdruck, Papier) /
Invitation card (offset print on paper); 29 × 20,8 cm

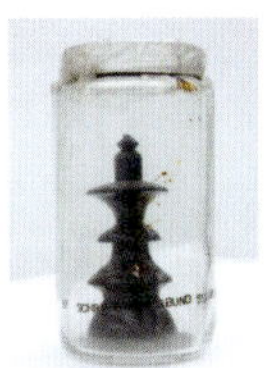

Schach-Kompott / Chess Compote, 1967–68
Objekt / Object; 14 × 7 cm
Photo: Csaba Aknay

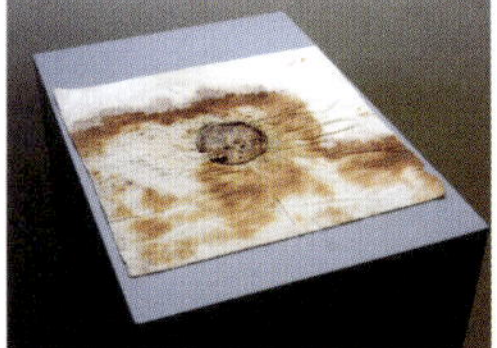

La Strada, 1969
Zitronenscheibe, Papier / A slice of lemon, paper; 21,5 × 21,5 cm
Photo: György Nyírő

La Strada, 1969
Silbergelatine-Abzug / Silver gelatin print; 12 × 18,1 cm

La Strada, 1969
Event-score (Vintage-Xerokopie) / Event score (vintage Xerox); A4

Alle Werke mit freundlicher Genehmigung des Künstlers und der acb Gallery / All works courtesy of the artist and acb Gallery

Gábor ATTALAI

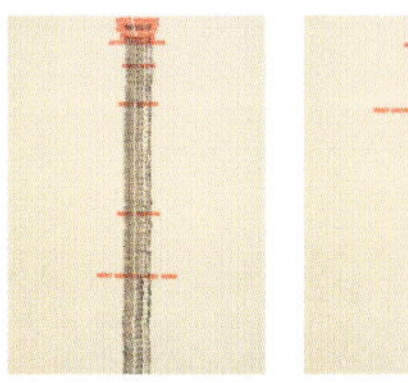

Antagonistic Relations between the Time-Numbers and the Time-Names I–II (Antagonistische Beziehungen zwischen Zeit-Nummern und Zeit-Namen) I–II, 1972
Tinte auf Papier / Ink on paper; jeweils / 70 × 50 cm / each | Photo: András Bozsó

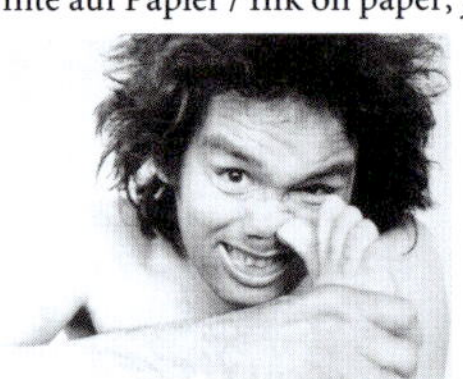

Idiotic Manner I–VI (Idiotisches Verhalten I–VI), 1973
6 Silbergelatine-Abzüge / 6 Silver gelatin prints; jeweils 14,5 × 19,5 cm / each
Photo: András Bozsó

Alle Werke mit freundlicher Genehmigung der Erben des Künstlers und der Vintage Galéria / All works courtesy of the heirs of Gábor Attalai and Vintage Galéria

Imre BAK

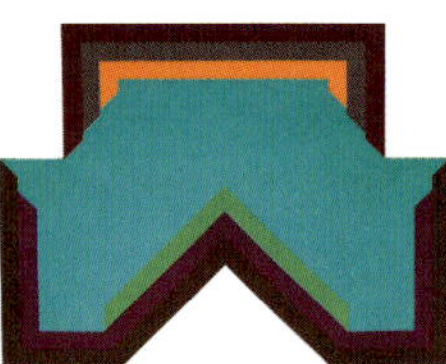

Fényes IV (Glänzend IV / Splendid IV), 1970
Acryl auf Leinwand / Acrylic on canvas; 130 × 170 cm
AX Sammlung / Collection, Budapest | Photo: Zsombor Szikora

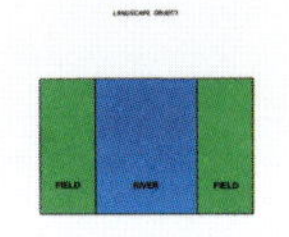

Landscape Object (Landschaftsobjekt), 1973
Tinte, Tempera und Letraset auf Papier / Ink, tempera and Letraset on paper
44 × 62,5 cm | Photo: Csaba Aknay

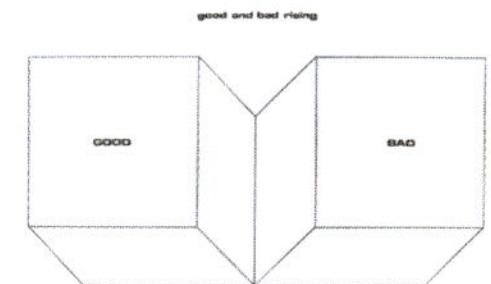

Good and Bad Rising (Auferstehung von Gut und Böse), 1973
Tinte und Letraset auf Papier / Ink and Letraset on paper; 43,5 × 62,5 cm
Photo: Csaba Aknay

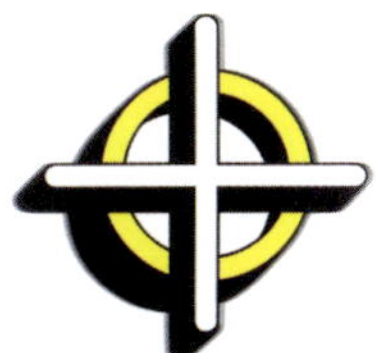

Kreis-Kreuz / Circle-Cross, 1979
Acryl auf Faserplatte / Acrylic on fibreboard; 120 × 120 cm
Grażyna Kulczyk Sammlung / Collection, Poznań | Photo: Csaba Aknay

Alle Werke mit freundlicher Genehmigung des Künstlers und der acb Gallery / All works courtesy of the artist and acb Gallery

Miklós ERDÉLY

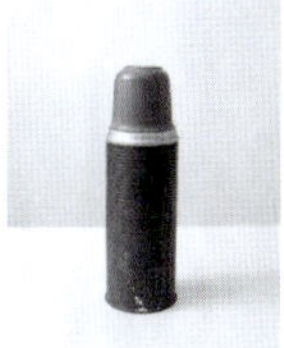

Der Schnee vom vergangenen Jahr / Last Year's Snow, 1970
Readymade: Thermosflasche / Vacuum flask; d: 9 cm, h: 25,5 cm
Péter Sáránszki Sammlung / Collection, Budapest
(EM Kat. Obk 4)
Photo: László Lugosi Lugo
Mit freundlicher Genehmigung der Erben von Miklós Erdély und der Miklós Erdély-Stiftung / Courtesy of the heirs of Miklós Erdély and the Miklós Erdély Foundation
Kisterem Gallery

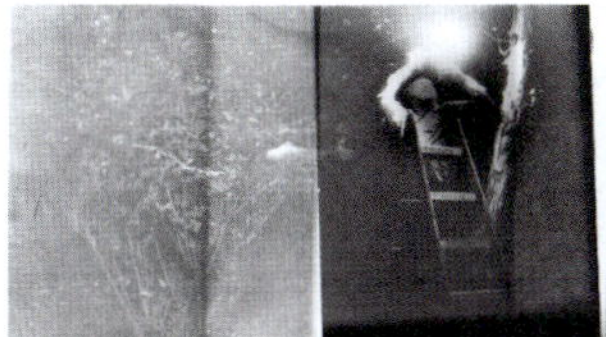
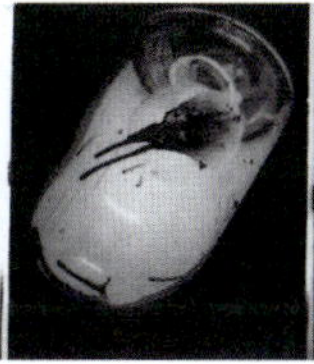

Abendaktion / Evening Action, um / around 1971–72
Silbergelatine-Abzug / Silver gelatin print; 88 × 29,4 cm
Nachlass von Miklós Erdély / Estate of Miklós Erdély
(EM Kat. Fom 6/2)
Photo: László Lugosi Lugo
Mit freundlicher Genehmigung von den Erben von Miklós Erdély und der Miklós Erdély-Stiftung / Courtesy of the heirs of Miklós Erdély and the Miklós Erdély Foundation
Kisterem Gallery

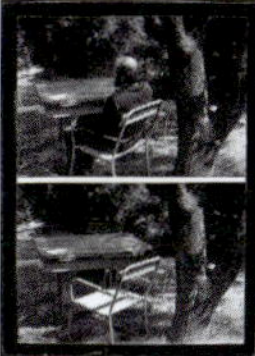

Metapher I / Metaphor I, 1972
2 Silbergelatine-Abzüge, jeweils 12 × 16,5 cm, montiert auf schwarzem Fotopapier / 2 silver gelatin prints, 12 × 16,5 cm each, mounted on black photo paper; 26,2 × 18,8 cm (Fotografiert von Dániel Erdély / Photos made by Dániel Erdély)
Nachlass von Miklós Erdély / Estate of Miklós Erdély
(EM Kat. Fom 10/A) | Photo: László Lugosi Lugo
Mit freundlicher Genehmigung der Erben von Miklós Erdély und der Miklós Erdély-Stiftung / Courtesy of the heirs of Miklós Erdély and the Miklós Erdély Foundation
Kisterem Gallery

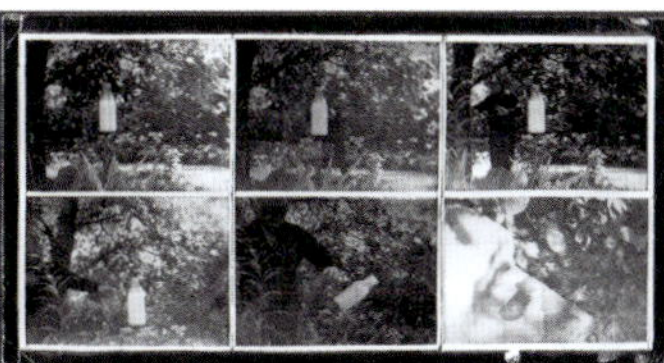

Metafora II / Metaphor II, um / around 1972
6 Silbergelatine-Abzüge, jeweils 9 × 12 cm, montiert auf schwarzem Fotopapier; 20 × 38 cm / 6 silver gelatin prints, 9 × 12 cm each, mounted on black photo paper; 20 × 38 cm (Fotografiert von Dániel Erdély / Photos made by Dániel Erdély)
Nachlass von Miklós Erdély / Estate of Miklós Erdély
(EM Kat. Fom 11) | Photo: László Lugosi Lugo
Mit freundlicher Genehmigung der Erben von Miklós Erdély und der Miklós Erdély-Stiftung / Courtesy of the heirs of Miklós Erdély and the Miklós Erdély Foundation
Kisterem Gallery

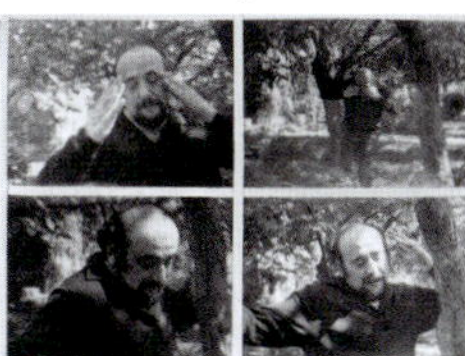

Metafora III / Metaphor III, um / around 1972
4 Silbergelatine-Abzüge, jeweils 9 × 12 cm, montiert auf Papier; 18 × 24 cm
4 silver gelatin prints; 9 × 12 cm each; mounted on paper, 18 × 24 cm
(Fotografiert von Dániel Erdély / Photos made by Dániel Erdély)
Nachlass von Miklós Erdély / Estate of Miklós Erdély
(EM Kat. Fom 12) | Photo: László Lugosi Lugo
Mit freundlicher Genehmigung der Erben von Miklós Erdély und der Miklós Erdély Stiftung / Courtesy of the heirs of Miklós Erdély and the Miklós Erdély Foundation
Kisterem Gallery

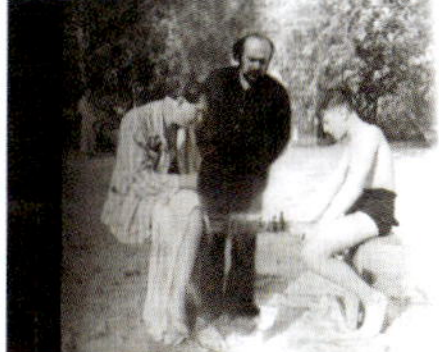

Werkfoto zum 3. Bild „Zeitreise" / Work photo to the 3rd picture of the "Time Travel" (III.), um / around 1976
Silbergelatine-Abzug / Silver gelatin print; 50 × 59,5 cm
Somlói-Spengler Sammlung / Collection, Budapest
(EM Kat. Fom 35/3MF) | Photo: András Bozsó
Mit freundlicher Genehmigung der Erben von Miklós Erdély / Courtesy of the heirs of Miklós Erdély
Kisterem Gallery

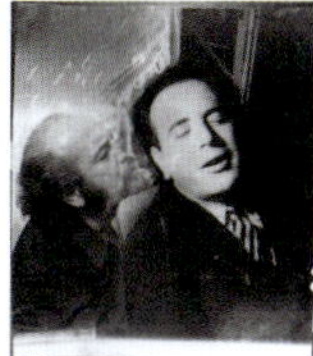

Werkfoto zum 5. Bild „Zeitreise" / Work photo to the 5th picture of the "Time Travel", um / around 1976
Silbergelatine-Abzug / Silver gelatin print; 49 × 59 cm
Somlói-Spengler Sammlung / Collection, Budapest
(EM Kat. Fom 35/5MF) | Photo: Annamária Szőke
Mit freundlicher Genehmigung der Erben von Miklós Erdély / Courtesy of the heirs of Miklós Erdély
Kisterem Gallery

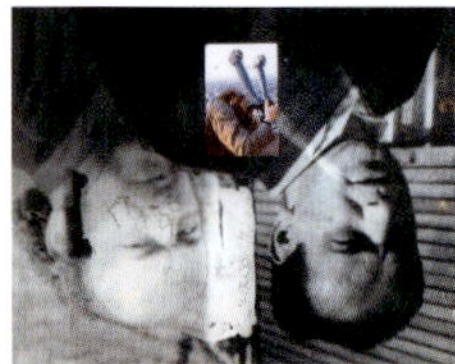

Zeitklammer / Time Bracket 1955–1972
Mitte, zweite Hälfte der Siebziger / Mid-, second half of the Seventies
Silbergelatine-Abzug, Collage / Silver gelatin print, collage; 50 × 70 cm
Somlói-Spengler Sammlung / Collection, Budapest
(EM Kat. Fom 36)
Photo: László Lugosi Lugo
Mit freundlicher Genehmigung der Erben von Miklós Erdély und der Miklós Erdély Stiftung / Courtesy of the heirs of Miklós Erdély and the Miklós Erdély Foundation
Kisterem Gallery

Tibor HAJAS

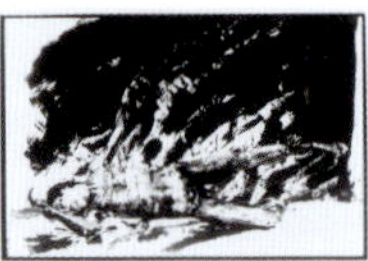
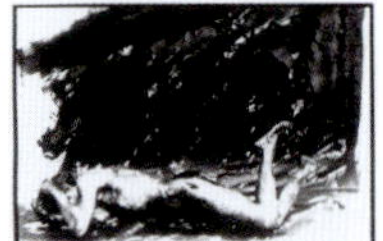
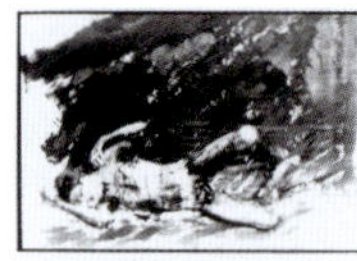

Fleischgemälde I–III / Flesh Painting I–III, 1978
3 Silbergelatine-Abzüge / 3 silver gelatin prints; jeweils / 18 × 24 cm / each
Photo: András Bozsó
Mit freundlicher Genehmigung der Erben des Künstlers und der Vintage Galéria / Courtesy of the heirs of Tibor Hajas and Vintage Galéria

Károly HALÁSZ

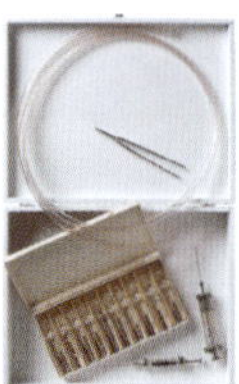

Museum – Museum der Gegenwart und Zukunft /
Museum – The Museum of Present and Future, 1977
Kanüle, Injektionsnadel, Ampullen / Syringe, hypodermic needle, phials; 20 × 30 × 8 cm
Photo: András Bozsó

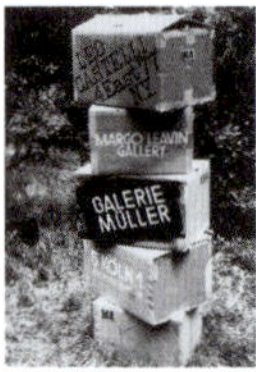

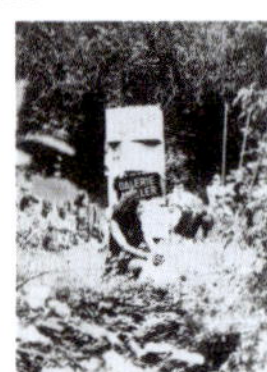

Informationsobjekte / Information Objects I–II, 1973
2 Silbergelatine-Abzüge / 2 silver gelatin prints; jeweils / 29,7 × 21 cm/ each
Photo: András Bozsó

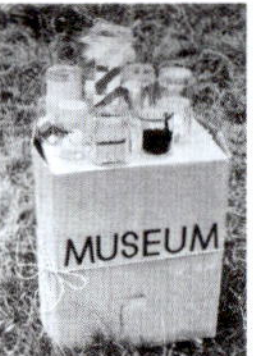

MUSEUM, 1973
Silbergelatine-Abzug / Silver gelatin print; 29,7 × 21 cm
Photo: András Bozsó

Alle Werke mit freundlicher Genehmigung des Künstlers und der Vintage Galéria / All works courtesy of the artist and Vintage Galéria

György JOVÁNOVICS

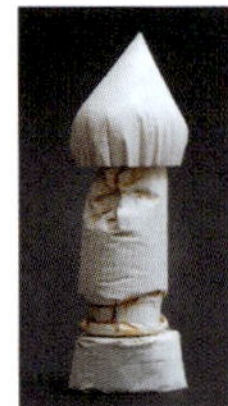

Petit Polichinelle, 1966
Gips / Plaster; h: 34 cm | Photo: Ágnes Bak – Bence Tihanyi

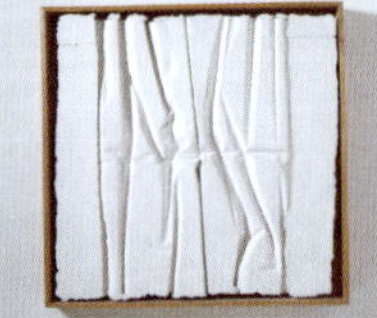

Vorhang zur EKSTATISCHEN MARIONETTE /
Fore-Curtain to the ECSTATIC MARIONETTE, 1979 *
Gips / Plaster; 130 × 130 cm | Photo: Ágnes Bak – Bence Tihanyi

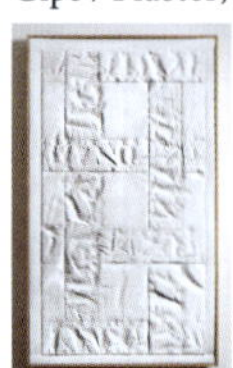

Relief K/3, 1980
Gips / Plaster; 125 × 71 cm | Photo: Ágnes Bak – Bence Tihanyi

Alle Werke mit freundlicher Genehmigung des Künstlers und der Kisterem Gallery / All works courtesy of the artist and Kisterem Gallery

Tamás KASZÁS

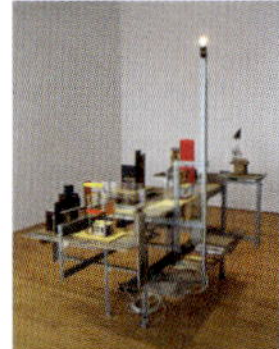

Diorama von der Kiosk-Siedlung /
Diorama of the Kiosk Village, 2013–2014
Mixed-Media-Installation, Maße variabel / Mixed media installation dimensions variable | Photo: Miklós Sulyok

Mit freundlicher Genehmigung des Künstlers und der Kisterem Gallery / Courtesy of the artist and Kisterem Gallery

Ilona KESERÜ

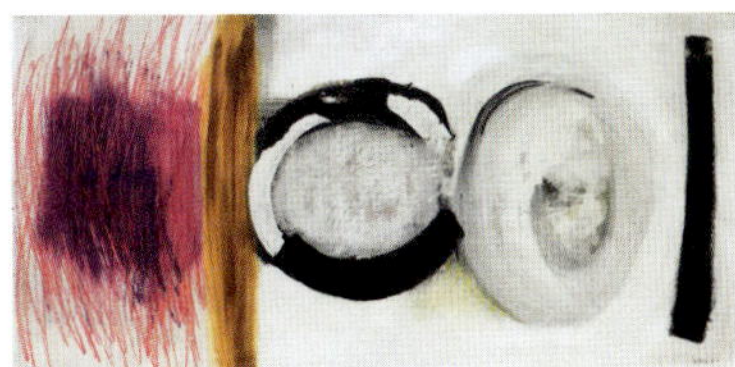

Gemälde Nr. 4 / Painting No. IV, 1965
Öl, Ölpastell, Email auf Holzfaserplatte /
Oil, oil pastel, enamel on woodfiber 63 × 125 cm
Photo: Gábor S. Horváth

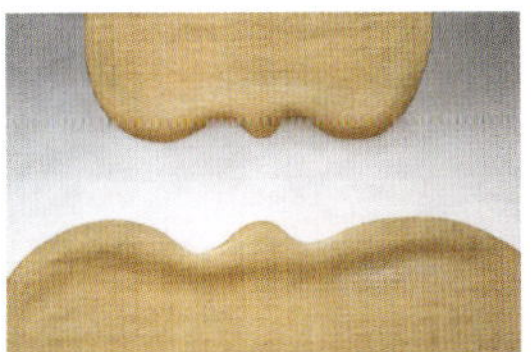

Annäherung II / Approach II, 1969
Öl auf geprägte Leinwand / Oil on embossed canvas; 120 × 170 × 4 cm
Kolozsváry Sammlung / Collection, Győr
Photo: Zsolt Szabóky

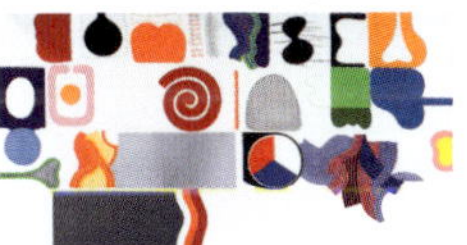

Botschaft / Message, 1968*
Öl auf Leinwad / Oil on canvas; 120 × 150 cm
László Gábor Sammlung / Collection, Budapest
Photo: Gábor S. Horváth
Alle Werke mit freundlicher Genehmigung der Künstlerin und der Kisterem Gallery / All works courtesy of the artist and Kisterem Gallery

Ádám KOKESCH

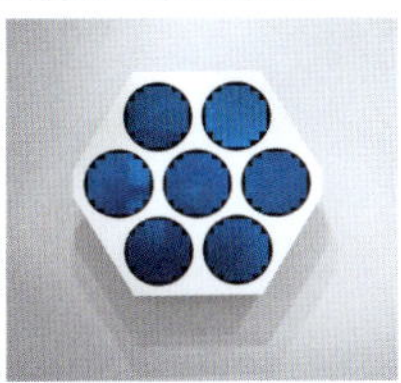

Ohne Titel / Untitled, 2013
Buntglas, Sperrholz, Acryl, Silikon / Stained glass, plywood, acrylic, silicone
87 × 85 × 20 cm | Photo: Miklós Sulyok

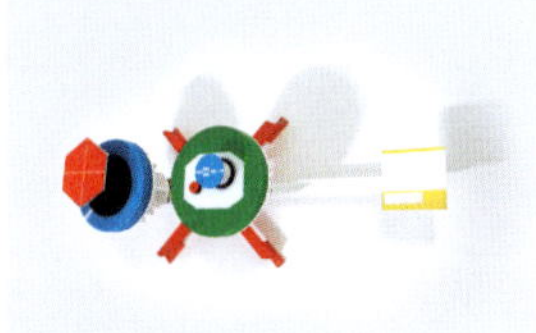

Ohne Titel / Untitled, 2014
Acryl, Plexiglas, Glas, Sperrholz / Acrylic, plexi, glass, plywood; 33 × 75 × 28 cm
Photo: Miklós Sulyok

Mit freundlicher Genehmigung des Künstlers und der Kisterem Gallery / Courtesy of the artist and Kisterem Gallery

Katalin LADIK

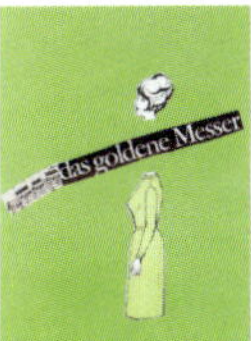

Das Lied von dem goldenen Messer, 1979
Collage; 34 × 24 cm | Photo: Csaba Aknay

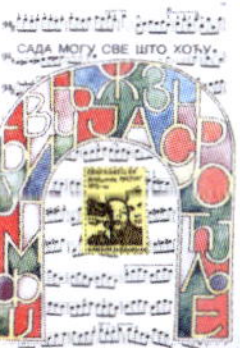

Die Meistersinger, 1980
Collage; 28,5 × 20,5 cm | Photo: Csaba Aknay

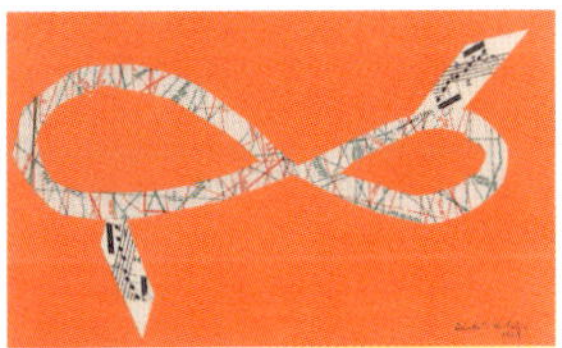

Duet, 1979
Collage; 21 × 30 cm | Photo: Csaba Aknay

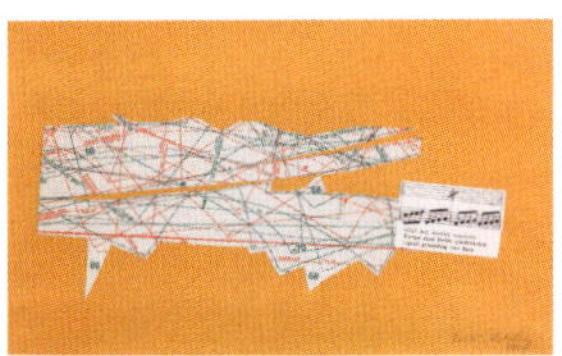

Mars de Triomphe '68, 1978
Collage; 26,5 × 32,5 cm | Photo: Csaba Aknay

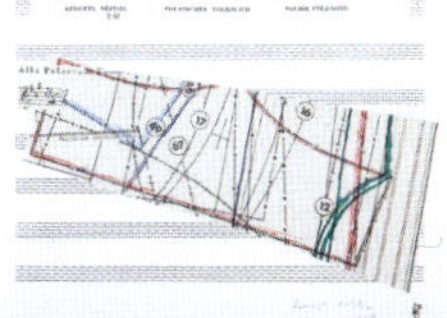

Polnisches Volkslied / Polish Folksong, 1978
Collage; 26 × 17 cm | Photo: Csaba Aknay

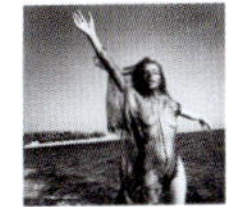
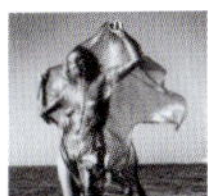

Pseudosculptura I–II, 1982
Foto-Performance / Photo performance
(Fotografiert von / Photo Tibor Somogyi Varga)
2 Silbergelatine-Abzüge / 2 silver gelatin prints; jeweils / 40,5 × 30 cm / each
I. László Vágó Sammlung / Collection, Budapest
Photo: Csaba Aknay

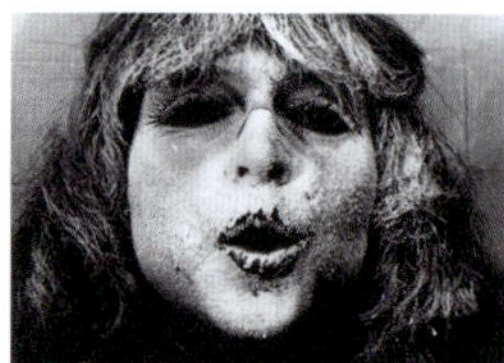

Poemask II, 1982
Foto-Performance / Photo performance
(Fotografiert von / Photos made by Gábor Ifjú)
7 Silbergelatine-Abzüge / 7 silver gelatin prints; jeweils / 18 × 13 cm / each
Emily Austin Sammlung / Collection, London
Photo: Csaba Aknay

Alle Werke mit freundlicher Genehmigung der Künstlerin und der acb Gallery / All works courtesy of the artist and acb Gallery

László LAKNER

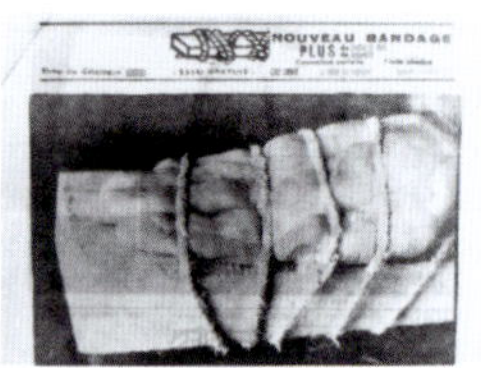

Neuer Verband / New Bandage, 1971
Silbergelatine-Abzug / Silver gelatin print; 21 × 29,7 cm
Photo: András Bozsó

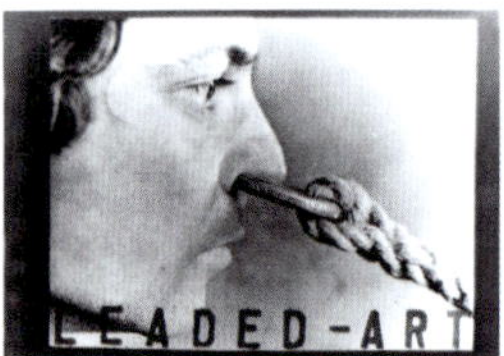

Leaded-Art, 1971
Silbergelatine-Abzug / Silver gelatin print; 21 × 29,7 cm
Photo: András Bozsó

Alle Werke mit freundlicher Genehmigung des Künstlers und der Vintage Galéria / All works courtesy of the artist and Vintage Galéria

LITTLE WARSAW

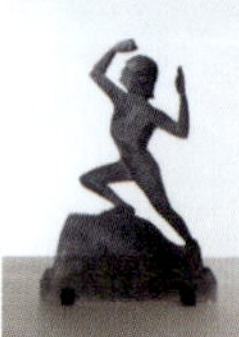

Kämpfer / Fighter, 2014
Fotografie auf Glasplatte, Magneten / Photograph on glass sheet, magnets
32,4 × 46,5 × 0,3 cm, Ed. 2/3.
Photo: Miklós Sulyok

Mit freundlicher Genehmigung der Künstler und der Kisterem Gallery / Courtesy of the artists and Kisterem Gallery

Dóra MAURER

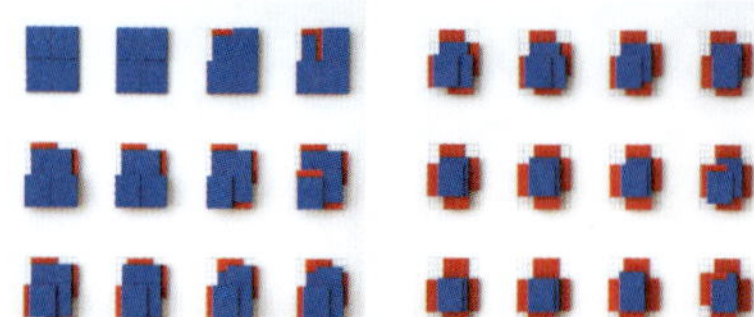

Displacements I–II (Verschiebungen I–II), 1974–75
Holzfaser, Papier, Acryl, Öl / Plywood, paper, acrylic, oil; jeweils
100 × 100 cm / each
Photo: Miklós Sulyok

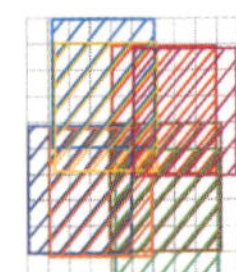
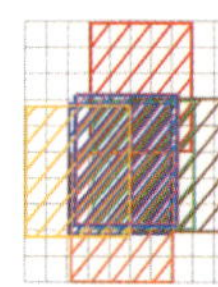
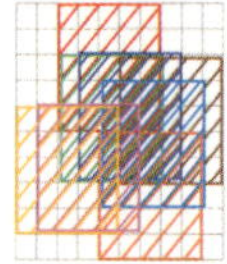
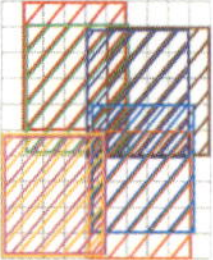

Displacements I–IV (Verschiebungen I–IV), 1972
Tempera auf Papier / Tempera on paper; jeweils / 64 × 42 cm / each
Photo: András Bozsó

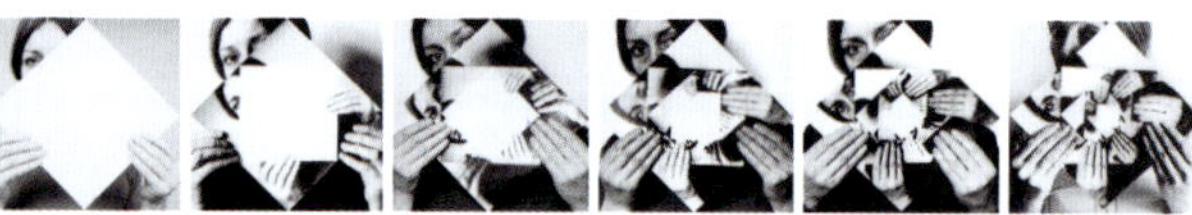

Sieben Drehungen I–VI / Seven Twists I–VI, 1977–78
6 Silbergelatine-Abzüge / 6 silver gelatin prints; jeweils / 20 × 20 cm / each
Szűcs Sammlung / Collection, Budapest
Photo: András Bozsó

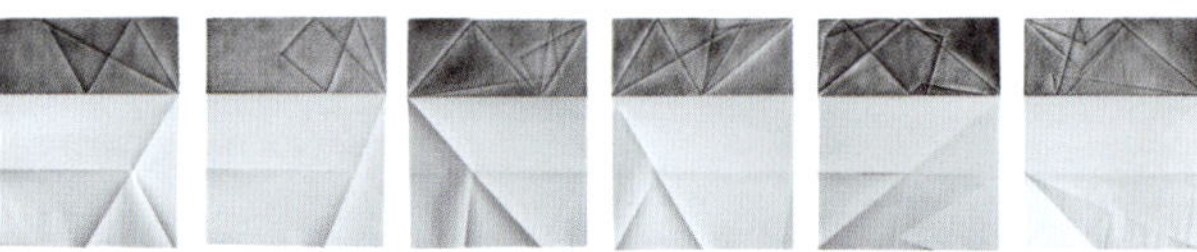

Verborgene Strukturen I–VI / Hidden Structures I–VI, 1977
Papier, Grafit, / Paper, graphite; jeweils / 65 × 50 cm / each
Photo: András Bozsó

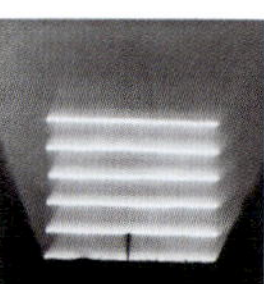
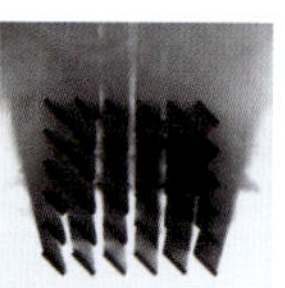
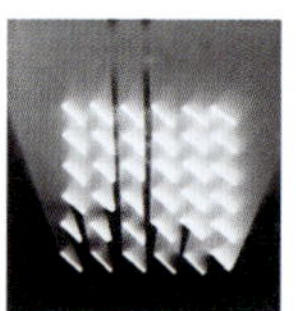

Schleusen I (a+b) / Sluices I (a+b)
Schleusen II (a+b) / Sluices II (a+b), 1980–81
Silbergelatine-Abzug, Silbergelatine-Fotogramm /
Silver gelatin print, silver print fotogram; jeweils / 48 × 43cm / each
Photo: András Bozsó

Alle Werke mit freundlicher Genehmigung der Künstlerin und der Vintage Galéria / All works courtesy of the artist and Vintage Galéria

István NÁDLER

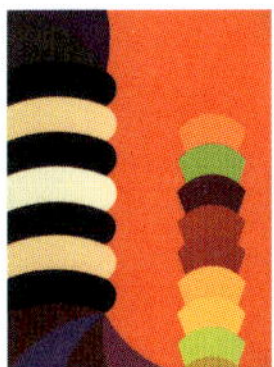

Säulen / Pillars, 1970
Tempera auf Leinwand / Tempera on canvas; 180 × 130 cm
Photo: Miklós Sulyok

Mit freundlicher Genehmigung des Künstlers und der Kisterem Gallery / Courtesy of the artist and Kisterem Gallery

Géza PERNECZKY

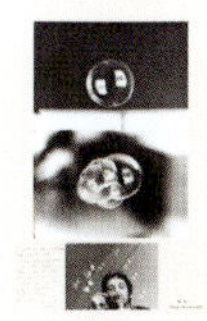

Art Bubble, 1972
Silbergelatine-Abzüge auf Papier / Silver prints on paper, 70 × 50 cm
Photo: András Bozsó

Mit freundlicher Genehmigung des Künstlers und der Vintage Galéria / Courtesy of the artist and Vintage Galéria

SOCIÉTÉ RÉALISTE

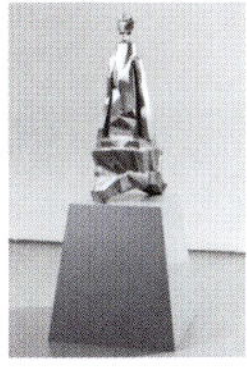

Mesomemorial: March of Victory, 2014
Aluminium; 100 × 40 × 40 cm
Photo: Csaba Aknay

Mit freundlicher Genehmigung der Künstler und der acb Gallery / Courtesy of the artists and acb Gallery

Dezső SZABÓ

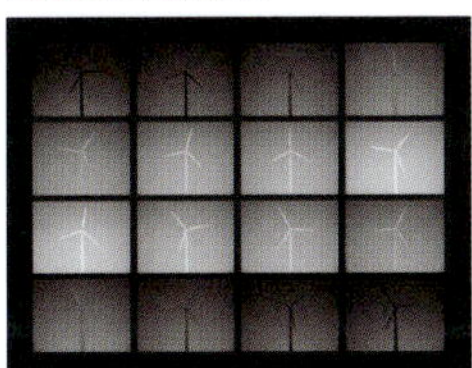

TURBO & STILL / TURBO STILLS, 2009
C-Print; 35 × 45 cm (Blatt / sheet: 55 × 65 cm), ED5

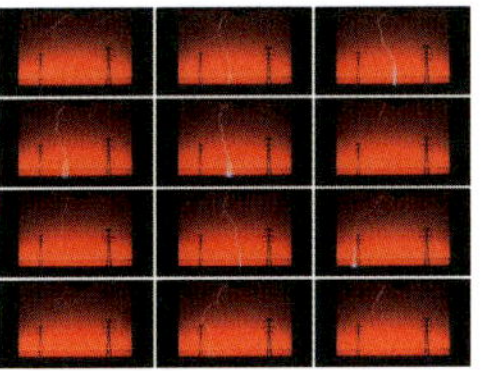

ELECTRIC FIELD, 2012
C-Print; 35 x 45 cm (Blatt / sheet: 55 × 65 cm), ED5

Alle Werke mit freundlicher Genehmigung des Künstlers und der Vintage Galéria / All works courtesy of the artist and Vintage Galéria

Péter SZALAY

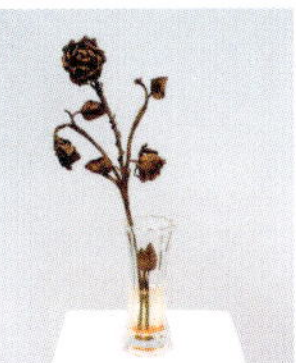

Gute Absicht / Good Intent, 2014
Eisen, Wasser, Glasvase / Iron, water, glass vase; 35 × 15 × 10 cm
Photo: György Orbán

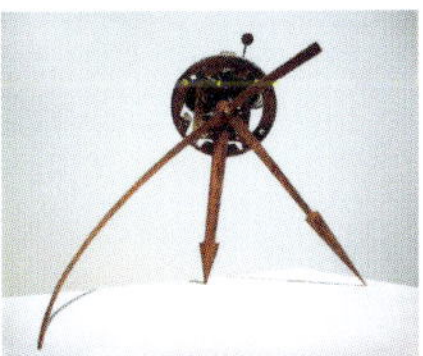

Statische Zeit / Static Time, 2011
Objekt / Object; 34 × 30 × 15 cm
Szűcs Sammlung / Collection, Budapest | Photo: Péter Szalay

Alle Werke mit freundlicher Genehmigung des Künstlers und der acb Gallery / All works courtesy of the artist and acb Gallery

Tamás SZENTJÓBY

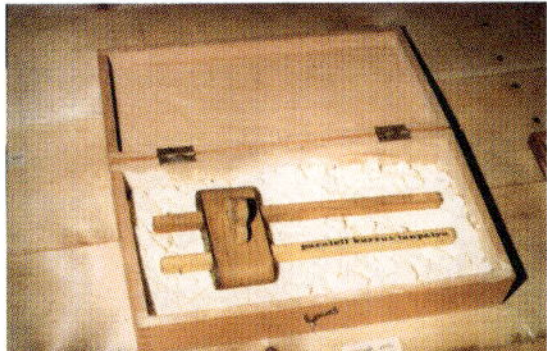

Emblem – Parallelkurs / Lehrbahn / Emblem – Parallel Course / Study Track, 1968
Holzkiste, Schreinerwerkzeug, Schwefelpulver, selbstklebende Buchstaben / Wooden box, carpenter tool, sulfur powder, self-adhesive letters; 6 × 37 × 16,3 cm
Photo: Tamás Stauby

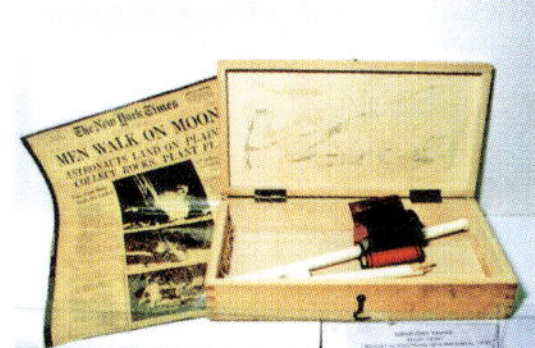

Mondlandung / Moon landing, 1969
Aktionsobjekt, während des ersten Mond-Spaziergangs gemacht / Action-object, made during the first moon-walk, Zerbrochener Stock, Film, Holzkasten, Zeitungsausschnitt / Broken stick, film, wooden box, news clipping; 6 × 30 × 16 cm | Photo: Tamás Stauby

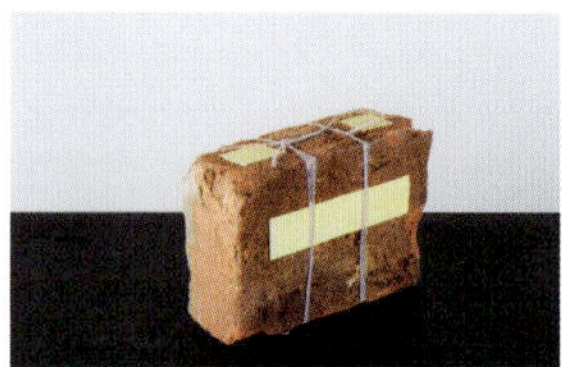

Tschechoslowakisches Radio 1968 / Czechoslovak Radio 1968, 1969
Mixed Media / Mixed media; 17 × 12 × 7 cm
Hella Pados Sammlung / Collection, Szombathely
Photo: László Lugosi Lugo

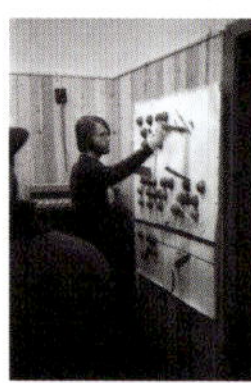

Schöne Dunkelheit – Audio-taktylisches Bildgedicht für Blinde / Beautiful Darkness – Audio-tactilist visual poem for the blind, 1970
Bildgedicht, Tonband, Eisen, Farbe, Karton, Holz; 140 × 140 cm und tragbares Tonbandgerät; 35 × 37 × 16 cm / Visual poem, tape, iron, paint, cardboard, wood; 140 × 140 cm and portable tape recorder; 35 × 37 × 16 cm | Photo: Dr. László Végh; Archiv Dr. László Végh / Ludwig Museum – Museum für Zeitgenössische Kunst / Dr. László Végh Archive / Ludwig Museum – Museum of Contemporary Art

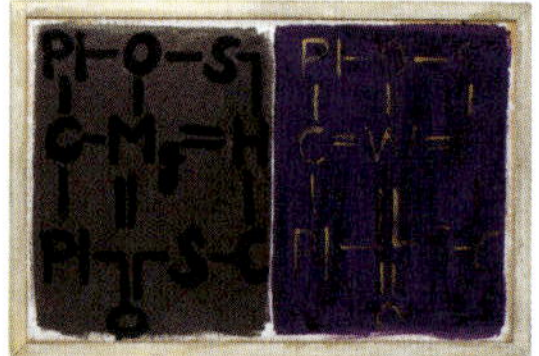

Die biochemische Wirkung auf das Vaterunser / The influence of biochemistry on Our Father, 1983
Öl auf Faserplatte / Oil on fibreboard; 53 × 83 cm
Grażyna Kulczyk Sammlung / Collection, Poznań | Photo: Lugosi Lugo László

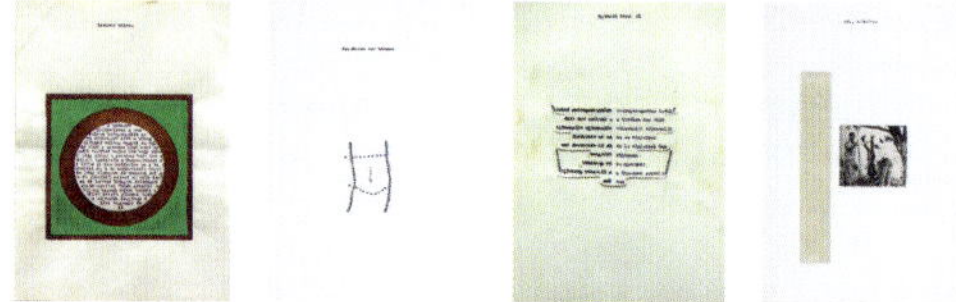

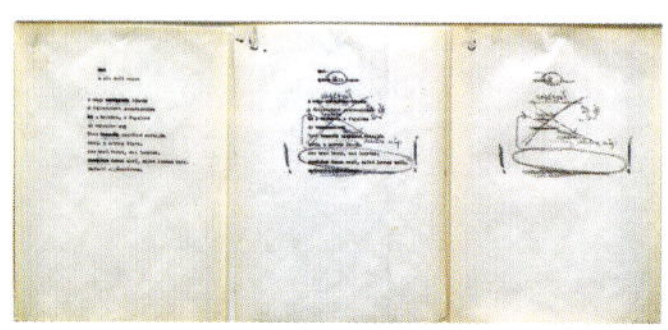

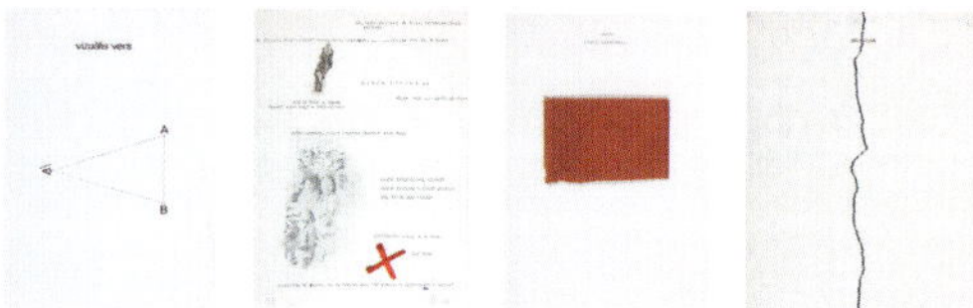

Allopoiesistas, 1966–69
9 visuelle Gedichte (Schreibmaschinenschrift und Mixed Media auf Papier) / 9 visual poems (typewriting and mixed technique on paper)
11 A4 Blätter / Sheets
Irokéz Sammlung / Collection, Szombathely | Photo: Csaba Aknay

Mit freundlicher Genehmigung von Tamás Szentjóby / Courtesy of Tamás Szentjóby

Endre TÓT

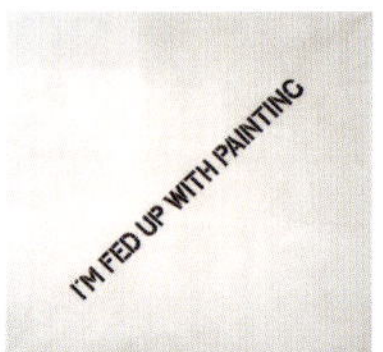

I'm fed up with painting, 1972
Öl auf Leinwand / Oil on canvas; 90 × 90 cm | Photo: Csaba Aknay

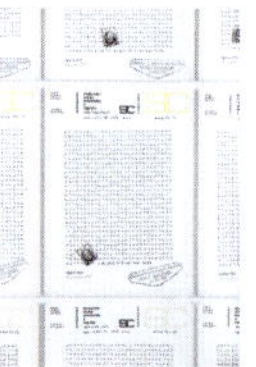

I am glad if I can type zeros, 1975
(Student Centre Gallery, Zagreb)
Schreibmaschinenschrift, Papier; 25 A4-Blätter / Typewriting, paper; 25 A4 sheets | Photo: Csaba Aknay

TÓTalJOYs / TÓTalJOYs, 1973–76
8 Fotos, unterschiedliche Größen / 8 photographs, dimensions variable
(Fotografiert von János Gulyás / Photos made by János Gulyás)
Photo: György Nyírő

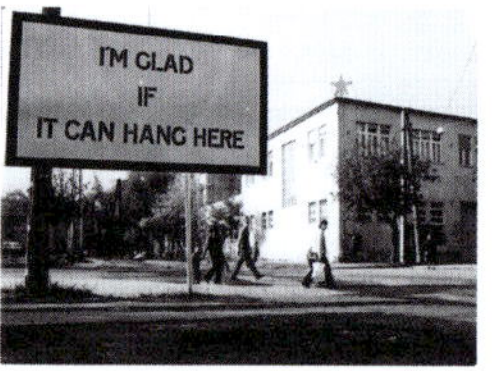

I'm glad if it can hang here
Silbergelatine-Abzug / Silver gelatin print; 9 × 12 cm

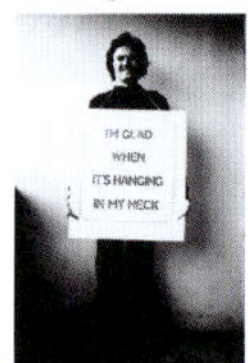

I'm glad when it's hanging in my neck
Silbergelatine-Abzug / Silver gelatin print; 18 × 11,7 cm

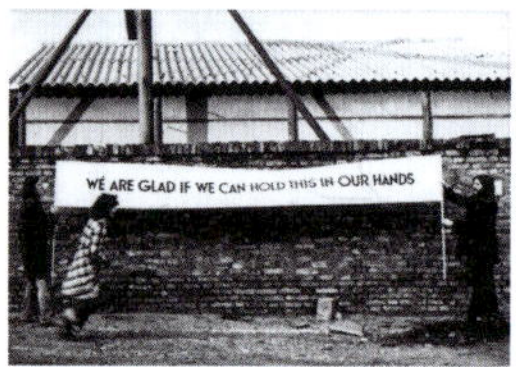

We are glad if we can hold this in our hands
Silbergelatine-Abzug auf Dokubrom-Papier / Silver gelatin print on Dokubrom paper; 11,6 × 14,7 cm

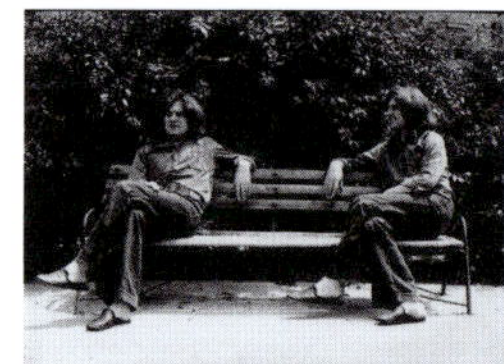

I am glad if I can look at you
Fotomontage / Photo montage; 18 × 23,9 cm

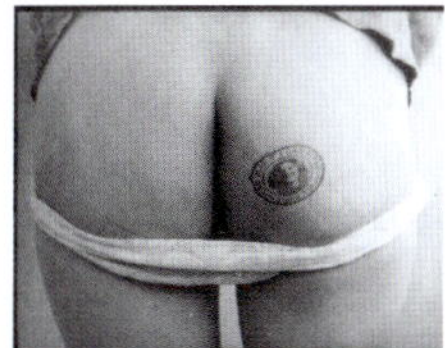

I am glad if I can stamp
Silbergelatine-Abzug auf Dokubrom-Papier / Silver gelatin print on Dokubrom paper; 10,2 × 12,1 cm

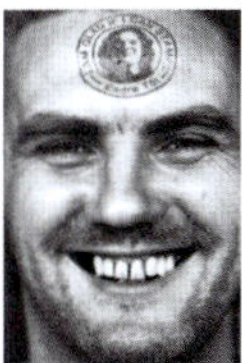

I am glad if I can stamp
Silbergelatine-Abzug / Silver gelatin print; 15,2 × 10 cm

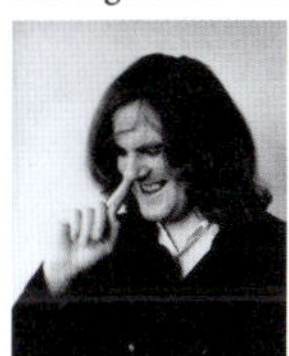

I am glad if…
Silbergelatine-Abzug / Silver gelatin print; 12 × 9 cm

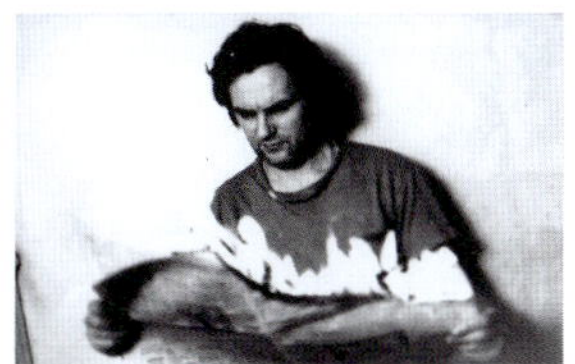

I am glad if I can read a burning newspaper
Silbergelatine-Abzug / Silver gelatin print; 11,8 × 18 cm

Alle Werke mit freundlicher Genehmigung des Künstlers und der acb Gallery / All works courtesy of the artist and acb Gallery

Gyula VÁRNAI

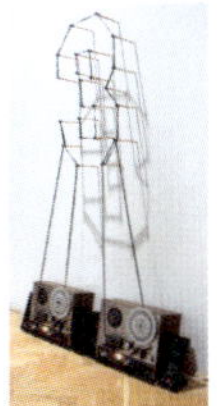

Philophonie / Philophony, 1999
Klanginstallation / Sound installation; 160 × 120 × 30 cm
Szűcs Sammlung / Collection, Budapest
Photo: Gyula Várnai

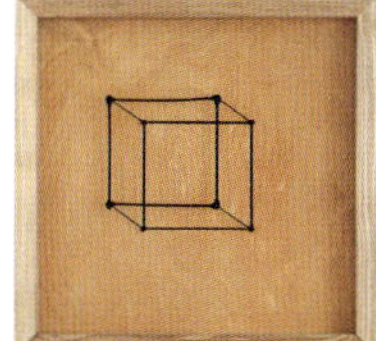

Raum und Zeit / Space and Time, 2012
Mobile; 50 × 50 cm
Ádám Kiss-Júlia Vecsenyi Sammlung / Collection, Budapest
Photo: György Nyírő

Alle Werke mit freundlicher Genehmigung des Künstlers und der acb Gallery / All works courtesy of the artist and acb Gallery

Gábor ERDÉLYI, András GÁLIK (Little Warsaw), Bálint HAVAS (Little Warsaw), Dezső SZABÓ

Die gegenständliche Welt / The World as Objectness, 2014
Ölgemälde / Oil painting [Zsigmond Károlyi: *ETALON*, 1992. Öl auf Leinwand / Oil on canvas; 80 × 60 cm], Vertrag / Contract; 7 A4 Blätter / 7 A4 sheets
Photo: Miklós Sulyok

Mit freundlicher Genehmigung der Künstler / Courtesy of the artists

*** Nicht ausgestellt / Not part of the exhibition.**

IMPRESSUM / COLOPHON

Dieser Katalog erscheint anlässlich der Ausstellung *BOOKMARKS – Neo-Avantgarde und postkonzeptuelle Positionen in der ungarischen Kunst von den 1960er Jahren bis heute*, Art Cologne, 16.–19. April 2015

This catalogue is published on the occasion of the exhibition *BOOKMARKS – Hungarian Neo-Avant-Garde and Post-Conceptual Art from the Late 1960s to the Present*, Art Cologne, 16–19 April 2015

Herausgeber / Editor: Katalin Székely

Konzeption / Concept: acb Gallery, Kisterem Gallery, Vintage Galéria

Gestaltung / Design: Zoltán Szmolka

Texte / Texts: Katalin Székely, Emese Kürti (14, 68)

Übersetzungen / Translations: Reuben Fowkes (HU-EN), Dániel Sipos (HU-EN, 68), Eva Zador (HU-DE)

Lektorat / Copy Editing: DISTANZ Verlag, Frederik Kugler (DE), Andrea Scrima (EN)

Fotonachweis / Photo Credits: Csaba Aknay (15, 22–23, 45–47, 63, 73–74, 80–81, 83–86), Ágnes Bak – Bence Tihanyi (33–35, 82), András Bozsó (17–19, 29, 31, 49, 53–55, 61, 80–82, 84–85), László Lugosi Lugo (25–27, 71, 81–82, 86), György Nyírő (75, 86–87), György Orbán (85), Miklós Sulyok (37, 43, 51, 56–57, 59, 79, 82–85, 87), Gábor S. Horváth (40–41, 83), Tamás Stauby (69, 85), Zsolt Szabóky (39, 83), Péter Szalay (67, 85), Zsombor Szikora (21, 80), Annamária Szőke (81), Gyula Várnai (77, 87), Dr. László Végh (70, 86)

Lithografie / Image Editing: max-color, Berlin

Produktion / Production Management: DISTANZ Verlag, Sonja Bahr

Gesamtherstellung / Production: optimal media GmbH, Röbel/Müritz

Vertrieb / Distribution
Gestalten, Berlin
www.gestalten.com
sales@gestalten.com

ISBN 978-3-95476-106-7
Printed in Germany

Erschienen im / Published by
DISTANZ Verlag
www.distanz.de

Mit der freundlichen Unterstützung von / Kindly supported by:
Prime Minister's Office Hungary, Maurice Ward Art Handling

Besonderer Dank / Special thanks: Künstler / artists, Daniel Hug, Péter Küllői, John Ward, AX Collection, Nóra Attalai, Emily Austin, Dániel Erdély, György Erdély, Simon Erdély, Irokéz Collection, Ádám Kiss – Júlia Vecsenyi, Anna Kiss Kovács, Grażyna Kulczyk, Kolozsváry Collection, Hella Pados, Péter Sáránszki, Zsolt Somlói – Katalin Spengler, Ferenc Szűcs, László Vágó und / and Katalin Aknai, Dávid Fehér, Orsolya Hegedüs, Róna Kopeczky, György Nyírő, Annamária Szőke / EMA, Mónika Zsikla